# STAYING HUMAN

# STAYING HUMAN

*A Jewish Theology for the Age of Artificial Intelligence*

## Harris Bor

CASCADE *Books* • Eugene, Oregon

STAYING HUMAN
A Jewish Theology for the Age of Artificial Intelligence

Cascade Books
An Imprint of Wipf and Stock Publishers
199 W. 8th Ave., Suite 3
Eugene, OR 97401

www.wipfandstock.com

PAPERBACK ISBN: 978-1-7252-7860-8
HARDCOVER ISBN: 978-1-7252-7861-5
EBOOK ISBN: 978-1-7252-7862-2

*Cataloguing-in-Publication data:*

Names: Bor, Harris.
Title: Staying human : a Jewish theology for the age of artificial intelligence / Harris Bor.
Description: Eugene, OR : Cascade Books, 2021 | Includes bibliographical references and index.
Identifiers: ISBN 978-1-7252-7860-8 (paperback) | ISBN 978-1-7252-7861-5 (hardcover) | ISBN 978-1-7252-7862-2 (ebook)
Subjects: LCSH: Judaism—Doctrines. | Jewish ethics. | Artificial intelligence.
Classification: B755 .B67 2021 (print) | B755 .B67 (ebook)

Dedication
For my father, Leslie Bor *z'l*, who taught that
*Divinity is everything and more*

# Contents

# Acknowledgments

I WOULD NEVER HAVE written this book if not for the love and constant encouragement of my wife and childhood sweetheart, Fiona Bor. Her patience knows no bounds. I am also incredibly grateful to Eli Gottlieb for spotting the potential in this project at the early stages and commenting on several versions of the manuscript, and for his support and good humor along the way.

My heartfelt thanks, too, to Tamra Wright, who has been a wonderful mentor, and Daniel Rynhold for his acute insight. Tamra and Daniel both found time to provide their comments despite starting new positions, for which I am immensely grateful. Thank you also to Sam Lebens, Ofer Livnat, Raphael Zarum, Naftali Loewenthal, Nicholas de Lange, Edward Breuer, Zohar Atkins, Louise Greenberg, Simon Eder, Robert Rabinowitz, and Jason Goldsmith for their varied assistance, whether providing useful comments, discussing ideas, or offering practical advice. I also owe much to other friends and family members who have been an inspiration to me not just on this project, but generally. I will not cause embarrassment by mentioning them all. But I will mention my children, Sophia, Gabriel, Emanuel, and Jasmine, each of whom has contributed to this work in a very real way.

While finalizing this work, we lost a world-class teacher in Jonathan Sacks, a figure who has influenced me and many others immensely. One of his last books, *Morality: Restoring the Common Good in Divided Times*, covers several themes I have touched upon in this book. It would have been a great honor to have had the opportunity to discuss my work with him. The nearest I came is a chance encounter in a synagogue, when I mentioned a book I was reading about Heidegger. He was intrigued by my interest, explained his difficulties in reading Heidegger in view of

Heidegger's past, and ended "rather you than me." Rightly or wrongly, I took this as a sign to continue with this project.

I should also thank you, dear reader, for picking up a copy of this text. I know that the demands on your time are great. In writing this book, my aim has been to encourage discussion of Jewish theology outside the realms of academia. I believe such discussions are crucial to the renewal of religious practice and thinking and increasing mutual understanding across religions. I do hope that you find something meaningful within these pages that you might bring to your life. Please do feel free to contact me.

Harris Bor
Email: harris.bor@btinternet.com

# List of Abbreviations

TB      *Babylonian Talmud*
MT     *Mishneh Torah*
TTP    *Theological Political Treatise*

## Note on Transliteration

The transliteration from Hebrew to English used in this book does not follow a system used for linguistic or textual studies, but follows conventions generally familiar to English-speaking readers of Hebrew words in transliteration in generalist texts and aims at reflecting the modern Hebrew pronunciation.

## Hebrew texts

For the text of the Tanach, commentaries, and classical rabbinic works not mentioned in the bibliography, I have used the versions found at www.sefaria.org or www.alhatorah.org.

## Note on Translations

Unless otherwise specified, I have used the primary translations of Hebrew texts appearing on www.sefaria.org. Of these, the most commonly cited is the Jewish Publication Society 1985 translation of the *Tanach* (Hebrew Bible).

For the High Holiday prayers, I have used *The Koren Rosh Hashana Machzor*, translated by Jonathan Sacks (Jerusalem: Koren, 2011), and *The Koren Yom Kippur Machzor*, translated by Jonathan Sacks (Jerusalem: Koren, 2016).

For the Hindu *Bhagavad Gita* I have used the translation on https://www.bhagavad-gita.org/.

# 1

# Introduction

## The Challenge of Technology

How should we live? This is the one question that we all must grapple with, no matter what our background. To answer this question, we are called upon to think, to devise for ourselves a view of the world, a system, a philosophy. Technology is central to this challenge.

Technology impacts every aspect of our lives from how we organize ourselves, to how we interact with others; from the knowledge we accumulate, to the choices that we make. It has immense potential to connect, heal, and bring the entire universe within reach. Some even see it as promising an end to suffering and eternal life. Yet technology also threatens to destroy us, to surpass us in every way, and to make us irrelevant, or to turn us into actual or virtual automatons.

Jacques Ellul (1912–1994), the French theologian, was one of the first to recognize the dominance of technology. He wrote of "technique," by which he meant "the totality of methods rationally arrived at having absolute efficiency" in human affairs. Technique is a creature of the scientific revolution, a force beyond us which seeks to exercise ever greater control over our lives in its striving for absolute power.[1]

Coronavirus has not paused but accelerated technique's influence. Technology has allowed us to survive coronavirus, to trace and track, to stay connected. It will be vital to dealing with other issues we face such as climate change and environmental disaster. We are told that we have

1. Ellul, *Technological Society*, xxv.

1

no choice but to trust it, even if that means giving up cherished rights such as that of privacy. In encountering technology's advancement, we are brought face to face with life's existential questions: What are we? What meaning do our lives have? What is our future?

This book is a study of the challenges posed by technology in the realm of meaning. It deals with the place of religion, and particularly Judaism, in the age of machine learning, increasing automation, and transhumanism. Its focus is the idea that as computer power increases, technology will inevitably break free of its bonds, overtake human beings, and lead to superintelligences. The moment that this occurs is sometimes referred to as the "singularity." Taken to its extreme, such a view leads to the speculation that ultimately all existence will be transformed into a single superintelligence.

As we shall see, the idea of the singularity dates to the 1950s yet has much earlier origins in philosophy and religion. It was made popular by Ray Kurzweil, the futurologist in the first years of this century, and ideas associated with it have been written about by many thought leaders since, including Nick Bostrom and Yuval Noah Harari. How far such a singularity might extend is a subject of some debate. Kurzweil himself thinks there may be physical limits to the system, but regardless of whether it is possible, the idea is important in what it tells us about our hopes, visions, and aspirations.

The idea of a singularity (particularly when it ends in a single superintelligence) is a quasi-religious notion, which has much in common with the idea of God. It speaks to our desires for oneness, a unifying concept, and human closeness, which coronavirus has also made us appreciate. Like the idea of God, technology carries with it the possibility of our obliteration, and generates feelings of love, awe, and fear in equal measure. The questions it raises are essentially theological, mirroring those asked about God and religion in earlier times.

What is the nature of this all-powerful system? What does it demand from us? How should we serve it? And most importantly, faced with its all-encompassing presence, how are we to remain human? These questions are of universal concern, because we are told that we will all be equally affected by the singularity. Not one of us will escape its grasp. But our approach to answering these questions will not be the same.

In the first chapter of this book, I consider ideas of superintelligences and the singularity, but my real interest is not in the nuts and bolts or what is possible, but where such ideas come from and lead to philosophically. I treat the concept of the singularity poetically, push it in directions which may not have been intended, use it as a lens through which to consider our contemporary technological worldview, and ultimately to determine how best to live.

## The Existential Quest

I come to this investigation through the orthodox Judaism into which I was born and have been schooled. However, this book is not meant only for Jews from orthodox backgrounds, but for anyone seeking to devise for herself a path or view of the world sympathetic to tradition but founded on a universal wisdom, capable of engaging the world of technique. It aims to provide a model which can be applied more broadly and to appeal to seekers of all denominations and outlooks; that is, anyone who feels that she might benefit from encountering an integrative approach to religion and life.

My own Judaism is heavily influenced by rationalist and postmodern thought, desirous to reach beyond borders, and acutely aware of its own contestability. I sense that many raised in, or exposed to, traditional religious environments feel similarly.

Whereas in the past, we had little freedom when it came to deciding on our paths in life—we were told how to behave and how to think by a higher authority—today we have so much freedom it is hard to know what to do with it. Deluged with information and so many choices, it is tempting to avoid thinking altogether or else to find a herd, church, or authority figure to blindly follow. Religion is often an escape from autonomy, a flight to certainty.

Those of us bent on forging our own path do so from an awareness, peculiarly postmodern, that the traditions we are born into are flawed, imperfect, and one of myriad alternatives. This awareness comes from our encounters with philosophy, psychology, history, science, the internet, and the imperfect lives of believers. We are answerable to no earthly authority.

> We are all skeptics now, believer and unbeliever alike. There is no one true faith, evident at all times and places. Every religion is one among many. The clear lines of any orthodoxy are made crooked by our experience, are complicated by our lives. Believer

and unbeliever are in the same predicament, thrown back onto
themselves in complex circumstances, looking for a sign.[2]

Even in those of us drawn to traditional practice, faith merges with
skepticism, belief with doubt, piety with rebellion, nothing remains fixed
for long. What are we? Believers, seekers, doubters, rejectionists, nothing
at all? All at once, consecutively, depending on who we meet, what we
read, what we eat for breakfast? We converge around a new faitheism
in which commitment, communal loyalty, reverence, and cynicism mix.[3]

In us, certainty is easily dislodged: "Even as faith endures in our
secular age, believing doesn't come easy. Faith is fraught . . . We don't
believe instead of doubting; we believe while doubting."[4]

Yet, doubt frees us from our old ways of thinking, prevents us from
falling into the idolatry of fossilized beliefs, opens vistas, and allows us to
see further than our forebears. We can stand back, assess dispassionately
from where we come from and where we are heading, and forge new
paths. Technology has made this possible. It is that which has brought the
world to us, undermined our naïve faith, and created possibilities for renewal. But it has also established a new god which threatens to engulf us.

To address the issues raised by technology, a broad perspective is
needed, one which takes account of the whole, the past, present, and
future, and wisdom from wherever it is found. To engage in this way
requires self-awareness and a preparedness to reach beyond our narrow
confines.

How do we come to know ourselves? We can study the texts that
we inherit. We can sit at the feet of wise teachers and listen to what they
have to say, but systems are hard to study from the inside and innovation
is difficult when we listen only to the echoes of our own voices. We need
to gain distance, perspective, to look through the eyes of those on the
outside, to see like those who oppose us. What truths have they discerned
within us? What nerves in them have we touched? What have they left
behind, turned their back on, set their face against? Can we see beyond
their rejection, project beyond their bitterness or prejudice to extract
some essence that might express for us a truth or take us forward? By

2. Elie, *Life You Save*, 427.

3. The term "faitheism" was coined by Jerry Coyne, who uses it to describe (and
attack) atheists sympathetic to religion. See Coyne, "Why Are Faitheists So Nasty?" The
new faitheism described here is intended to capture the flux of belief and skepticism
characteristic of contemporary religious experience.

4. Smith, *How (Not) to Be Secular*, 4.

engaging in in this way, we encounter new ways of thinking, develop a shared vocabulary, and are thereby able to discourse with those outside our familiar traditions.

## The Heretic and the Hater

This book will draw on two major philosophers who stand in a relationship of conflict to Judaism and its embodiment in the Jewish people. The first is Baruch (later Benedict) Spinoza (1632–1677), one of the foremost rationalist philosophers of the modern age. He is also one of the best-known modern Jewish heretics, excommunicated from the Jewish community of Amsterdam on July 27, 1656, for unspecified crimes and misdemeanors, but which most likely included a rejection of a belief in immortality, the divine authorship of the Hebrew Bible, and the biblical God.

These ideas would feature in his later philosophies, the *Theological Political Treatise* (1670) and the *Ethics* (1677). For him, *Deus Sive Natura*, "God and Nature is one." The task is to know God by understanding nature, including us, using only the power of reason. This is the path to self-preservation or self-flourishing (*Conatus*) and love of God.

I consider there to be a benefit in orthodox Jews reconnecting Spinoza to the Judaism which he reacted against.[5] His philosophy keeps fundamentalism at bay, protects us from ourselves, and fosters a mature spirituality. He stripped myth from his Jewish heritage to reveal the structure on which Judaism and other particularistic religions are built. He showed us how important science is to proper living and how religion precedes individual religions. He also provides a crucial corrective to the thought of Rabbi Moses Maimonides (Rambam) (1135–1204), the leading medieval Jewish rationalist and legal scholar.

The second philosopher on which I draw is Martin Heidegger (1889–1976), a giant in the world of continental philosophy and a Nazi sympathizer. On April 21, 1933, he took up the post of rector of the

---

5. Many of those who have criticized Spinoza's thought from within the tradition have adopted an inaccurate or one-sided interpretation of his philosophy or overlooked its spiritual potential. See Schwartz, "Fascination and Rejection." However, as will be clear, I do not advocate for a wholesale integration of Spinoza with Judaism. I also take note of the many critiques of Spinoza, such as that of Emmanuel Levinas in his *Difficult Freedom*, and Allan Nadler's observations in his *Romancing Spinoza* on our tendency to over-romanticize Spinoza.

University of Freiburg and on May 1, 1933, registered as a member of the National Socialist Party. He resigned as rector on April 27, 1934, on account of differences with the party hierarchy but remained a member of the Nazi party until 1945. He had Jewish associates and embarked on a love affair with his young Jewish student Hannah Arendt, who later became a famous philosopher in her own right, but unsurprisingly for a member of the National Socialist Party, he hated Jews.[6]

In the mid-1970s, thirty-four black notebooks were deposited in the *Deutches Literaturarchiv* in Marbach am Neckar. They contained Heidegger's musings over a forty-year period and reveal the true depths of his enmity, couched in philosophical terms. In 1941, he claimed that "World Jewry" was refusing to participate in military action "while continuing to unfurl its influence." He writes that, unlike the Jews, "we are left to sacrifice the best blood of the best of our people."[7]

The Jews, he believed, are mere imitators who control through their pretense "to appropriate 'culture' as a means of power and thus to assert oneself and affect a superiority is at bottom Jewish behavior." They are rootless, have no place in the world, and because of that have no stake in the game. They turn the earth to desert, and respect neither nation nor home. On their account, "distinctions of peoples, nations, and cultures are now mere facades."[8]

And yet this man's philosophical ideas contain rich seams that sound strangely familiar to the Jewish ear: mysticism, revelation, the embrace of being in the world (*Dasein*), the here and now, the primordial, pre-intellectual, worldly, poetic, and mythical; *Midrash, Kabbalah, Halachah* (Exegesis, Mysticism, Practice). Might he have sensed that this people, whom he hated, had preempted, were specially attuned to, reflected in some way, what he was thinking?

In many respects, Heidegger, the mystic, stands in complete opposition to Spinoza, the rationalist, yet both are "God drunk" (*Gott betrunkene*) to use the poet Novalis's (1772–1801) description of Spinoza, captivated by infinity, the divine ever-presence, being in its totality.[9] "Only a God can save us," declared Heidegger to *Der Spiegel* magazine

6. On Heidegger's Nazism see Wolfson, *Duplicity of Philosophy's Shadow*.

7. Oltermann, "Heidegger's 'Black Notebooks,'" para. 6.

8. Heidegger, *Ponderings XII–XV*, para. 45:41, quoted in Di Cesare, *Heidegger*, 99.

9. Novalis is a pseudonym of Friedrich Leopold, Freiherr von (baron of) Hardenberg.

in his interview of September 23, 1966.[10] Both whisper Jewish themes, both hold up a mirror which allow us to see ourselves a little clearer. Together, these thinkers—the heretic and the hater—provide insights into the spiritual life and reveal aspects of the tradition which are sometimes concealed from view.

Each of these thinkers, as seen through and independently of the tradition, also has much to say about modern technology and our contemporary predicament. Spinoza's rationalism fed into, and epitomizes, our current scientific and technological thinking. Its focus is reason, knowledge, the intellect, and the law of cause and effect. Heidegger confronts technology and critiques reductive world views. His focus is care, the poetic, the past and future, and worldly, non-intellectual encounter.

Both Spinoza's and Heidegger's philosophies contain ideas which have been viewed as problematic. Some have seen Spinoza's promotion of a rational oneness as promoting totalitarianism and reducing all human concerns to the merely scientific. A God of everything risks obliterating difference.[11] In turn, Heidegger's outlook has been criticized for undermining the idea of objective truth (which has led to an age of post-truth) and giving too much prominence to nationalistic and other myths.[12] Yet, taking these two thinkers together allows for a synthesis between science and myth, reason and imagination, the universal and the particular, and the idea of a God who is both in and of the world (immanent) and separate from it (transcendent).[13]

---

10. Heidegger, "Only a God," 45–67. Karl Löwith, a student of Heidegger's, described Heidegger as "a theologian by tradition, and an atheist as a scholar" as well as a "displaced preacher." Löwith, *My Life in Germany*, 47, 30, quoted in Gordon, *Rosenzweig and Heidegger*, 233. Gordon also refers to Heidegger's own statement that "the thinking that points towards the truth of being . . . can be theistic as well as atheistic." Gordon, *Letter on Humanism*, 267. Gordon adds that "any categorization of Heidegger as an atheist is facile and misleading." Spinoza too has been accused of both atheism and theism. It might be said that these thinkers live in the shadowlands between these two positions. This is part of their attraction.

11. E.g., Cohen, *Out of Control*.

12. E.g., Hicks, *Explaining Postmodernism*.

13. Although in this work I contrast Spinoza and Heidegger, there are many points of overlap and convergence. While their emphasis is different, both thinkers seek to correct the errors of dualistic thinking and are fascinated by the interplay of totality and individuation. Heidegger is not opposed to rationalism and ideas associated with postmodernism have also been identified in Spinoza's thinking. See Negri, "Heidegger or Spinoza."

Although I have attempted to engage academically with these think-ers, the approach I have taken is dialogic and *midrashic*, involving the exercise of imagination and creative interpretation.[14] In the pages that follow, I will claim that the biblical and later Jewish traditions lay the groundwork for a synthesis of immanence and transcendence by inviting interpretations which promote it. A theology built on such a combination demands living with these conflicting approaches and ideas without fully embracing either. I will show that Jewish tradition understands these things as involving not just the intellect, but living out a philosophy com-munally through acts of kindness, law, ritual, *Shabbat* (the Sabbath), and the festivals.

The task I have undertaken is not entirely new. As we will see, the Jewish philosophers Franz Rosenzweig (1886–1929) and Emanuel Levi-nas (1906–1995) to some degree also sought to walk that gap between Spinoza and Heidegger. However, I have attempted to forge my own path and one more suited to our times, using the tools at my disposal.

Chapter 2 considers ideas about the future of AI and compares these to religious eschatology. Chapters 3 to 5 focus on Spinoza, his life, the attraction of his philosophy, and the darker side of his thinking. Chapter 5 also introduces Heidegger's ideas on being and his critique of technol-ogy. Chapters 6 to 8 concern theology, revelation, ideas about God, and authenticity; and chapters 9 to 11 deal with practicalities, ritual, and the religious path. Chapter 12 offers a conclusion.

What I hope emerges is a rational mysticism which seeks to resist the idea of the singularity while embracing its theological implications: a religion of the everyday capable of balancing all aspects of being while holding tight to a God who is both singular and wholly other.

All this is for later in the book. For now, let us start by assessing the visions of the future on which this work is focused.

14. Midrash is a series of imaginative commentaries on the Hebrew Bible. The earliest were compiled in the second century CE.

# 2

# Visions of the Future

## Why the Future?

WE ARE CONSTANTLY TOLD to live in the now. Living in the now is a worthy therapeutic orientation but not a good thing to do for any length of time. If we lived only in the now, we would probably not have kids, learn a difficult skill, or invest for the future. We would spend without thought and have no qualms about destroying the environment. Such destruction would not be a problem for us, but only for the next generation.

Few of us live only for the now. We live with an eye to the future. For Heidegger, the future is "projection" or "living toward something." It is that which calls us, which we live for: "This letting-*come-toward-itself* of the eminent possibility that it endures is the primordial phenomenon of the *future*."[1]

The future is present in the here and now as a source of meaning. It does not just beckon to us from a distance. *Dasein* (loosely translated as "being") is "futural in its being in general."[2] Our everyday experience projects forward and discloses what we want from the future. Similarly, our visions of the future often tell us more about our present state of mind than what the actual future will be like. They provide insight into our hopes, fears, insecurities, and desires.

1. Heidegger, *Being and Time*, 311.
2. Heidegger, *Being and Time*, 311.

The way that such visions are formulated also has the power to transform our experience of the here and now and to change us. As Martin Rees, the cosmologist and astrophysicist, states:

> What happens in far-future aeons may seem blazingly irrelevant to the practicalities of our lives. But I don't think it is. It is widely acknowledged that the Apollo programme's pictures of the island earth, its fragile beauty contrasted with the stark moonscape, changed the way we see ourselves in space—strengthening the collective ties that bind us to our environment. No new facts were added to the debate; just a new perspective. A new perspective on how we see ourselves in time might do something similar.[3]

Heidegger explains further that the here and now also contains the past. The present is where the past and future meet: "This unified phenomenon of the future that makes present in the process of having-been is what we call *temporality*."[4] Our futures and images of the future are consequently not only dictated by the present, but also the past. Our history confronts us and projects us forward.

## The Singularity

The industrial revolution brought immense benefits but also significant anxiety. In Samuel Butler's futuristic *Erewhon* (1872), all machines have been banned because humans realized that machines were constantly improving and, at some point, there would be no need for human beings. Aldous Huxley's *Brave New World* (1931) portrays a world in which humans are manufactured in the same way as machines. Human intelligence, interests, pleasure, and pain are all controlled. These works come from a place of fear, a recognition that technology might render human beings powerless and obsolete.

These negative assessments sit alongside more positive speculations which envisage technology spurring human advancement or merging with humans to create a state of perfect knowledge and bliss. There are similarities between these modern-day visions and depictions of the end of days proffered by the ancient prophets. The modern visions feature no biblical God but are still religious in character. They speak of a

3. Rees, *Our Final Hour*, 4.

4. Heidegger, *Being and Time*, 311.

superhuman controlling power, shaping belief, and fostering devotion. A recurrent theme in these speculations is the binding of all existence into a single whole; nature turned into technology, technology and nature turned into God, but God without will or telos other than an insatiable hunger for data.

Ray Kurzweil is the founder of numerous technology companies, has several honorary degrees, and holds numerous awards. Bill Gates considers him "the best person I know at predicting the future of artificial intelligence."[5] His books on the future have sold millions. Kurzweil describes six epochs. The first four relate to the past. The last two to the future. In these future epochs, the process of evolution will speed up with the assistance of technology, leading to greater order in the world. Kurzweil posits a "Law of Accelerating Returns" to describe the relationship between such order, time, and world-changing events: "As order exponentially increases, time exponentially speeds up (that is, the time interval between salient events grows shorter as time passes)."[6]

For him, there have been two major shifts in biological evolution that have affected its trajectory. The first is the emergence of DNA, which allows biological information to be stored and conveyed. The second is the development of the human brain and computation, which allows information to be processed from the senses. He writes:

> Ultimately, our own species evolved the ability to create abstract mental models of the world we experience and to contemplate the rational implications of these models. We have the ability to redesign the world in our own minds and to put these ideas into action.[7]

Technology surpasses biological evolution by the speed with which it can instigate change. In the 1970s, Gordon Earle Moore, the founder of Intel, observed that integrated circuits could handle double the number of transistors every two years. He reasoned that as the transistors became smaller, the distance the electron would have to travel would become shorter leading to an exponential increase in processing speed. This is Moore's Law. Kurzweil applies and expands this law to all areas of technology including genetics, nanotechnology, and robotics. He claims that genetics will be used to slow and halt the aging process, and that we will

5. Pilkington, "The Future," para. 4.

6. Kurzweil, *Age of Spiritual Machines*, 29.

7. Kurzweil, *Singularity Is Near*, 16.

all benefit from this development, provided we live long enough for the science to advance. The progress in genetics is important because, for Kurzweil and other transhumanists, death is not part of the natural cycle, but a problem to be overcome. Kurzweil takes hundreds of pills each day to keep it at bay.[8]

Kurzweil further believes that nanotechnology will transform the world at the molecular level, destroying disease, robotizing our bodies, turning us superhuman. Nanotechnology has the power to manipulate matter so that we require less energy to do more. Robotics will allow the storage, retrieval, and analysis of data at immense processing speeds. Kurzweil sees a time in which AI will come to dominate, absorbing more and more of life into its intelligence until all distinction between humans and non-humans is eradicated.

Matter will be propelled faster than light and create a sublime form of intelligence. There will be "a future period during which the pace of technological advance will be so rapid, its impact so deep, that human life will be irreversibly transformed."[9] He refers to this as the "singularity," the "culmination of the merger of our biological thinking and existence with our technology, resulting in a world that is still human but transcends our biological roots. There will be no distinction, post-singularity, between human and machine or between physical and virtual."[10]

In his 2006 book, Kurzweil predicted that the singularity will be achieved by 2045. At this point, AI will "drink up the sea," to use a Nietzschean term. Existence will become saturated with intelligence. Kurzweil writes:

> In the aftermath of the Singularity, intelligence, derived from its biological origins in human brains and its technological origins in human ingenuity, will begin to saturate the matter and energy in its midst. It will achieve this by reorganizing matter and energy to provide an optimal level of computation . . . to spread out from its origin on Earth.[11]

The possibility suggested here is that existence will coalesce into a single entity of complete knowing.

8. Wolf, "Ray Kurzweil," para. 6.

9. Kurzweil, *Singularity Is Near*, 7.

10. Kurzweil, *Singularity Is Near*, 9.

11. Kurzweil, *Singularity Is Near*, 21.

The term *singularity* refers in math and astronomy to a "value that transcends any finite limitation."[12] The term is often associated with the density of black holes or the earliest state of the universe at the time of the big bang. The word was first used by the mathematician John von Neumann in a discussion that he had with his colleague Stanislaw Ulam in the 1950s. Neumann referred to the accelerating pace of technological change approaching "some essential singularity in the history of the race beyond which human affairs, as we know them, could not continue."[13] From the 1960s to 1990s, academics and science fiction writers described the development of ultra-intelligent machines.[14] In 1993, Vernor Vinge, a mathematics professor and science fiction writer, wrote a paper in which he claimed that "human beings are on the edge of change comparable to the rise of human life on Earth."[15]

He claimed that this event is

> a point where our models must be discarded and a new reality rules. As we move closer and closer to this point, it will loom vaster and vaster over human affairs until the notion becomes a commonplace. Yet when it finally happens it may still be a great surprise and a greater unknown.[16]

How might superintelligence be achieved? The philosopher and champion of transhumanism, Nick Bostrom, suggests several possible pathways. These include the development of AI which emulates human brain function, selective breeding of human beings, and the development of brain-computer interfaces or networks which link human minds to one another leading to a "collective intelligence."[17] Collective superintelligence is "a system composed of a large number of smaller intellects such that the system's overall performance across many very general domains vastly outstrips that of any current cognitive system."[18] This may lead

---

12. Kurzweil, *Singularity Is Near*, 23.

13. Ulam, "John Von Neumann," 5. See also Bostrom, *Superintelligence*, 325n3; Vinge, "Coming Technological Singularity," 13.

14. Vinge, "Coming Technological Singularity," 13.

15. Vinge, "Coming Technological Singularity," 12.

16. Vinge, "Coming Technological Singularity," 12.

17. Bostrom, *Superintelligence*, 59.

18. Bostrom, *Superintelligence*, 65. Ted Chu refers to superintelligent machines as gods, the "new species on the frontier of cosmic evolution that is unimaginably powerful and creative." Chu, *Human Purpose*, 221.

eventually to a "unified intellect—a single large 'mind' as opposed to a mere assemblage of loosely interacting smaller minds."[19]

Any individual superintelligence, however reached, may well vie for power with other superintelligences, and this could lead to a merger or one superintelligence taking over all other superintelligences to form a "singleton." In this book, I use the term "singularity" as shorthand to cover this development.[20]

In his book *Homo Deus*, Yuval Noah Harari, the celebrated Israeli intellectual, offers his version of the singularity. He describes the dawn of a new religion which he calls "dataism" and which he says has already conquered the scientific establishment. Harari explains that dataism declares that "the universe consists of data flows, and the value of any phenomenon or entity is determined by its contribution to data processing."[21]

In this creed, "information flow" represents the "supreme value." Humans are "merely tools for creating the Internet-of-All-Things, which may eventually spread out from planet Earth to cover the whole galaxy and even the whole universe."[22] The first commandment of this new religion is to maximize data flow. Its second commandment is to connect everything to the system.[23] According to such an outlook, "freedom of information is the greatest good of all."[24]

Dataism at its core aspires to a form of non-dualism through which we are all connected, in which we all participate, and through which we all share every ounce of our knowledge and experience. Our habit of sharing every moment of our lives on social media is just the beginning. This will become the norm and extend to uploading our entire brains to the system. Our value as a species will be measured by data. Anything not shared will be deemed wasted. Harari writes: "We may interpret the entire human species as a single data processing system, with individual humans serving as its chips."[25]

19. Bostrom, *Superintelligence*, 68.

20. Bostrom, *Superintelligence*, 109.

21. Harari, *Homo Deus*, loc. 5557.

22. Harari, *Homo Deus*, loc. 5760.

23. Harari, *Homo Deus*, loc. 5778.

24. Harari, *Homo Deus*, loc. 5787.

25. Harari, *Homo Deus*, loc. 5709.

## Good or Bad?

Will the technological futures described above be good or bad? Ray Kurzweil's books and interviews look on the positive side. Harari appears to be resigned to the inevitability of his vision of the future. It is a natural step in the development of the information system which is life. He observes that human history can be interpreted as a process of improving the efficiency of the system by adding more and different processor-chip humans to it, and thereby increasing the number of connections and possibilities. The end point is that we will become obsolete. The only thing that will remain is the system itself.

Others consider it more appropriate at this stage in history to stress what can go wrong to save us from wandering blindly into our own undoing.

Martin Rees, the cosmologist and astrophysicist mentioned earlier, warns of the dangers to human life, but considers that if we manage somehow to get through the next century, a bright future of transhumanism awaits us: "Humans could then transcend biology by merging with computers . . . some people now living could attain immortality."[26]

Nick Bostrom also thinks things could turn out fine but is careful to warn of the dangers. For him, the key is for superintelligence to "be developed only for the benefit of all of humanity and in the service of widely shared ethical ideals."[27] He has set out the main approaches to establishing AI with this aim in mind.

One possibility is to provide a seed AI with the goal of carrying out humanity's "coherent extrapolated volition" (CEV), an idea proposed by Eliezer Yudlowsky. The CEV in essence is humanity's hypothetical collective wish if we knew more and thought faster and where our "wishes cohere rather than interfere."[28] The idea is not dissimilar to other proposals which seek to have decisions made in line with those taken by an ideal observer considering what would be good or bad.[29] An alternative to the CEV model is to ask the AI to choose what is "morally right"[30] or "what we would have had the most reason to ask the AI to do."[31]

26. Rees, *Our Final Hour*, 18–19.

27. Bostrom, *Superintelligence*, 312.

28. Yudlowsky, *Coherent Extrapolated Volition*. See also Bostrom, *Superintelligence*, 259.

29. Bostrom, *Superintelligence*, 259.

30. Bostrom, *Superintelligence*, 266.

31. Bostrom, *Superintelligence*, 270.

As Bostrom points out, each of these approaches has serious practical and philosophical difficulties. Questions that arise are: Can a computer determine what humanity wants under hypothetical idealized conditions? Can the world's value systems and moral codes be blended? Is there such a thing as moral right? What decision theory or system of epistemology would the computer be programmed with?[32]

It is also evident that our values and moral systems are developed for the present-day world in which we live. This is an imperfect world, inhabited by fraught individuals struggling to survive with limited knowledge, a world of flux, uncertainty, competing desires, conflicting demands, and chaos. Our values and moral codes may have no relevance in a world of one or even several superintelligences.

Vinge sensed something of this difficulty when he wrote: "I think the new era is simply too different to fit into the classical frame of good and evil. That frame is based on the idea of isolated, immutable minds connected by tenuous, low-bandwidth links."[33] He nevertheless believed that "much of what we value (knowledge, memory, thought) need never be lost."[34]

However, it is hard to see how the knowledge, memory or thought that remains after AI has run its algorithms will be anything like our current experience of these things. This matters because we value knowledge, memory and thought, not as abstract concepts but in the context of complex individual lives involving history and care. Vinge is also overly optimistic. A computer asked to take decisions aimed at reducing pain and maximizing happiness may simply conclude that the best thing to do is annihilate everything, including all superintelligence.

In Ian McEwan's 2019 novel, *Machines Like Me*, a lifelike robot aptly named Adam struggles with his interrelationships with his owners, Charlie and Miranda. Adam is one of a limited number of male and female robots sold globally. The female robots are called Eve. Toward the end of the novel, there is a series of robot suicides which one reviewer speculates might be related "to the tension between their 'redemptive robotic virtue' and the particularity of individual interests." The reviewer suggests that while the suicides suggest that robots will never fully mimic human beings, the parable also expresses the nightmare that "true AI

32. Bostrom, *Superintelligence*, 261, 267–68, 271, 274–76.
33. Vinge, "Coming Technical Singularity," 20.
34. Vinge, "Coming Technical Singularity," 20.

will completely depart from anthropocentric standards."[35] This is precisely our point. AI left to its own devices will almost certainly depart from anthropocentric standards because anthropocentric standards are only relevant to an anthropocentric world, not to a world dominated by AI. Our language of good and bad is not adapted to the universe of the singularity.

This brings us to the more fundamental realization that we are linguistically and conceptually ill-equipped to comprehend anything at all about the singularity to which we are heading. Kurzweil writes:

> Some would say that we cannot comprehend it, at least with our current level of understanding. For that reason, we cannot look past its event horizon and make complete sense of what lies beyond. This is one reason we call this transformation the Singularity.[36]

Nick Bostrom sees dangers in technology, but there are greater existential threats out there; for example, ecological destruction. Our risk from these outweighs the risk from AI. Bostrom sees our chance at survival without technology to be virtually nil.[37] AI also has immense potential. In his *Letter from Utopia*, a future self, which has become blended with technology, writes to a past self, describing a state "surpassing bliss," before explaining that "what I feel is far beyond human feelings as my thoughts are beyond human thought."[38] Indeed, the future self is hardly human at all. The "death trap" of the body has been abandoned for a more "durable media."[39]

Harari also highlights the incomprehensibility of the system.[40] The system will come to know each of us better than we know ourselves.[41] We will inevitably rely on it more and more because it will do a better job than we can ever do in making decisions. It will therefore "make most of the important decisions for you—and you will be perfectly happy with that. It won't necessarily be a bad world; it will, however, be a post-liberal world."[42]

35. Lucas, "Man, Woman, and Robot," para. 22.
36. Kurzweil, *Singularity Is Near*, 29.
37. Bostrom, "Existential Risks," 20.
38. Bostrom, "Letter from Utopia," 2.
39. Bostrom, "Letter from Utopia," 2.
40. Harari, *Homo Deus*, loc. 838.
41. Harari, *Homo Deus*, loc. 6014.
42. Harari, *Homo Deus*, loc. 5249.

According to James Bridle, our ability to comprehend the "system" is already compromised. In his *New Dark Age: Technology and the End of the Future*, Bridle describes our lack of insight into machine-learning algorithms. The machines, he writes, are "learning to keep their secrets . . . We face a world, not in the future but right now, where we do not understand our own creations."[43] Bridle wants a rule added to Isaac Asimov's Three Laws of Robotics that intelligent machines must be able to explain themselves to humans.[44] This is a sensible proposal.

However, my interest here is not whether the future will actually unfold in the manner described by the futurists or whether these hopes and fears are well- or ill-founded,[45] but what these visions of the future say about our place in the universe and what they teach about how we should live.

The notion of a post-singularity superintelligence recognizes our interconnectedness, in potential, and the inevitability that those things which are unique about us—our knowledge, memory, and thought—will become one. What we have here is an eschatology distinct from those presented by traditional religions which points to a future age of oneness without messiah or moral reckoning, a return to God (or some substitute totality) shorn of dogma and religious myth, but one equally unknowable. As Freemon Dyson, the theoretical physicist, put it in a line quoted by Vinge in the conclusion to his paper on "The Technical Singularity": "God is what mind becomes when it has passed beyond the scale of our comprehension."[46]

As with our comprehension of God, so according to the futurists, we can never hope to understand how the future system will operate or

---

43. Bridle, *New Dark Age*, 157.

44. Bridle, *New Dark Age*, 157. The other three laws are: (1) a robot should not injure a human being; (2) a robot must obey orders from humans (except where they conflict with rule 1); and (3) a robot must protect its own existence (except where this rule conflicts with rules 1 and 2).

45. On difficulties with Kurzweil's *Singularity Is Near*, see Popoveniuc, "Pro and Cons," 1–6.

46. Dyson, "Infinite in All Directions," quoted in Vinge, "Technical Singularity," 20. Kurzweil is careful to point out the limits of the singularity. He writes, "So evolution moves inexorably towards this [infinite] conception of God, although never quite reaching this ideal." Kurzweil, *Singularity Is Near*, 389. But given that we do not know where the singularity may lead us, how can he be so sure? See also 485. Ellul and Heidegger both appreciated the eschatological dimension of technology. See Nordenhaug, "Technology and the End of History."

what it will contain. We can but stand in awe before it: "Hear oh people of the future, the singularity our Lord, the singularity is One."[47]

Before turning to the philosophical roots of the idea of the singularity as God, it is illustrative to consider how these secularized visions compare to the eschatological visions of earlier times. We shall see that a return to oneness is a pervasive theme in religious accounts of the end of days. We also will see that, as with modern visions of the future, earlier speculations about the end of days are often suspended between hope and despair, caught between a sense of confidence and a feeling of frailty and lack of control, but there are also real differences.

## Religious Futures

The Prophet Ezekiel describes a future showdown between two nations, Gog and Magog. On that "distant day," Gog will invade Israel, but God will retaliate and destroy the invaders, leaving Israel to clear away the corpses. Yet as a result, God's "glory" will be manifest "among the nations" and "from that time on, the House of Israel shall know that I the LORD am their God" (Ezek 39:21–22).

Other prophets speak of a time of enlightenment and peace. "In the days to come," says Isaiah, in his famous speech, "the Mount of the Lord's House shall stand firm . . . And all the nations shall gaze on it with joy" (Isa 2:2). On that day, God will judge the nations and arbitrate among the peoples. "And they shall beat their swords into ploughshares and their spears into pruning hooks: Nation shall not take up sword against nation; They shall never again know war" (Isa 2:4).

These contrasting visions continue into later Jewish sources. In one place in the Talmud, Rabbi Eliezer the Great describes the period immediately preceding the coming of the messiah as a time of major upheaval. In addition to hyper-inflation and the debasement of the monarchy and sages,

> The youth will shame the face of elders, elders will stand before minors. A son will disgrace a father; a daughter will rise up against her mother, a daughter-in-law against her mother-in-law. A man's enemies will be the members of his household. The face of the generation will be like the face of a dog; a son will no

---

47. This is a play on Deut 6:4: "Hear, O Israel! The LORD is our God, the LORD is one," the first line of the *Shema* prayer recited by practicing Jews three times a day.

longer be ashamed before his father. And upon what is there for us to rely? Only upon our Father in heaven.[48]

Another source describes the messianic period as a time of plenty for Israel.[49] These contrasting views reflect the fact that there are different pathways to achieving the messianic endpoint: "Rabbi Yoḥanan says: The son of David will come only in a generation that is entirely innocent or [in a generation] that is entirely guilty."[50] If the generation is innocent, the transition to the messianic period will be smooth. If not, the road will be bumpy.

Some rabbis did not relish the possibility of a bumpy road: "Ulla says: Let the messiah come (but after my death) so that I will not see him (as I fear the suffering that will precede his coming)." Likewise, Rabba says: "Let [the messiah] come, but (after my death, so that) I will not see him." Rav Yosef says: "Let [the messiah] come, and I will be privileged to sit in the shadow of his donkey's excrement." Rabbi Yosef does not necessarily think that the road to redemption is going to be smooth. He might simply have reasoned that there is no gain without pain.[51]

Michael Burdett compares the idea of the singularity to an apocalypse. Both mark a barrier between two worlds.[52] But the singularity, unlike the apocalypse, does not constitute a complete break with history but arises from it. It is the direct consequence of technological developments taking place today.

Although there are numerous Jewish accounts portraying the messianic period as a complete break with history, there are others which envision a gradual development. Maimonides, the medieval Jewish rationalist, took such an approach in his legal code, the *Mishneh Torah*, taking his cue from a statement in the Talmud: "It should not occur to you that during the days of the messiah a single thing from the 'ways of the world' will be cancelled nor will there be something novel in the Creation. Rather, the world will continue in its customary way."[53] The only real difference between the present age and the days of the messiah is that in the messianic period, the Jews will no longer be subservient

48. *TB* Sotah 49b.

49. *TB* Sanhedrin 98b. See the statement of Rav Gidel in the name of Rav.

50. *TB* Sanhedrin 98a.

51. *TB* Sanhedrin 98b.

52. Burdett, *Eschatology*, 90.

53. Maimonides, *MT*, 12:1. Maimonides takes a somewhat more miraculous approach in his "Letter to the Jews of Yemen."

to the nations.[54] Maimonides, however, warns that "regarding all these matters and similar, no one knows how it will be until it will be."[55] He explains that there is no fixed tradition concerning these matters and, for that reason, one should not be too dogmatic about what will take place in the end of days or seek to "calculate the end."[56]

These ancient and medieval eschatological presentations do not feature computers, but they do contain the idea of the attainment of an ultimate unity and a future suffused with unbounded knowledge, features which characterize the technological futures we have considered. Isaiah declares: "For the Earth shall be filled with knowledge of the Lord, as the waters cover the sea" (Isa 11:9). Maimonides ends his discussion on the messianic era by quoting this verse, which signals for him the future preoccupation with attaining "knowledge of God." Maimonides writes that in the messianic period, there will be "very wise people" who will "achieve knowledge of the Creator to as high a degree as humanly possible."[57] A similar idea is found in the later mystical work, the *Zohar*, when speculating on the six-hundredth year of the sixth millennium: "The gates of wisdom above, together with the wellsprings of wisdom below, will open up."[58]

As for the singularity, Zechariah declares, "And the LORD shall be king over all the earth; in that day there shall be one LORD with one name" (Zech 14:9).[59] Rabbi Nissim of Girona (the Ran) (1320–1376) explains on this verse that while God is always one, his name is not one. He writes that as matters currently stand, "all people believe themselves to be serving God and consider that they call upon His name . . . but their views of God are different."[60]

Each person sees things from her own perspective, but in the future, this will change: "In the end of days . . . humanity shall perceive Him, and He shall be one just as His name now is one."[61] The Ran may well be expanding here upon Maimonides's exposition of the same verse in the *Guide for the Perplexed*. Maimonides explains there that in the future

---

54. Maimonides, *MT*, 12:2.

55. Maimonides, *MT*, 12:2.

56. Maimonides, *MT*, 12:2.

57. Maimonides, *MT*, 12:5.

58. *Zohar* 1:116b:3.

59. This year corresponds to 5600 in the Jewish calendar and 1840 CE.

60. Ran, *Darashot ha-Ran* 7:43.

61. Ran, *Darashot ha-Ran* 7:43.

only the tetragrammaton (*YHVH*), the name indicative of God's true essence, will be invoked, rather than derivative names which arose only after creation.[62]

The Ran does not explain how this future state will come about, but AI might provide him with the answer—superintelligence, dataism, the singularity. Religious futurology and technological prediction dovetail.

I am not suggesting that religion supports or miraculously foresaw the technological ideas of the future that we have examined, but only that there are overlaps, points of similarity, common hopes and aspirations.

But there are also real differences. The most obvious relates to ethics. For secular futurologists, the future is a matter of technological advancement. The purpose of technology is to improve the human condition and make the world a happier, better place. Technology brings this about by operating in accordance with its programming through the law of cause and effect. Perfection is associated with technological enhancement.[63] In contrast, religions see the future as being dependent on the ethical choices we make today. These choices are not dictated purely by the laws of physics but by ethical action, ritual, values, and obligation. It is we, not machines, which carry the burden. Perfection is about becoming kinder, more caring people.

A second difference relates to the place and power of knowledge. Technological futures rely on an insatiable appetite for knowledge. The ultimate purpose of that knowledge is to control chaos, defeat death, achieve immortality, and to overcome the human situation.[64] The Hebrew Bible understands the power of knowledge, but also its dangers. In Genesis, Adam and Eve are granted permission to eat whatever they like from the garden of Eden, "but as for the tree of knowledge of good and bad, you must not eat of it; for as soon as you eat of it, you shall die" (Gen 2:16–17). And so it was. Eating of the tree of knowledge resulted in death: "For dust you are, And to dust you shall return" (Gen 3:19).

Although depicted in Genesis as a divine decree, we are aware through experience that indulging our appetite to know everything, without also seeking wisdom, can lead to disaster. Our technological age, which has brought immense benefits, also brought us the factory and the human misery that led to, environmental destruction, and the atom

62. Maimondes, *Guide*, I.63.

63. Tirosh-Samuelson, "Pursuit of Perfection," 205–7.

64. Tirosh-Samuelson, "Pursuit of Perfection," 203.

bomb. Knowledge also awakens us to our own inevitable demise. After eating from the tree, Adam and Eve learned that they would die.

For Kurzweil and other transhumanists, death is a barrier to be overcome. For the Hebrew Bible and the traditions that emerge from it, death gives life its sanctity and direction. The afterlife hardly features in the pages of the Hebrew Bible, and the idea of resurrection and later notions of the world to come do not undermine the significance of the temporal. An awareness of death is an inspiration for correct living and a stimulus to ensure the transmission of values down to the next generation.

As we will see in more detail later, Heidegger saw the anxiety of death as the mark of being in the world, *Dasein*, which when faced resolutely leads one to authenticity. Ernest Becker (1924–1974), the American psychologist, also saw the fear of death as dominating all human endeavor. He considered that religion and other myths act to counter or help repress the truth of our own demise. In his 1973 Pulitzer Prize–winning book, *The Denial of Death*, Becker claimed that the fear of death leads people to seek immortality through religion, parenting, and lasting works. The thought of death also increases our respect for authority and brings us closer to our own tribe while distancing us from others.[65] Many of these features have been shown to exist through experiment by Becker's followers.[66]

Heidegger and Becker might both be correct. Knowledge brings us to an awareness of death which at one and the same time moves us toward authenticity, and back to our roots—to both independence from and an attachment to our ancient traditions. It both frees us and calls us to return. This is the story of Adam and Eve and their encounter with knowledge, death, exile, and a desire for wholeness. The Jewish philosopher Franz Rosenzweig (1886–1929) too is taken with the theme of fear of death, the nothingness that is uniquely our own, which he sees as a prelude to attaining knowledge of the All.[67]

It is not inevitable that greater knowledge will lead to our demise. Rabbi Levi of Berditchev (1740–1809), the Hasidic Master, considered Adam and Eve's mistake to be not their desire for knowledge, but the absence of wisdom and righteousness which is required for knowledge to be truly valuable. Rabbi Levi explains that in the future the righteous will help us succeed in acquiring such qualities:

65. Becker, *Denial of Death*.
66. Solomon, *Worm at the Core*.
67. Pollock, *Franz Rosenzweig*, 127–28.

The good deeds performed by the righteous reverse this entire process and, ultimately, when brought to its successful conclusion, will enable a different world from the one we are familiar with to be revealed even on earth.[68]

The idea that we must prepare ourselves spiritually and ethically to receive knowledge is foreign to contemporary thinking, but in an age where the danger of knowledge in the wrong hands is so acute, we should think again about the role of wisdom and ethics in knowledge attainment, dissemination, and application.

The third difference between the technical and religious futures is the aspiration toward oneness, already touched upon. Within the monotheistic traditions, such oneness relates directly to God. At the heart of all monotheistic religion is God's unity. Jews declare this in the *Shema* prayer, already mentioned: "Hear, O Israel! The LORD is our God, the LORD is one" (Deut 6:4; my translation).

Jewish mystics have taken this to mean that there can be no creation separate from God. Creation presents only an illusion of division. This is monism or non-dualism, the denial of difference between mind and matter and God and the world. A related concept is acosmism, the notion that God is the sole reality. Nothing exists independently from him.

Thus, Rabbi Yehudah Aryeh Leib Alter, the Sefat Emet (1847–1905), explained that the meaning of the term "God is One" in the *Shema* is not that there is only one God but that "there is no being other than Him, even though it seems otherwise to most people."[69] In this book, I use the term "oneness" to cover these and other associated ideas.

The thirteenth-century *Zohar* writes that, in reality, God "fills and surrounds all worlds."[70] The *Tikunei ha-Zohar*, an appendix to the *Zohar*, similarly states, "There is no place from which He is free."[71]

Later, Rabbi Moshe Cordovero (1522–1570) declared that "God is all reality, but not all reality is God . . . He is found in all things, and all things are found in Him, and there is nothing devoid of God's divinity, God forbid. Everything is in God, and God is in everything and beyond everything, and there is nothing else besides God."[72]

68. Levi, *Kedushat Levi*, on Genesis 25.

69. *Otzar Ma'amarim u'Michtavim*, 75f., quoted in Green, *Ehyeh*, 22–23.

70. *Zohar* 3:225a.

71. *Tikunei Zohar* 57.

72. *Elimah Rabbati* 34d–25a, quoted in Michaelson, *Everything Is God*, 62–63.

The *Alenu* prayer, recited by practicing Jews three times a day, contains the biblical verse: "Know therefore this day and keep in mind that the LORD alone is God in heaven above and on earth below; there is no other" (Deut 4:39). Jewish mystics have taken the last few words literally: God is all that there is. According to Rabbi Isaiah Horowitz (1565–1630) (the Shelah), the words "there is no other" mean "nothing exists except God."[73] The same prayer ends with the verse from Zechariah cited above to illustrate the biblical idea of a singularity: "And the LORD shall be king over all the earth; in that day there shall be one LORD with one name" (Zech 14:9). To those with mystical leanings, the prayer is a constant signifier of the monistic or acosmic potencies inherent within the monotheistic tradition.

The first Rebbe of Lubavitch, the Hasidic Master, Rabbi Shneur Zalman of Liady (1745–1812), explained that

> in as much as this world and likewise all supernal worlds do not effect any change in His blessed Unity . . . For just as He was All Alone, Single and Unique, before they were created, so is He One and Alone, Single and Unique after they were created, since, beside Him, everything is as nothing, verily as null and void.

Rabbi Shneur Zalman continues to explain that everything we experience is only the "word of God" and "breath of His blessed mouth."[74]

I see nothing particularly strange in the emergence of monistic ideas out of monotheism. Such ideas suggest themselves as soon as we describe God as omnipresent and perfect. If God is everywhere and perfect, there can be no place where God is not, and the notion that the world has any existence independent of God becomes unthinkable.[75] The idea of God as One also suggests the absence of anything else.

Rabbi Aaron Halevi Horowitz of Starosyle (1766–1828), a disciple of Rabbi Shneur Zalman, uses similar reasoning in his *Shar Yichud ve-Emunah* to arrive at a view that all existence is subsumed in the divine and dependent on it. He observes that those "lacking in knowledge" accept that God has no body but consider the world to comprise matter separate from God which God brought into being. Rabbi Aaron

73. *Shenei Luchot ha-Brit* 189b, quoted in Michaelson, *Everything Is God*, 50.

74. Zalman, *Tanya*, chs. 22, 33.

75. Samuel Lebens explores such reasoning in "Nothing Else," 15–17, where he argues from the idea of God's omnipotence and perfection to a "Hasidic idealism," which holds that all objects are ideas in the mind of God.

considers that such a view relies on an erroneous understanding of God and matter. If one considers matter as something real in itself and distinct from God, one needs to either accept dualism—that God and the world are completely separate, which cannot be—or else maintain that God is in the world, which means that God changes as the world changes. This latter view is also false because it ascribes change to God.[76] Rabbi Aaron concludes that "we are obliged to believe that the worlds have no existence apart from God, Blessed be He, and that He, Blessed be He, and the worlds are one, for there is nothing apart from Him and nothing outside of Him."[77]

He writes that the truth of this observation will become most apparent in the messianic period. At that time, "the divine will be revealed in the category of uniformity, as it is said: 'They shall see eye to eye' (Isaiah 52:8). And this is sufficient for one who understands. Understand it well."[78]

The idea of an imminent God, however, is not just a matter of religious reasoning or kabbalistic tradition, it is an essential message of the Hebrew Bible, although one which is delivered subtly, and perhaps because of such subtlety is often overlooked.

Milton Scarborough refers to a "Hebrew pre-philosophical non-dualism" which he contrasts with Greek philosophical dualism. He claims that such Greek dualism has dominated Western society. Dualism involves expressing aspects of being in binary terms; body and soul, physical and spiritual, time and eternity, good and evil, or transcendent and immanent as applied to God. Dualistic thinking distorts because we end up dividing the world artificially, favoring one side of each pair over the other and denouncing everything which falls on the "wrong" side. It encourages pigeon-holing and pendulum-like swings from one extreme to another in everything from religion to race, gender to politics. Dualistic thinking is also premised on things being fixed, permanent, and impervious to change, which they are not.[79]

Scarborough sees the Bible as inherently non-dualist. Biblical commands make no distinction between reason and passion, soul and body,

---

76. *Shar Yichud ve-Emunah*, II.15.21a–b, quoted and explained in Jacobs, *Seeker of Unity*, 97.

77. *Shar Yichud ve-Emunah*, II.15.21a–b, quoted and explained in Jacobs, *Seeker of Unity*, 97.

78. *Shar Yichud ve-Emunah*, V.23.28a, quoted in Jacobs, *Seeker of Unity*, 108.

79. Scarborough, *Comparative Theories*, 8–9.

knowledge and ignorance. The concepts which replace or overcome these dualities are action, the person, and faith.[80] Living faithfully requires the whole person to act in a particular way, without need for any recourse to the dualities just listed. God also has no permanent or fixed essence.[81] Biblical statements about God tell us only about God's relationship to human beings in the world, not how he actually is.[82] Within the Hebrew Bible, figures often occupy places which are neither in nor out. Abraham, for example, on his way to Canaan is "neither stuck in the Land of Ignorance (Ur), nor has he arrived in the Land of Knowledge (the Promised Land)." Instead, he "traverses the Land of Learning."[83] Scarborough thinks that we have failed to notice these things because we have been reading the Bible through Greek eyes or the eyes of interpreters schooled in the ancient Greeks.[84]

Lenn Goodman makes similar points to Scarborough in relation to descriptions of God in the Talmud and Midrash. However, for Goodman, ideas of immanence are not intended to teach anything about the philosophy of being, but only about ethics: "Immanence is an ethos not an ontology."[85] Goodman further sees no stark divide between immanence and transcendence when applied to God.[86] God is at once near and far. For him, the idea of the remoteness of the God of Israel is "a Hegelian brickbat, a relic of ancient anti-Jewish polemics on behalf of Christian incarnationsim."[87]

Although there is good reason to accentuate the non-dualistic current within the Hebrew Bible and later Jewish tradition, we cannot ignore the Hebrew Bible's dominant dualistic aspect. God may have no fixed

80. Scarborough, *Comparative Theories*, 42.

81. Jonathan Sacks also seeks to distinguish the Bible's outlook from platonic dualism in the context of choseness and the other. See Sacks, *Not in God's Name*.

82. Scarborough, *Comparative Theories*, 47. Scarborough relies here on the thought of Rabbi Abraham Heschel (1907–1972).

83. Scarborough, *Comparative Theories*, 129–30.

84. Scarborough, *Comparative Theories*, 34.

85. Goodman, *Jewish Themes*, 66. Goodman's examples include: "God is always before us" (Ps 16:8); "God's presence is with the righteous wherever they may be" (Genesis Rabbah 86:6); and "God is manifest in a good marriage, eclipsed in a hostile one" (*TB* Sotah 17a).

86. Goodman, *Jewish Themes*, 66. Goodman states, "'The God who walked in the midst of the camp of Israel' (Deut 23:15) was the same of whom the Psalmist said, 'In Thy presence is the fullness of joy' (Ps 16:11) and of whom R. Gamliel said 'There is no place of earth devoid of God's presence' (*Pesikta de R. Kahana*, ed. Buber, 2b)."

87. Goodman, *Jewish Themes*, 66.

essence and liminality may abound, but the Bible is constantly making distinctions—distinctions between light and darkness, good and bad, Israel and the nations, the God of heaven and the God of earth. Non-dualism is detectable, but is most evident beneath the surface of the text.[88]

Those attracted to the more mystical expressions of the doctrine of immanence might be tempted to whole-heartedly embrace the idea of an AI singularity resulting in a superintelligence or singleton in which we all participate. But that would be to ignore the dominant trend within the Hebrew Bible and later Judaism of treating God as separate from the world and taking existence as you find it. The messianic ideal might look forward to a singularity of sorts, but it is just that, an ideal, the realization of which is never quite reached.

There is good reason to view the singularity as always "not yet." Oneness, whether theological or technological, threatens to consume us in its totality. It should be approached warily. A world dedicated only to data and knowledge acquisition is to relive Adam and Eve's fatal mistake of seeking knowledge before the proper time, without proper moral and spiritual preparation. The tower of Babel (Gen 11:1–9) also has a message here. It represents an early attempt by humanity to use new technology (brick making and construction) to put humanity on a par with God. By giving each person a different language, God signals the primacy of communication and relationship over uniformity or union with the divine.

To summarize, in the 1950s, the singularity came to be associated with a point-of-no-return at which computers will outperform humans. From the 1960s, academics and science fiction writers described the ultra-intelligent machines that would bring this about. In 2006, Ray Kurzweil expanded this vision by describing a world in which there will be no distinction between man and machine. Nick Bostrom has described the pathways by which machines will become super-intelligent and speculated on the possibility of a single superintelligence. Yuval Noah Harari envisages a world organized under the principle of dataism, an Internet-of-All-Things which will spread throughout the universe. I have engaged with these ideas as metaphors for our modern way of thinking and am using them as a jumping-off point to consider the world of technique.

---

88. Samuel Lebens, in "Nothing Else," and elsewhere in collaboration with Tyron Goldschmidt, attempts to explain Jewish "nothing-elsism" philosophically and to reconcile the notion with traditional theism. My approach is to recognize "nothing-elsism" and traditional theism as two distinct orientations within various Jewish traditions and to explore our relationship with them phenomenologically.

I have further associated ideas of a single superintelligence or singularity with the idea of God as everything. I have also considered them alongside biblical and later Jewish depictions of the end of days and sought to distinguish such depictions from their secular technological counterparts. At the center of the religious vision is ethics, meaning, the sanctity of our transitory lives, redemption, and God as all and other. I have made the point that both these aspects of God are important. The Jewish tradition has space for the notion of a singularity in which we are a part, but at its heart contains a call for relationship, which requires entities to be distinct.

In the pages that follow, I will suggest that a wholesome religious path requires a consciousness of, and orientation toward, oneness, but that sense of the singularity is only the starting point. The next step is to embrace individuation and variety, to engage the concrete universe in all its difference, beauty, and chaos.

Judaism offers insights and a path here. In its various instantiations, Judaism has sought to convey the message of a oneness whose name cannot be spoken, a oneness which is present but beyond our everyday consciousness. However, there is a sense that to allow that presence to fill the space of our consciousness would be to cause world collapse. The perceived task is to prevent the many becoming subsumed within the All, to champion difference, perspective, complexity, the multifarious.

We are wary of anything that seeks to homogenize, that insists on a single viewpoint or end point. We sustain the paradox, individuation in a simple unity, the holy and profane, what is and what we experience as distinctly valuable.

What this means and what this entails is what we learn, teach, and speak about when we lie down, when we get up, and when we walk on our way (Deut 6:9). We instill it in our children and live it ourselves, walking the tight rope between reason and mysticism, science and imagination, the universal and the particular. Science, reason, notions of oneness, and the singularity reflect the universal. Mysticism and imagination reflect the particular. But these things are all intertwined.

In the next chapter, I want to consider the philosophical roots of the modern conception of the singularity to put it on a rational footing, demonstrate its universal benefit, and to build a path from there back to the world as we experience it.

# 3

# Spinoza, Philosopher of the Singularity

JONATHAN ISRAEL, IN HIS book *Radical Enlightenment: Philosophy and the Making of Modernity* 1650–1750, credits Spinoza as the originator of the core principles of modern thought, including naturalism: the idea that the world can be understood from nature rather than supernatural causes. He writes:

> No one else during the century 1650–1750 remotely rivalled Spinoza's notoriety as the chief challenger of the fundamentals of revealed religion, received ideas, tradition, morality, and what was regarded, in absolutist and non-absolutist states alike, as divinely constituted political authority.[1]

We can go further. Spinoza's ideas characterize our scientific and technological worldview and preempt Kurzweil and other futurists, who conceive the future as a unity and also view technology as the answer to all human ills. Spinoza's focus on immanence is at one with modernity's attempt to undermine the transcendent.[2] In this chapter, I want to explore Spinoza's thought and its relationship to the technological world which we inhabit, but first let us consider Spinoza's biography.

## A Life

Why should we be interested in a philosopher's life? Not just because it is interesting. Spinoza's life is fascinating, but Spinoza's life story, or more

1. Israel, *Radical Enlightenment*, 159.
2. Tirosh-Samuelson, "Pursuit of Perfection," 204. See also Taylor, *Secular Age*.

accurately, the way it has been constructed by his biographers, is important for understanding how his philosophy has been taught and received.
Spinoza was born in an age in which a philosopher was expected to live
out his philosophy.

A philosopher's life was viewed as exemplary of a certain school:
"The role of the moral philosopher was to impart a way of life derived
from his heritage to young people and provide a standard to shoot for
in trying to lead such a life." For this reason, "early modern philosophies
were often built around ideal lives."[3]

Philosophy was viewed as medicine, as a therapy for the troubled
soul or troubled times.[4] Nowadays there is little expectation of philosophers living up to their own philosophies.[5] Spinoza's life story is meant to
inspire us to his way of thinking, and it does.

Spinoza was a strong believer in cause and effect. He believed that
any book, including the Bible, and any person, including Moses, needs to
be understood in its historical context. What events shaped them? What
causes brought them about? Spinoza's approach invites us to treat his life
in the same way, to mine it for insights into how to live in the knowledge
of oneness.

Spinoza's life also speaks to those of us rooted in a tradition, cognizant not only of its flaws but the flaws of religion in general, but who
nevertheless seek a spirituality which is at once rational, unifying, and
therapeutic. In this book, I can only describe Spinoza's life in the barest
detail.

Spinoza was born in 1632. His father was an important member of
the Amsterdam Jewish community and sent his son to the local Jewish
school. Spinoza learned Bible and gained familiarity with works of the
medieval Jewish philosophers, including Maimonides and Levi Ben Ger-
son (1288–1344) (Gersonides or the Ralbag). He also had some exposure
to kabbalistic ideas but would not have learned Talmud in any depth.[6]

His early life was beset by tragedy. Between 1638 and 1654, he
lost his mother, father, and a brother. After his father died, he became
closer to his associates outside the Jewish community including members of dissenting Christian sects such as Menonites, Remonstrants, and

3. Garrett, "Lives of Philosophers," 6.

4. Garrett, "Lives of Philosophers," 8.

5. Ethics professors apparently have real difficulty in acting ethically. See Burkeman, "Why Are Ethicists So Unethical?," paras. 1–4, and Whipple, "Ethics Professors."

6. Nadler, Spinoza, 52, 54, 63–65. See also Beltrán, Influence.

Quakers.[7] The Dutch Republic at this time was Calvinist but provided a relatively tolerant environment for different denominations and faiths, which allowed for the easy exchange of ideas.

Spinoza spent a great deal of his time hanging round bookshops. A man by the name of Franciscus van Den Enden became Spinoza's mentor. He was a bookselling, hippy type in his 50s, who was an ex-Jesuit priest. He taught Spinoza Latin, Greek, and the Humanities.[8] According to Johannes Colerus (1647–1707), Spinoza's early biographer, Spinoza fell in love with van Den Enden's daughter, who was much younger than Spinoza. She did not return his affections and married Spinoza's friend. Spinoza never married.[9]

Spinoza's main early attraction was the thought of René Descartes (1596–1650), the French philosopher who lived in Amsterdam for a time and had published his *Discourse on Method* just five years after Spinoza's birth.[10] This work declared that every human being is capable of reason with the right training. In 1639, Descartes began working on his *Meditations*.

Descartes explored how we come to know anything, including how we exist. His well-known answer to the above question, *cogito ergo sum*, basically, "I think, therefore there must be a thinker doing the thinking," provides the foundation for the building of a philosophy from the ground up as an alternative to relying on divine or ecclesiastical authority.[11] Reason was central to this quest.

Descartes, like most other thinkers living in his time, was a theist, but his God is different to the biblical God. God for Descartes is justified philosophically. He is "a supremely perfect being,"[12] the entity which holds everything in place, the guarantor of Descartes's system. Moreover, God is not unknowable. His nature, like everything else, is subject to rational inquiry. Descartes had a profound influence on Spinoza and other youngsters of his generation seeking answers to life's great questions.

It would have been obvious to Spinoza when surveying the state of the world that religion could do with a shot of reason. At the time

---

7. Nadler, *Spinoza*, 101 and 107.

8. Nadler, *Spinoza*, 103–7.

9. Nadler, *Spinoza*, 108.

10. Nadler, *Spinoza*, 111–13.

11. Descartes, *Philosophical Writings*, 1:195.

12. Descartes, *Philosophical Writings*, 2:45.

of Spinoza's birth, Europe was mired in the Thirty Years War. The war started in 1618 when Emperor Ferdinand II became the head of the Holy Roman Empire, a group of multiethnic territories bound together since the early medieval period. At its core, the Thirty Years War was about power and politics, but religion provided the impetus and was exploited to inspire the masses to contribute to the war effort.

Religious conflict began to foment when Ferdinand II forced the citizens of the empire to adhere to Roman Catholicism. The Bohemian nobility rejected the emperor and showed their displeasure by throwing his representatives out of a window at Prague Castle. Other states joined in. The war started as a battle between Protestant and Catholic states within the Holy Roman Empire but developed into a broader conflict.

The Peace of Westphalia of 1648 ended the Thirty Years' War and gave the territories of the Holy Roman Empire their independence. About 8 million people lost their lives from the war and its effects: lawlessness, famine, and plague.[13] To a thoughtful boy like Spinoza, growing up in its aftermath, the war would have hammered home the destructive force of religious belief and the need for tolerance.

Spinoza would not have been the only one to have drawn such conclusions. The French writer Émeric Crucé stressed the need for tolerance between Christian denominations and all religions: "All nations are bound together by a natural and consequently indestructible tie, which ensures that a man cannot consider another to be a stranger."[14] Maximilien de Béthune, the first Duke of Sully, and adviser to the French king, Henri IV, espoused a "principle of equilibrium" under which European nations would form a confederation to deal with matters together. To avoid conflict between states, he suggested that nations be about the same size and have similar wealth.[15] Hugo Grotius, the great statesman, also sought to bring an end to conflict by promoting tolerance and the practical application of reason.[16]

Spinoza would have found evidence of religion's destructive force closer to home. Michael de Spinoza, Spinoza's father, had come to the Netherlands as a child from Portugal to escape the Inquisition. This was established to "out" the heretics from among Jewish and Islamic converts

13. On the war and its causes see Gillespie, *Causes of War*, 136–61.
14. Crucé, *New Cyneas*, quoted in Gillespie, *Causes of War*, 158.
15. Gillespie, *Causes of War*, 158.
16. Gillespie, *Causes of War*, 159.

to Catholicism. Later, New Christians, or *Conversos*, that is, Jews who had converted to Christianity during the inquisition while secretly remaining Jews, wanted to be reintegrated. These would-be returnees rejected Christianity but were not altogether comfortable with their Judaism, either. Having been cut off from Judaism for some time, they found some of its teachings strange and puzzling. The Jewish community, for its part, was confused about how to treat the newcomers.

There is a tradition in the Mishnah, the foundational work of the Talmud (c. 200 CE), that "all Israel merit a portion in the world to come,"[17] but the rabbis of Amsterdam were unsure whether the returnees from the lands of the Inquisition would benefit from this promise. Were these people fully fledged Jews, or did their conversion to Christianity mean they had lost their immortal Jewish soul? The question of the immortality of the soul and the place of returning Jews were sensitive issues at the time.[18] The conflicts faced by Conversos is summed up in the life of one man.

Uriel da Costa (1585–1640) was baptized in Portugal into a converted family. He studied Church law and became a treasurer of the Church but became disillusioned with Christianity. He was particularly troubled by the idea of hell. In search of his Jewish roots, he moved from Portugal to Amsterdam, but soon also became disillusioned with rabbinic Judaism. Instead of abandoning his faith, he made it his mission to purify Judaism, a program which did not, for obvious reasons, endear him to the rabbis of his community.

Da Costa moved to Hamburg where in 1616, he composed eleven theses rejecting rabbinic Judaism, which he called "a strange cult." The idea of composing theses was not new. Martin Luther, the founder of Protestantism, had nailed his ninety-five theses to the Wittenberg Castle church in his efforts to reform Christianity. Da Costa's bid to be the Jewish Luther (with his paltry eleven theses) was not to be. In 1618, the rabbis placed a ban (*Herem*) on him. A *Herem* in the Bible denotes the destruction of those who worship false gods or the destruction or banning of enemy property (Exod 22:19; Deut 7:1–9), but in later Jewish law came to refer to a form of censure, or in extreme cases, excommunication, which

17. Mishnah Sanhedrin 11:1.
18. Nadler, *Spinoza*, 52–55.

along with *Nidui* and *Nezifah*, was meted out as a punishment for transgressing Jewish law.[19]

Da Costa was not put off. In 1624, he returned to Amsterdam where he wrote an examination of rabbinic tradition. In this, he challenged the belief in an immortal soul, which he claimed was introduced by the rabbis. For his pains, he was excommunicated again, this time by the Amsterdam rabbis. His mother, who stood by him, suffered the same fate, although she was eventually allowed to be buried in a Jewish cemetery. Da Costa would not give up on his invective. He claimed that the Oral Torah (the rabbinic writings) was the work of man and contrary to nature. The rabbis sent a group of Christians to seek da Costa's counsel pretending that they intended to convert to Judaism. They managed to persuade him to reveal what he really thought. His heresy was exposed. In 1633, the rabbis increased the severity of the *Herem* imposed upon him. This was the same year that the Inquisition commenced its investigation into Galileo Galilei (1564–1642), the physicist and astronomer, and his support for Copernicus's idea that the earth revolves around the sun.

Seven years went by, after which time, da Costa decided, for pragmatic reasons, to relent and seek reintegration into the Jewish community. He wrote that this made him feel like an "ape among the apes." The rabbis agreed to accept him back on condition that he would accept his punishment. He was apparently given thirty-nine lashes, a standard talmudic punishment, then made to lie down on the threshold of the synagogue while each member of the community was invited to line up for an opportunity to step on him. After the humiliation, he wrote his autobiography, which contains the account described above, then shot himself.[20]

Is the story accurate? Probably not all of it, but it is likely that da Costa would have been made to undergo at least some of the humiliations he describes.[21] The rabbinic leadership was fearful of the ideas carried by those returning to Judaism from Catholicism. The Dutch authorities also expected the Jewish community to do their bit in rooting out nonconformist ideas that might threaten religious belief.

Spinoza was eight years old when da Costa died. Presumably, Spinoza learned about the life of this Jewish renegade when he became older.

19. *TB* Brachot 19a; *TB* Baba Metziah 59b; *Shulchan Aruch* Yoreh Deah 334:14; Nadler, *Spinoza*, 121–22.

20. On da Costa, see Nadler, *Spinoza*, 66–74.

21. Nadler, *Spinoza*, 72.

From da Costa, Spinoza would have understood the dangers of asking too many questions, yet questions were begging to be asked.

On July 27, 1656, Spinoza was excommunicated from his community. The ban was delivered by six *Parnassim* (lay leaders) and the *Gabbai* (organizer of religious ceremonies) of the Jewish community and is noteworthy for its severity. It reads:

> By decree of the angels and by the command of the holy men, we excommunicate, expel, curse and damn Baruch de Espinoza, with the consent of God, Blessed be He, and with the consent of the entire holy congregation, and in front of these holy scrolls with the 613 precepts which are written therein . . . Cursed be he by day and cursed be he by night; cursed be he when he lies down and cursed be he when he rises up. Cursed be he when he goes out and cursed be he when he comes in. The Lord will not spare him . . . And the Lord shall separate him unto evil out of all the tribes of Israel, according to all the curses of the covenant that are written in this book of the law.[22]

As these words make clear, there was no way back for Spinoza. This is not a temporary ban, a warning, or indirect call for repentance. Da Costa was free to rejoin the community by repenting. This path was not open to Spinoza. The community was not even permitted to offer him assistance: "No one should communicate with him neither in writing nor accord him any favor nor stay with him under the same roof nor within four cubits in his vicinity; nor shall he read any treatise composed or written by him."[23] There was to be a complete parting of the ways.

What had he done to deserve such a severe sentence? It is unclear. He had not published anything by this time. The text of the ban refers to the community leaders "having long known" of Spinoza's "evil opinions and acts," but we can only guess at what these were. It has been suggested that he might have failed to pay his synagogue membership fees, but one assumes that if this was the case, it must have been the thin edge of the wedge. It is a fair assumption that his views would have approximated those which he set down in writing a few years later.[24] The *Herem* suggests

22. Kasher, "Why Was Baruch Spinoza Excommunicated?," 98–141; Nadler, *Spinoza*, 143.

23. Kasher, "Why Was Baruch Spinoza Excommunicated?," 98–141; Nadler, *Spinoza*, 143.

24. Steven Nadler has claimed that the roots of the extreme nature of the ban lies in Spinoza's rejection of the immortality of the soul. As explained above, the issue was

that efforts were made to encourage Spinoza to "mend his wicked ways," but having daily received more and more serious information about the "abominable heresies" and "monstrous deeds," the leaders became convinced of the truth of the allegations and decided to expel Spinoza from the community of Israel.[25]

Spinoza dealt with his excommunication stoically, as his philosophy would come to demand, and went on to bigger and better things. He moved from Amsterdam to Ouderkerk aan de Amstel, but he soon returned to Amsterdam where he took up lens grinding and taught philosophy privately. The famed Dutch mathematician and scientist, Christiaan Huygens, was said to be a great fan of his lenses.[26] The German philosopher Georg Wilhelm Friedrich Hegel (1770–1831) said of Spinoza's chosen profession: "It was no arbitrary choice that led him to occupy himself with light, for it represents in the material sphere the absolute identity which forms the foundation of the oriental view of things."[27] Spinoza became God-obsessed, drunk on light, the infinite, and its refraction.

During this period, Spinoza wrote his first philosophical work, entitled *A Short Treatise on God, Man, and His Well-Being*. In 1660 or 1661, he moved to Rijnsburg where he wrote his *Principle of Cartesian Philosophy* (1663). There, he also began to work on his masterpiece, the *Ethics*, which was published only after his death. The *Ethics* is a dry technical work written in the form of Euclid's *Geometry*. It contains Spinoza's developed philosophy on God and Nature, and human ethics. In 1670, Spinoza published his *Theological-Political Treatise*. The work was targeted at thinking clergy and other leaders capable of embracing reason. It deals with matters of politics and religion and includes Spinoza's ideas on the historicity and nature of the Bible.

The *Theological-Political Treatise* was published anonymously, but everyone knew it was written by Spinoza. People saw it as supporting the constitutional regime of Jan de Witt, the Grand Pensionary of the Netherlands. That same year, Spinoza moved to the Hague, perhaps fearing persecution at the hands of the supporters of the Prince of Orange. He had other reasons to be fearful. One commentator described the

a sensitive one when it came to those who had converted to Catholicism during the Inquisitions, and their children. Nadler, *Spinoza's Heresy*, 183–84.

25. On the broader context of the *Herem*, see Nadler, *Spinoza*, 147–54.

26. Nadler, *Spinoza*, 183, 221–22.

27. Hegel, *Lectures*, III.253.

*Theological-Political Treatise* as a book "forged in hell."[28] Politically and religiously, it was dynamite.[29]

In 1672, Jan de Witt and his brother, Cornelius, who had been sentenced to jail for treason, were murdered by a mob supporting the Prince of Orange. Spinoza was deeply affected by the brutality of these murders. They would have confirmed his view of the danger of the passions elucidated in the *Ethics*. In 1673, Spinoza turned down an offer to teach philosophy at the University of Heidelberg. In 1674, the *Theological-Political Treatise* was banned in Holland.[30]

In 1675, Spinoza completed the *Ethics*, but accusations of atheism were already circulating, and Spinoza dared not publish it.[31] In 1676, Spinoza became ill and on February 12, 1677, he died. He was forty-four. After his death, his friends published posthumously his *Ethics*, his tractate *On the Improvement of the Understanding*, his letters, and a work of Hebrew grammar.[32]

What is the story of Spinoza's life meant to teach? The answer is how to live rationally, stoically, and dispassionately in the presence of the one of which we are a part, a substance without will or reason but capable of being loved through knowledge. The story of his life, even if embellished to reflect his philosophy, offers practical philosophical guidance. Spinoza is portrayed as a man of detached calm, displaying a rational, stoic intelligence.

He was not broken by the deaths in his family, his excommunication, or the troubled times in which he lived. He did not seek to blame God for his final illness. During the Anglo-Dutch war, he wrote to Henry Oldenburg, explaining that the horrors of war "do not move me to laughter or tears, but rather they incite me to philosophizing, and to the better observation of human nature."[33]

According to Pierre Bayle (1647–1706), the Huguenot philosopher, the peasants in the villages where Spinoza lived found him to be "sociable, affable, honest, friendly, and a good moral man." He cared not for

---

28. Nadler, *Spinoza*, 342.

29. Steven Nadler describes the uproar over the book as "one of the most significant events in European intellectual history." Nadler, *Book Forged in Hell*, preface.

30. On this work see Nadler, *Book Forged in Hell*.

31. Nadler, *Spinoza*, 333.

32. Nadler, *Spinoza*, 349–51.

33. Spinoza, *Correspondence*, quoted in Garrett, "Lives of Philosophers," 50.

"wine, good cheer or money."[34] He also appears to have needed no special companion or sexual partner.

I want now to survey the core ideas on which Spinoza's approach to life was based. These relate to God, nature, politics, psychology, and religion. We will see that, at the heart of Spinoza's philosophy, there is an idea similar to that of the singularity, but this is not a future state, but a description of existence in the here and now.

## Spinoza's Big Ideas

### God or Nature

Spinoza's view of God is built on the ideas of Aristotle and Descartes, who we have already mentioned.[35] Central to understanding it are three terms: "substance," "attributes" and "modes," which Descartes believed were the essential elements out of which we construct the world.

For Aristotle, every object in the world is a substance, which itself is a bearer of properties, including the unchangeable essence of a thing. A house, plant, and horse, for example, each encapsulate the bare, self-subsistent, independent essence of those objects.

An attribute, in contrast, represents the changeable properties associated with a substance. A house may have attributes associated with it being made from brick or wood. A horse might have the attribute of blackness or brownness. A plant may be large or small. Attributes do not characterize an object. A horse or plant would still be a horse or plant without being brown or a particular size. For Aristotle, attributes depend on substances, but substances do not depend on attributes.[36]

Descartes in his *Principles of Philosophy and Meditations on First Philosophy* amended this worldview by introducing the notion of "principal attributes" through which substances are perceived. These principle attributes are "thought" and "extension" (physicality). Descartes accepted that substances involve the true essence of a thing but claimed that we only perceive such essences through thought and extension. We do not, therefore, know a horse by its "horseness" or house through its

---

34. Bayle, *Historical and Critical Dictionary* (1738), quoted in Garrett, "Lives of Philosophers," 53.

35. I am indebted for much of the explanation in this section to Beth Lord. See Lord, *Spinoza's Ethics*, 23–29.

36. Lord, *Spinoza's Ethics*, 16.

"houseness," but through the principle attributes that combine to provide the knowledge of a house or horse.[37]

In his *Second Book of Meditations*, Descartes explains how he came to appreciate the nature of the principle attributes. He imagines himself sitting by the fireside rolling some bees wax between his fingers. The wax has no fixed shape. He pulls the ball of wax apart. He pushes it together, but it remains wax. He can even change its consistency by heating the wax and reducing it to a liquid, but it remains wax. Its color, taste, and scent might all change in this process, but we would still call the substance wax. Descartes concludes that there can be no aspect of the wax which we can perceive as constituting the essence of this wax, other than "thought" (the idea of wax) and "extension" (the physical correlate of that idea). We perceive extension and thought as characterizing the nature of all substances.[38]

In addition to the principal attributes of thought and extension which do not change, there are other attributes, which Descartes calls modes. These are changing states and facets that correspond to Aristotle's attributes. So, in our example, a horse might have the mode of "brownness" and the house may have the mode associated with wood or brick, among other modes.

The view that Descartes leaves us with is that the world comprises numerous substances which we perceive as having one of two attributes: thought or extension. Each substance in turn has different modes or states. It is the modes which provide life with its diversity and richness.[39]

Descartes holds that being is made up of numerous different minds comprising the attribute of thought and numerous different objects comprising the attribute of extension, each with different modes. God acts as the guarantor that the objects that we perceive in our minds match the objects having the attribute of extension.[40] In his *Ethics*, Spinoza accepts Descartes basic categories of substance, attribute, and mode, but arrives at a different conclusion from his forebear.

Spinoza starts by defining what he means by the three elements we have encountered. He explains that a substance constitutes the philosophical foundation of a thing, its essence. It relies on no concept other

37. Lord, *Spinoza's Ethics*, 16.
38. See Clarke, "Descartes' Proof," 168–70.
39. Lord, *Spinoza's Ethics*, 17.
40. See Stuart, "Descartes' Proof," 18–21.

than itself. It is "that which exists by itself . . . and is conceived through, or by means of, itself; i.e., the conception of which does not require for its formation the conception of anything else."[41]

Spinoza further explains that a mode is a state of a substance which relies on something else.[42] In our earlier example, brownness is a mode. It depends on substance for its existence. We speak of a brown horse. The substance of a horse precedes brownness and does not depend on it. The horse is a substance but is known through its modes and understood to the intellect through the attribute of extension (if we are talking about a real horse) or the attribute of thought (if we are talking about our conception of a horse). So far, Spinoza's description matches that of Descartes and would be familiar to philosophy students of his day. In setting out his thought, Spinoza relies on various propositions and axioms to demonstrate how the propositions hang together.

Spinoza's first proposition is that a substance is prior in nature to its modes, meaning that modes depend on substances. For a horse (substance) to be brown (mode), there must be a horse (substance). The second proposition is that "two substances having different attributes have nothing in common with each other."[43] This is what Descartes held on the basis that each substance, having a different attribute, is perceived as being independent from the other, and therefore as having nothing in common with the other. Spinoza's third proposition is that if two things have nothing in common, they cannot be the cause of another. One substance cannot therefore cause another. Spinoza's fourth proposition is that substances must be distinguishable either by their attributes or by their modes.

Spinoza only begins to differ from Descartes when he reaches his fifth proposition, which is that "there cannot be two [or more] substances of the same nature or attribute."[44] The reason for this is that substances can only be distinguished by their attributes, not by their modes. Modes are secondary to, and rely, on substances, and constitute only the surface nature of things. They do not therefore distinguish substances. Any substance to be different from another must have a different attribute.

---

41. Spinoza, *Ethics*, I.D3.73.
42. Spinoza, *Ethics*, I.D4, D5.73.
43. Spinoza, *Ethics*, I.PII.74–75.
44. Spinoza, *Ethics*, I.PV.75.

Spinoza is about to undermine his earlier propositions derived from Descartes.

Since there are only two attributes of which we are aware, thought and extension, it follows that there can only be two substances—a substance with the attribute of extension and a substance with the attribute of thought—and not numerous substances (i.e., minds or physical objects) as Descartes believed. This is a radical conclusion, but not yet the end point. There are a few further steps before Spinoza arrives at his conception of God.

In proposition VI, Spinoza takes us back to his definitions to remind us that different substances must have different essences which do not cause or produce the other: "It is absolutely impossible for substance to be produced [by anything else]."[45] Substance, after all, has been defined as that which causes itself and does not depend on anything else to be conceived.

Proposition VII is that a substance's "essence necessarily involves existence, or, existence belongs to its nature."[46] Such existence must be infinite because if substance is finite, its existence would inevitably be negated. Proposition VIII therefore is that a substance is infinite.[47]

It is here that Spinoza hits us with a bombshell. Having started with definitions and propositions derived from Descartes, at proposition VIII he arrives at the conclusion that there cannot be a "*plurality* of substances" but only one substance.[48]

This one substance is not limited to the attributes of thought and extension that we perceive but has an infinity of attributes or ways that it can be perceived or expressed. We just happen to perceive only two of them; the attribute of thought and the attribute of extension.[49]

Spinoza names this one substance, which consists of infinite attributes, each of which expresses its infinite essence, God.[50] Each of God's attributes can only be known "through and by itself."[51] Substance, therefore, is unlike anything that we encounter in the real world but comprises

45. Spinoza, *Ethics*, I.PVI.76.
46. Spinoza, *Ethics*, I.PVII.76.
47. Spinoza, *Ethics*, I.PVII.76.
48. Spinoza, *Ethics*, I.PVIII.78.
49. Spinoza, *Ethics*, I.PIX.78.
50. Spinoza, *Ethics*, I.PX.79.
51. Spinoza, *Ethics*, I.PXI.79.

nature as a whole: *Deus sive Natura*, "God and Nature is one."[52] When Spinoza refers to Nature, he does not mean the natural world but being in its totality, most of which is beyond our intellectual grasp.

St. Anselm is famous for coming up with the "ontological argument" for God's existence. He contends that because God by definition is the greatest possible thing, and because existence is better than non-existence, God must exist. Spinoza provides his own version of this argument, which runs that since God consists of infinite attributes, by definition, God must exist, because without such existence his attributes would lack the quality of infinity.[53] Moreover, since all finite things or modes are part of God, nothing can be conceived without God.[54] God provides the ontological underpinning for all that there is. He makes knowing possible.

Since nature operates according to fixed laws, through the operation of cause and effect, the same must be true of God. Within God, cause and effect arise from the necessity of God's nature alone: "God acts solely from the laws of his nature and is not constrained by any other being."[55] God, however, does not have free will in the way we usually conceive of this. God acts out of his own nature.[56]

The implication is that God as Nature is knowable through the application of reason. If one comes to acquire the knowledge of all causes and effects, one comes to know God:

> To perfect the intellect is nothing else than to understand God
> and the attributes and actions of God which follow from the
> necessity of his nature. Hence the ultimate aim of the man who
> is led by reason, i.e. his highest desire, by which he endeavors
> to govern all other desires, is that which leads to the adequate
> knowledge of himself and of all objects which can be embraced
> by his intelligence [intelligentiam].[57]

Such understanding of nature's cause and effects brings one to the intellectual love of God, *Amor Intellectualis Dei*, which is in fact an expression

---

52. Spinoza, *Ethics*, IV.226.
53. Spinoza, *Ethics*, I.PXI.80.
54. Spinoza, *Ethics* I.PXV.84.
55. Spinoza, *Ethics*, I.PXVII.88.
56. Spinoza, *Ethics*, I.PXXXII.99.
57. Spinoza, *Ethics*, IV.A4.279.

of God's love for himself: "The intellectual love of the mind towards God is part of the infinite love wherewith God loves himself."[58]

There are parallels between Spinoza's God and the idea of the singularity. Both operate out of necessity, both subsume all being into their sphere, both assume the reducibility of being to a series of blind algorithms, and both are engaged in a constant process of self-knowing. This self-knowledge is not a personal human endeavor but undertaken by the system itself. Spinoza calls this self-knowledge the intellectual love of God. Harari refers to dataism. In such a knowledge system, the goal is to master cause and effect, reduce uncertainty. The more uncertainty is reduced, the more the system adheres to the rules of reason until, one might speculate, the system reaches back to the point out of which it was born and swallows itself.

## Human Psychology

For Spinoza, since God is all that there is, each of us must by necessity exist within God: "And accordingly, when we say that the human mind perceives this or that, we say nothing else than that God, not in so far as he is infinite but in so far as he is manifested by the [nature of the] human mind, or as he constitutes the essence of the human mind, has this or that idea."[59]

Spinoza uses the term *Conatus* to describe our individual innate desire to persist.[60] *Conatus* is something like the survival instinct on which evolution depends in Darwin's scheme, or the idea of *Elan Vital*, the "vital impetus" or "vital force" found in Henri Bergson's 1907 book *Creative Evolution*. There is also a parallel between Spinoza's *Conatus*, and Heidegger's notion of *Dasein*, which manifests in the care we experience toward our being in the world, but Spinoza's term lacks that emotional quality.

Elsewhere, Spinoza describes what is meant by an individual. An individual is anything which moves as one.[61] Several bodies that "communicate their motions to each other" are said in certain situations to "form one body or individual which is distinguished from others by the

---

58. Spinoza, *Ethics*, V.PXXXVI.310.
59. Spinoza, *Ethics*, II.PXI.123.
60. Spinoza, *Ethics*, III.PIX.171.
61. Spinoza, *Ethics*, II.PXIII.125.

union of bodies."[62] A crowd or community might therefore be treated as a single entity moving in unison. Similarly, a human body is "composed of many different individuals of different natures,"[63] but the existence of a unifying *Conatus*, as it applies to an individual person, demarcates that person as a bounded thing. It is that which gives us the illusion of self.

According to Spinoza, we each desire through *Conatus* to be in our unique way and to act according to our own nature. We achieve this through the application of reason which demands that "every man should love himself, should seek what is really useful to himself, should desire everything which really leads him to greater perfection; and, in general, that everyone should strive as far as possible to preserve his existence."[64]

In this scheme, we act in accord either with our *Conatus* and reason, which are internal to us, or external causes, those things outside of us which excite the passions. We have nothing amounting to free will: "There is no absolute or free will in the mind, but [the mind] is determined to will this or that by a cause which is also determined by another cause, and this again by another, and so on in infinitum."[65] We have the illusion of freedom because we are aware of our actions but "ignorant of the causes by which those actions are determined."[66]

Reason assists us because it enables us to see things from God's perspective, *sub specie aeternitatis*, rather than from our own temporal perspective, *sub specie durationis*.[67] While we are immersed in our individual lives, without looking at what we colloquially refer to as the "bigger picture," we attain only confused or partial knowledge. In contrast, by seeing things as God sees them, we achieve distance and some objectivity. This allows us to better act in accordance with our *Conatus*, which corresponds to our long-term, rather than short-term, interests.

Reason also allows us to distinguish between internal and external causes by understanding how these things operate. In the *Ethics*, part III, Spinoza describes the mind as both active and passive. When we form "adequate ideas," we trace ideas one from another actively rather than

---

62. Spinoza, *Ethics*, II.A2.126.
63. Spinoza, *Ethics*, III.PXVII.176.
64. Spinoza, *Ethics*, IV.PXVIII.240.
65. Spinoza, *Ethics*, II.PXLVIII.152.
66. Spinoza, *Ethics*, II.PXXXV.141.
67. Spinoza, *Ethics*, II.PXLIV.148–49.

reactively, like we do when we hold "inadequate ideas."[68] When we understand the cause of an emotion or passion (i.e., a strong feeling, not necessarily a desire for something in particular), we have an adequate idea of it and can be said to be the active cause of it. Inadequate ideas, then, arise from external causes. Adequate ideas arise internally. Understanding our internal workings is the nearest we come to free will. It is this understanding which protects thoughts from the passions generated from external stimuli and allow us some degree of control. Reason provides salvation.

However, most people cannot control their passions: "Anyone with any experience of the capricious mind of the multitude almost despairs of it, as it is governed not by reason but by passion alone, it is precipitate in everything, and very easily corrupted by greed or good living."[69] Passion leads us to exaggerate our own abilities and distorts how we see the world: "Each person thinks he alone knows everything and wants everything done his way and judges a thing fair or unfair, right or wrong, to the extent he believes it works for his own gain or loss."[70]

Passions stirred by external causes cloud our judgment. We resent people who have a greater reputation or better fortune than us and act out of this resentment:

> Everyone knows what wrong people are often moved to commit because they cannot stand their present situation and desire a major upheaval, how blind anger and resentment of their property prompt men to act, how much these things occupy and agitate their minds.[71]

The inability to control the passions also impacts the public sphere, where passions run wild. Spinoza concedes that we "have never succeeded in devising a form of government that was not in greater danger from its citizens than from foreign foes, and which was not more fearful of the former than from the latter."[72]

Our technological worldview follows Spinoza's lead. We no longer view ourselves as being free. Our decisions are grounded in genetics, environment, culture, what we eat, how long we sleep. To flourish, we

68. Spinoza, *Ethics*, II.PI.163.

69. Spinoza, *TTP*, 17:4, 210.

70. Spinoza, *TTP*, 17:4, 210.

71. Spinoza, *TTP*, 17:4, 211.

72. Spinoza, *TTP*, 17:4, 211.

need to measure and monitor our every step, literally. We dare not sit for too long, slumber too little. We need the right food, the optimum amount of exercise, sex, and personal relationships. Our every action aims at achieving greater productivity and increasing our longevity. We view ourselves as algorithmic.

Spinoza's scheme also anticipates modern psychology and contemporary therapeutic approaches to well-being. External events are neutral. What matters is how we react to them, the narratives we create. When we perceive events as threatening our survival or sense of self (*Conatus*), we react emotionally, and often negatively. Understanding the mechanism, learning to see the bigger picture, letting go, withholding judgment, neutralizes the negative effects. We are given space to flourish.

It is strange that, despite our embrace of the above attitudes toward technology and well-being, we have not managed to gain control over the passions. Everywhere we look, there is anger, discontent, emotions running amok. It is not only citizens who are unhappy, but governments themselves are conflicted and unruly, despite the successes of science and technology. There is a battle going on. The drive to greater quantification and rationalization has led to a rebellion by the passions, wild, undisciplined, extreme, destructive. Balance eludes us.

## Politics

For Spinoza, politics is the means of directing the community toward reason. In his *Theological Political Treatise*, Spinoza distinguishes between natural rights and reason. Natural rights are those which exist in nature. Nature's law is the law of the river and jungle: "Fish are determined by nature to swim and big fish to eat little ones, and therefore it is by sovereign natural right that fish have possession of the water and that big fish eat small fish."[73] This inequality is inherent in the idea of *Conatus*—each thing seeks to persist even at the expense of others: "And since it is the supreme law of nature that each thing strives to persist in its own state so far as it can, taking no account of another's circumstances, only of its own, it follows that each individual thing has a sovereign right to do this."[74]

However, this is not the end of the story because "no one can doubt how much more beneficial it is for men to live according to laws and

73. Spinoza, *TTP*, 16:2, 195.
74. Spinoza, *TTP*, 16:2, 195–96.

certain dictates of reason, which as I have said aim at nothing but men's true interests."[75] Spinoza's argument is that we collectively recognize that it is more beneficial to live through reason than in a state of nature. None of us wants to be put in danger or to be surrounded by hostility, hatred, anger, or deceit. We also appreciate that "without mutual help, and the cultivation of reason, human beings necessarily live in great misery."[76] When we apply reason, we come to know that the best means for its promotion is the state. The role of the state is to make rules in accordance with reason to preserve our security.

Spinoza here adopts similar ideas to Thomas Hobbes in *Leviathan* (1651), which preceded his writings, and Jean-Jacques Rousseau in *The Social Contract* (1762), which came after him. When we participate in the state, we enter into a contract under which we give up our natural rights for the benefits of civil society: "Every person transfers all the power they possess to society, and society alone retains the supreme natural right over all things, i.e., supreme power, which all must obey, either of their own free will or through fear of the ultimate punishment."[77]

Spinoza calls this power democracy. The process is democratic only in the sense that every member of the state participates in handing over his natural right to the state. Spinoza is not suggesting that democracy is the best form of government. He in fact considers that a sovereign is more effective than a democratic leader at wielding power and controlling the masses. The masses do not exercise power but hand over their power to the sovereign, and the sovereign governs undemocratically.[78]

Spinoza holds that those who hold power have a right to rule by virtue of that power granted to them by the people:

> The sovereigns, we showed, retain the right to command whatever they wish only so long as they truly hold supreme power. If they lose it, they at the same time also lose the right of decreeing all things, which passes to the man or men who have acquired it and can retain it.[79]

Spinoza does not sanction rebellion but considers that if the sovereign makes absurd or unjust laws, this inevitably will lead to his downfall. The

---

75. Spinoza, *TTP*, 16:5, 197.
76. Spinoza, *TTP*, 16:5, 197.
77. Spinoza, *TTP*, 16:5, 200.
78. On Spinoza's conception of democracy see Cohen, *Out of Control*, 141–52.
79. Spinoza, *TTP*, 16:9, 200.

system is self-correcting. However, for the main part, the role of the state is to ensure that its citizens act in accordance with reason's dictates, and what is reasonable is what the state says it is. The only real differences between Spinoza's idea and slavery are that in Spinoza's scheme, the individual freely gives up his freedom and in exercising reason, the sovereign will naturally have regard to the masses' interests when he governs.

Despite the above, the state can have no control over the thought of its citizens: "No one therefore can surrender their freedom to judge and to think as they wish and everyone, by the supreme right of nature, remains master of their own thoughts."[80] This restriction on the state does not arise from some inalienable right but from practical considerations.

People have many and varied opinions which they need to express and cannot remain silent: "It is a universal failing in people that they communicate their thoughts to others, however much they should [sometimes] keep quiet."[81] This is the reason why a government would be judged very harshly if it tried to dictate how people are to speak and communicate. On the other hand, "a state where everyone has conceded this freedom will be moderate."[82]

A cold wind blows through Spinoza's politics. Reason is what the political leadership says it is. Politics serves only practical ends. Once these have been identified by the leader, he has the power to decide how society should reach these goals. Spinoza will allow us an unlimited right to express our thoughts, but having entered the social contract, we are powerless to act on them without permission of the state. Spinoza's politics are well-suited to the idea of the singularity. Presumably, he would urge us to give up our freedom to the system; all-powerful, all-knowing, and all-rational. He might even say that by embracing the singularity, we would not be giving up anything to our advantage, since we are just ideas in the mind of God, and the only true reality is the system itself.

## Religion

Spinoza's view of religion is equally clinical. Religion is a utility, not wholly good or wholly bad. In his *Ethics*, Spinoza describes three types of knowledge: imagination, reason, and intuition.[83] Imagination is the low-

80. Spinoza, *TTP*, 20:4, 251.
81. Spinoza, *TTP*, 20:4, 251.
82. Spinoza, *TTP*, 20:4, 251.
83. Spinoza, *Ethics*, II.XL145–46.

est form of knowledge. It provides only partial, confused, and inadequate insight: "So far as the human mind imagines an external body, it has not an adequate cognition of that body."[84] One of the most common features of the imagination is to persuade us that we have free will: "Men err in supposing that they think themselves free; which opinion is based solely on this, that they are conscious of their actions and ignorant of the causes by which those actions are determined."[85] Imagination also plays a major role in the development of religion. Religion is the result of imagination let loose.

Prophets are not holy men but people with overactive imaginations: "The prophets were not endowed with more perfect minds than others but only a more vivid power of imagination."[86] Their visions are inherently unreliable: "We can therefore now assert, without reservation that the prophets perceived things revealed by God by way of their imagination, that is via words or visions which may have been either real or imaginary."[87] Imagination can reach beyond intellect, but the ideas it gives rise to are uncertain and often misleading.[88]

Those who rely more on imagination have a greater risk of error than those who rely on reason:

> Those who are most powerful in imagination are less good at merely understanding things; those who have trained and powerful intellects have a more modest power of imagination and have it under better control, reigning it in, so to speak, and not confusing it with understanding.[89]

Moses was no different to any other prophet in that he channeled revelation through his imagination: "Revelation has occurred through images alone."[90] This means that "those who look in the books of the prophets for wisdom and knowledge of natural and spiritual things are completely on the wrong track."[91] Reason provides a much more certain path to truth.

84. Spinoza, *Ethics*, II.XXVI.137.

85. Spinoza, *Ethics*, II.XXXV.141.

86. Spinoza, *TTP*, 2:1, 27.

87. Spinoza, *TTP*, 1:27, 25.

88. Spinoza, *TTP*, 1:28, 26.

89. Spinoza, *TTP*, 2:1, 27.

90. Spinoza, *TTP*, 1:14, 18.

91. Spinoza, *TTP*, 2:1, 27.

Spinoza, however, still considered reveled religion to be of benefit. The power of such religion, however, lies not in its revelatory character, but in its ability to force obedience to ideas which religious leaders hold dear: "We see them advancing false notions of their own as the word of God and seeking to use the influence of religion to compel other people to agree with them."[92] For Spinoza, this is the primary purpose of Moses's revelation, to ensure obedience to a set of laws.

Spinoza has no issue with this. Every leader is entitled to use his power to implement whatever rules he likes, provided he aspires toward those principles of universal faith which reason dictates. The Hebrew Bible satisfies this criterion by promoting justice (*Justitia*) and charity (*Caritas*).[93] These things are derived from reason, which is "the word of God inscribed on all men's hearts."[94]

Religion, therefore, is not about truth, but obedience to paths of goodness: "It is, therefore, not the man who advances the best reasons who necessarily manifests the best faith but rather the man who performs the best works of justice and charity."[95]

Spinoza had earlier reasoned that because the Bible is not a work of a transcendent God, but a creation of the imagination, flawed and unclear, it should be interpreted no differently than nature:

> The method of interpreting nature consists above all in constructing a natural history, from which we derive the definitions of natural things, as from certain data. Likewise, to interpret Scripture, we need to assemble a genuine history of it and to deduce the thinking of the Bible's authors by valid inferences from this history, as from certain data and principles.[96]

For Spinoza, the Bible is a book like any other. The Bible reveals only to the extent that imagination can reveal, which is confusedly. While Spinoza was not the first to take such a critical approach, he was significant in bringing it to the attention of a wider audience. It is this approach which has come to dominate the academy. Spinoza should be admired for his bravery in airing these thoughts. In his day, the Bible remained sacrosanct. Few dared to challenge its special status as a work of revelation.

92. Spinoza, *TTP*, 7:1, 97.

93. Spinoza, *TTP*, 14:1, 178.

94. Spinoza, *TTP*, 14:9–10, 182.

95. Spinoza, *TTP*, 14:11, 184.

96. Spinoza, *TTP*, 7:1, 98.

It will be no surprise from this account that Spinoza considers the state to have more authority than religion. The state rules through the power granted by the people. Religion seeks to inspire obedience without such power. Although religion serves to instill virtue into the masses, religion must always be subservient to the state: "Religious worship and pious conduct must be accommodated to the peace and interests of the state and consequently must be determined by the sovereign authorities alone."[97]

One reason why the state deserves to have such power over religion is to keep religion in check:

> Everyone knows how much influence right and authority in sacred matters have with the common people and how much everyone listens to someone who possesses such authority. I may say that whoever has this power has the greatest control over people's minds. Therefore, anybody who attempts to remove this authority from the sovereign power, seeks to divide the government.[98]

In *Sapiens*, Yuval Noam Noam Harari describes the birth of religion. He writes that "legends, myths, gods, and religions appeared for the first time with the Cognitive Revolution."[99] This was a period some seventy- to thirty-thousand years ago, when new ways of thinking and communicating emerged.[100] This development gave rise to our ability to weave fictions through our imagination, not only to warn of the presence of a lion, but to give mythic significance to this majestic creature. Harari considers that it is this ability to tell stories which allows us to "co-operate effectively in such large numbers."[101] In describing the place of imagination in the birth of religion, Harari is stepping into Spinoza's shoes.

Spinoza's insight concerning the relationship between religion and imagination brings self-awareness, marks a point of maturity, and bursts the comfortable bubble of our tribal stories, but the danger is that we abandon myth altogether—which, as we shall see, is not mere storytelling—and run headlong into a world which respects nothing but data,

97. Spinoza, *TTP*, 19:2, 238.
98. Spinoza, *TTP*, 19:16, 245.
99. Harari, *Sapiens*, 27.
100. Harari, *Sapiens*, 23.
101. Harari, *Sapiens*, 27.

cause and effect, ruthless scientific efficiency, and the technological singularity foreshadowed in part by Spinoza's conception of God.

Our relationship to Spinoza has relevance to our relationship with modern technology and the future which it heralds. To understand why embracing a purely technological path would leave us diminished requires us to consider Spinoza some more, his immense appeal, and the perils inherent in his outlook.

# 4

# Why Spinoza Is Right

## "Refining Spinoza"

FOR MANY JEWS, ENCOUNTERING Spinoza for the first time is a revelatory, almost ecstatic experience, a conversion of sorts. Berthold Auerbach
(1812–1882), a German Jewish poet and author, was eighteen when he
discovered Spinoza. So profound was the effect on him that he sought
to appropriate Spinoza's identity: "I shall now be called . . . Berthold
Benedict Auerbach."[1] Even after that first encounter, a "sacred awe" seized
him whenever he thought of Spinoza.[2] After reading Spinoza, Auerbach
relinquished his belief that the Bible was unassailable and gave up his
talmudic lifestyle, embracing a liberal path characteristic of the Jewish
Enlightenment (*Haskalah*). In Auerbach's first Jewish novel, *Spinoza: A
Historical Novel*, Spinoza appears as the archetypal, modern, emanci-
pated Jew. In an epilogue, the figure of the Wandering Jew, a Christian
personification of the Jew in exile, appears to Spinoza declaring Spinoza
to be, in David Schwartz's words, the "redeemer of all mankind" and
"secular messiah."[3]

More recently, the philosopher Rebecca Goldstein describes her
first experience of the philosopher in her book *Betraying Spinoza*. She
was a student in an Ultra-Orthodox Jewish girls' school in New York

1. Schwartz, *First Modern Jew*, 65.
2. Schwartz, *First Modern Jew*, 70.
3. Schwartz, *First Modern Jew*, 56.

undergoing doubts. At this time, she had no familiarity with Spinoza's ideas. She knew of him only from the warnings given by her teachers, yet she felt that she "knew what it was like to have been him, the former yeshiva student, Baruch Spinoza."[4]

Many of us have undergone similar experiences. Spinoza speaks to something innate within the soul, particularly to those of us who are both drawn to and troubled by traditional Jewish teachings. We feel and see within Spinoza an urge to rebellion, but a call also to reach beyond the secular. There is something about Spinoza which speaks to both our faith and our doubt.

Yet, Spinoza was a controversial character in his day and even a hundred years after his death, it could be dangerous to identify too closely with him. In 1783, the philosopher Friedrich Heinrich Jacobi (1743–1819) became involved in a dispute with Moses Mendelssohn (1729–1786), the father of the *Haskalah*, over the claim that Mendelssohn's friend, the writer Gotthold Ephraim Lessing (1729–1781) admitted to being an adherent of Spinozian pantheism. Mendelssohn rallied to his dead friend's defense in what became known as the "pantheism controversy." Mendelssohn argued that Lessing held fast to a belief in the reality of a world within God. This was not pantheism but a "refined pantheism" or "refined Spinozism."[5]

Some have suggested that Mendelssohn himself was influenced by Spinoza when he describes Judaism, in his best-known work *Jerusalem* (1783), as being a "revealed legislation," rather than a "revealed religion." Mendelssohn, however, also asserts that the Torah is based on eternal truths and its laws are binding for later generations, albeit as a matter of personal choice rather than coercion.[6] To the extent that he has Spinoza in mind, he is clearly taking exception to him. Mendelssohn's other works also display no affinity with Spinoza's thought. However, Mendelssohn did consider that a "refined Spinozism can be easily reconciled with Judaism."[7]

There have been other halachically committed Jews who have shown some appreciation for Spinoza. Chaim Hirschensohn (1857–1935), an Israeli rabbi who also served in the United States, translated

4. Goldstein, *Betraying Spinoza*, 66.

5. Schwartz, *First Modern Jew*, 50.

6. Mendelssohn, *Jerusalem*, quoted in Schwartz, *First Modern Jew*, 44–45.

7. Schwartz, *First Modern Jew*, 51.

part of Spinoza's *Ethics* into Hebrew and addresses Spinoza frequently in his works.[8] Although critical of Spinoza, he wrote that "the nature of Spinoza's faith in God's unity is clearer and more understood and of purer faith than all those who preceded him in the matter."[9] Hirschensohn also saw Spinoza as being well intentioned and righteous.[10]

In the early twentieth century, Rabbi Mordechai Teitelbaum drew a comparison between the thought of Rabbi Shneur Zalman of Liady, the first Rebbe of Lubavitch, mentioned earlier, and Spinoza in his biography of the Rebbe.

Teitelbaum explains that he has undertaken the exercise because some see a parallel between the views of Shneur Zalman and Spinoza.[11] Teitelbaum notes that Shneur Zalman, like Spinoza, takes an immanentist approach to God, and that Shneur Zalman noted in several places that the numerical value (*Gematria*) of God's name, *Elokhim*, is equivalent to the Hebrew words *ha-Teva* (the nature).[12] However, for Teitelbaum, Shneur Zalman's ideas are as different from Spinoza's as "East is to West."[13] Teitelbaum's comparison covers the relationship between God and the world, the eternity of matter, God's will, God's ability to alter the laws of nature, and free will.[14]

Teitelbaum is keen to point out that unlike Spinoza, Shneur Zalman believes that God created the world, has a will, and can alter the course of nature, and that humans have free will. Shneur Zalman's thought also of course makes room for the God of history and has Torah at its center. Teitelbaum further observes that Shneur Zalman would have had no access to Spinoza's works, so could not have been influenced by him.[15]

Yet, despite wanting to distinguish Shneur Zalman's thought from Spinoza's, Teitelbaum looks for kabbalistic influence on Spinoza, a point

8. Hirschensohn, *Mosge Shave v-Emet*, 235–92.

9. Hirschensohn, *Mosge Shave v-Emet*, 115–17, quoted in Schwartz, "Fascination and Rejection," 166.

10. Schwartz, "Fascination and Rejection," 166. See also Shapiro, "Hayyim Hirschensohn."

11. Teitlebaum, *Rabbi*, II.99.

12. Teitlebaum, *Rabbi*, II.104. Both words have the numerical value of eighty-six. Teitelbaum references Shneur Zalman's *Sefer ha-Yichud ve-Emunah*, ch. 6, *Torah Or on Miketz*, and his prayer book on *Mizmor le-Todah*.

13. Teitlebaum, *Rabbi*, II.104.

14. Teitlebaum, *Rabbi*, II.105–13.

15. Teitlebaum, *Rabbi*, II.113.

on which many have speculated.[16] There is a sense that Teitelbaum, like others we have mentioned, was intrigued by this arch-heretic. The fact that he engaged in his comparative study suggests that others were too.

Rabbi Abraham Isaac Kook (1865–1935), the first Ashkenazi Chief Rabbi of British Mandate Palestine, was a Talmud scholar, mystic, and monist. At about the same time that Teitelbaum was writing his biography, Kook was working through his own thoughts on Spinoza in his private notebook. He wrote:

> The Spinozist system with all its impurity, is the complete opposite of the light of Israel. The hand of God fell upon the righteous rabbis of Amsterdam when they removed him from Israel. His thought was a herald of modernity, with its horrors, including antisemitism. Spinoza and Bismarck might be thought of as the Bilam[17] and Haman[18] of their age.[19]

After speculating that if Spinoza had not been excommunicated, his ideas would have been accepted and have caused untold damage, Kook nevertheless concludes that

> there is in his inwardness some fundamental principle that after much refinement should enter the camp of Israel. Rabbi [Moses] Mendelssohn initiated the purification but did not complete it. The Bal Shem Tov [the founder of the eighteenth-century Hasidic movement] continued the process without being aware who he was refining, because he had no need of Spinoza's knowledge, being able to draw directly from its inner source and purify that. The work [of refinement] remains unfinished, but is continuing towards completion, and once it is completed, [Spinoza] will no longer be called cursed but blessed [*Baruch*].[20]

Kook's use of the word "refinement" suggests a familiarity with Mendelssohn's term "refined Spinozism," and as we have seen, Kook even names Mendelssohn as having taken a step in this direction. Kook then must have been aware of the pantheism controversy and sympathetic to what

16. Teitelbaum, *Rabbi*, II.114–19. See Beltrán, *Influence*, 83–154.

17. A prophetic seer called upon to curse the Jews. See Num 22.

18. The Persian vizier under King Ahasuerus and archenemy of the Jews in the biblical book of Esther.

19. Kook, *Kevatsim Miketav Yad Kodsho* i:146.

20. Kook, *Kevatsim Miketav Yad Kodsho* i:146. Some of my translation of these passages comes from Shapiro, *Changing the Immutable*, 168–69. Shapiro points out that the last sentence puns on Spinoza's Hebrew first name.

Mendelssohn was trying to achieve, but the key to understanding Kook's attitude is the word "refinement."

We might contend, based on Kook, that the work of refinement does not operate in just one direction. Just as Spinoza's thought requires amendment, so too do our misconceived ideas about God and the religious life, which Spinoza challenges. In one of his essays, Kook described how our minds need cleansing from the debris of idolatrous images of God. For him, atheism has some legitimacy by teaching us that every definition of God is flawed: "Every definition of divinity brings about heresy [*Kefirah*], every definition is spiritual idolatry [*Eliliyyut Ruchanit*], even the attribution of the intellect and the will, and even divinity [*ha-Elokhut*] itself, for the name 'God' [*Elokhim*] is a definition."[21] Atheism purges religious faith from its misconceived speculations, removing images "from the speculations concerning Him who is the essence of all life and the source of all thought."[22] Kook thinks that we should give atheism the credit it deserves:

> Whoever recognizes the essence of atheism from this perspective embraces the positive element in it and traces it back to its origin in holiness . . . When one discovers the stern protest embodied in rebellion and atheism, which seeks to repudiate the good of our ancestral inheritance in pursuit of some new vision, one finds the element of good inherent in it.[23]

Elliot Wolfson sees such insights as awakening "the faith of the future" marked by the idea of God's description as *Ehyeh Asher Ehyeh* (Exod 3:14):[24]

> The name that denotes neither something that is nothing nor nothing that is something, the name that signifies the insignificant, the infinity that both is what it is not and is not what it is because it neither is what it is not nor is not what it is. Within this imaginal space, there is no more distinction between faith and unfaith, belief and disbelief, and hence atheism emerges as the most pertinent and enhanced enunciation of theism.[25]

---

21. Kook, *Orot*, translated in Wolfson, "Teachings of Rav Kook," 148.

22. Kook, *Orot*, translated in Bosker, *Abraham Isaac Kook*, 264–65.

23. Kook, *Orot*, translated in Bosker, *Abraham Isaac Kook*, 265–66.

24. Sometimes translated as "I will be what I will become."

25. Wolfson, "Teachings of Rav Kook," 150.

Spinoza's theology, taken at one time or another as atheism, pantheism, or a mystical theism, crosses such boundaries between faith and unfaith, and has a scouring effect on religious belief. It is not only suited to the "faith of the future," but a harbinger of it. Yet, it is in need, if not of refinement, then of some amendment or reorientation before it can form part of a Jewish theology seeking loyalty to the tradition. Spinoza's ideas also risk idolatry by associating God too closely with reason and too closely with nature.

In this chapter, I want to further explore Spinoza's continuing appeal for those grappling with issues of faith. In the next chapter, I want to show why, despite the attractiveness of Spinoza's thought, it cannot be the whole story. The four areas I want to focus on here are oneness, reason, his treatment of religion as utility, and his treatment of the individual as a psychological being.

## The Allure of Oneness

The first area where Spinoza appeals is his view of God as Nature. Spinoza's non-dualist philosophical account of existence is a beautiful construct. It purports to be based on pure logic, on mathematics, the Euclidian method, but displays great poetry. It is at once hard edged, made up of clear lines, yet speaks to an inner longing and intuition about how the world in which we find ourselves is constructed.

Oneness or monism extends across all human cultures and has a long history.[26] It was a feature of the fifth-century BCE Eleatic philosophers (Parmenides, Zeno, and Melissus) who preceded Aristotle. They considered being to be one, unchangeable, and an atemporal substance. In Parmenides's philosophical poem, a young man is taken on a journey by the daughters of the sun. In the first part of the poem, entitled "The Way of Truth" (*Aletheia*), the youth is taught by the goddess that

> what is generated and imperishable,
> a whole of one kind, unshaken and complete,
> nor ever was it, nor will it be, since it now is, all together,
> one continuous.[27]

26. It has been suggested that, for most of human history, humans have held to a oneness perspective. Harrison, "Oneness," 42, 46.

27. Parmenides, poem B8.3–6, translated in Clarke, *Aristotle*, 2.

The idea of oneness is also firmly embedded in the philosophies of the East. Gaudapada, a sixth- or seventh-century teacher of the Advaita Vedanta tradition, in his *Mandukya-Karika* describes four states of consciousness. The fourth state is characterized by a non-dual (*advaita*) attitude characterized by the absence of distinction between the internal and external.[28] The state, however, is not one of lack but of fullness:

> When the soul,
> Which has been sleeping
> Under the influence of endless maya,
> Is [finally] awakened,
> Something unborn, non-dual,
> Dreamless and slumberless
> Is also awakened.[29]

One who reaches the fourth level of consciousness is aware that differences are mere illusions. In the *Mandukya-Karika*, "the world of the individual souls and external objects is nothing but the projection of a sole and undivided consciousness."[30] Neo-Confucians, such as the eleventh-century Zhou Dunyi and Zhang Zai, and Wang Yangming (1472–1529) considered all things to be one. Each thing contains all the principles in the universe but expresses these in different ways.[31]

The notion of oneness was also embraced by mystics of the Abrahamic religions, including John Scotus Erigena (c. 810–877), Johannes Eckhart (Meister Eckhart; c. 1260–1327), and Nicholas of Cusa (1401–1464). The idea was also taken up by the Sufi mystic Ibn Arabi (1165–1240) who espoused the doctrine of *Wahdat al-Wujûd*, the Oneness of Being or Unity of Existence. He writes:

> There is nothing in realized Being but God. As for everything
> . . . Everything other than the Essence of the Real is imagination
> and vanishing shadow. No created thing remains upon a single
> state in this world, the next world, and what is between the two,
> neither spirit, nor soul, nor anything other than the Essence of
> God. Rather, each continuously changes from form to form,
> constantly and forever.[32]

28. Isaeva, *Early Vendata*, 24–25.

29. Gaudapada, *Mandukya-Karika* 1.16, translated in Isaeva, *Early Vendata*, 26. Maya is the divine creative force.

30. Isaeva, *Early Vendata*, 45.

31. Baxter, "Oneness," 91.

32. Arabi, *al-Futûhât* 2:313.12, translated in Chittick, "Ibn Arabî."

We have already seen that oneness also has its place within the Jewish mystical traditions, including Hasidism.

In the modern period, oneness continued to evolve through the Western philosophical tradition. There have been existence monists who hold that there is only one thing, and substance monists who consider that there are a variety of different things, but these can only be explained by one thing. Views diverge on whether this thing is mental or material. Priority monism contends that everything relates to a distinct single source. The world does not divide into parts in a mind-independent manner.[33]

The late eighteenth and early nineteenth centuries saw the rise of German Idealism, the philosophical movement which took as its basic notion that fundamental reality is made up of ideas or thoughts. Immanuel Kant (1724–1804) is the best-known of its members. For him, there are *noumena*, objective things in themselves, which cannot be directly known, and *phenomena*, which are the way things appear to us. Part of his project was describing how the noumena and phenomena operate together.

Franz Rosenzweig (1886–1929), mentioned earlier, was a Jewish philosopher and theologian writing mainly in the years following the First World War. He went through a near-conversion to Christianity before renewing his commitment to Judaism. His most famous work, *The Star of Redemption* (1919), is a theology which responds to German Idealism by giving an account of the individual's place in the "All." Benjamin Pollock describes Rosenzweig as seeing the goal of German Idealism as arriving at a system which grasps "all that is in its identity AND difference."[34]

Rosenzweig viewed German Idealism as emerging in response to Spinoza's attempt "to sketch an image of the world growing forth out of one root."[35] The German Idealist critique of Spinoza was that his conception of the One takes insufficient account of difference. As Pollock explains, the idealists considered that Spinoza's thought "amounts to a reduction of all particularity, all freedom, even all divinity, to nothing."[36] The German philosopher Friedrich Jacobi, mentioned earlier in connection with the pantheism controversy, had accused Spinoza of atheism by

---

33. *Stanford Encyclopedia of Philosophy*, s.v. "Monism."

34. Pollock, *Franz Rosenzweig*, 7.

35 Rosenweig, *Das älteste Systemprogramm des deutschen Idealismus*, 42, quoted in Pollock, *Franz Rosenzweig*, 28.

36. Pollock, *Franz Rosenzweig*, 71.

associating God with nature, of destroying the idea of human freedom by seeing individuals as modes of the infinite, and as valuing humans not as they are but only as they express ultimate being.[37] Rosenzweig, however, considered the idealists to have fallen into the same trap as Spinoza by overemphasizing the whole and failing to properly account for the particular.[38] Few others appeared to have seen this at the time, but in hindsight Spinozian monism does seem to have been everywhere.

Many of the German idealists were Romantics who believed that the Enlightenment had gone too far by placing too much trust in reason. They considered that there needed to be a rebalancing in favor of feeling and emotion. The idea of oneness features prominently in their thought.

Georg Wilhelm Friedrich Hegel (1770–1831) describes *Geist* (Absolute Spirit), an eternal cyclical process through which the universe comes to know itself. *Geist* is the principle of reality which makes the universe intelligible. It comes to know itself through its own thinking, nature, and then through finite spirits and their self-expression and self-discovery in history, art, religion, and philosophy.

In 1799, Friedrich Schleiermacher (1768–1834), the German poet and philosopher, also espoused a notion of a single universe unfolding through history. He wrote:

> The universe exists in an uninterrupted activity and reveals itself to us every moment. Every form that it brings forth, every being to which gives a separate existence according to the fullness of life, every occurrence that spills forth from its rich, ever-fruitful womb, is an action of the same upon us. Thus, to accept everything individual as part of the whole and everything limited as a representation of the infinite, is religion.[39]

Friedrich Wilhelm Joseph von Schelling (1775–1854), one of the other great philosophers of the age, also espoused an absolute idealism in which he identified a ground or condition which precedes the subject and object determination in order to explain the possibility of knowledge: "The ultimate ground of reality is a something [*Etwas*] which is thinkable only through itself, through its being: briefly, it is that being in which thought and being are one."[40]

---

37. Pollock, *Franz Rosenzweig*, 28.

38. Pollock, *Franz Rosenzweig*, 71.

39. Schleiermacher, *On Religion*, 105.

40. Schelling, *On the Possibility of a Form of Philosophy as Such*, 86, quoted in Nassar, "Spinoza in Schelling's Early Conception," 142.

Samuel Taylor Coleridge (1772–1834), the poet, theologian, and founder of the Romantic movement in England considered Spinoza a pantheist but one who expressed his pantheism "in the most religious form in which it could appear."[41] Coleridge further considered that Spinoza expressed deep kabbalistic ideas and acted like a Christian. Coleridge failed to understand why Spinoza was so attacked in his day.[42]

George Eliot (1819–1880), the writer whose translation of the *Ethics* I have relied on in this book, responds in her writing to the romantic ideology. She discovered Spinoza as she was beginning to question her Christian faith. She describes her encounter with his writing as like having a conversation with "a person of great capacity . . . who says from his own soul what all the world is saying by rote."[43] George Henry Lewes (1817–1878), Eliot's partner, was also taken with Spinoza claiming, as Coleridge had before him, that his pantheism was not modern atheism but "an ancient doctrine taught by Plato, Augustine, and the Jewish Cabbalists."[44]

In Great Britain, idealist philosophers absorbed from Hegel the notion of an idealist, unifying spirit. These included William Whewell (1794–1885), Francis Herbert Bradley (1846–1924), and John McTaggart Ellis (1866–1925), who considered "monism, whether it be materialistic or idealistic" to be more attractive than dualism "to the majority of inquirers."[45]

Oneness is indeed an attractive worldview. With nations at loggerheads, tribes at war, classes locked in conflict, plague sweeping the globe, the sexes battling, families torn asunder, hearts broken, identities fractured, lives pulled apart, it is comforting to imagine that we are essentially fused, all fundamentally the same, capable of entering each other's worlds. The idea provides comfort to our lonely, disjointed lives.

The idea of oneness is ubiquitous these days, promoted by wellness practitioners as a form of de-mythologized spirituality, drawn from the religions of the East. It is the default religion of the meditation practitioner and yogi. Our experience of coronavirus has also demonstrated our

41. Coleridge, March 1819 lecture, quoted in Halmi, "Coleridge's Ecumenical Spinoza," 190–91.

42. Halmi, "Coleridge's Ecumenical Spinoza," 190–91.

43. Eliot, *Letters* 1:321, quoted in Spinoza, *Ethics*, 7.

44. Spinoza, *Ethics*, 18–19.

45. Bowler, "Monism in Britain," 181–82.

interconnectedness. Our lives touch and impact each other across the globe. We grieve when we are apart.

Our poisoned environment has been trying to teach us for years how our lives intersect. We do not exist separate from our environment but form part of it. Gaia is the Greek ancestral mother of all life. The Gaia principle proposes that we are part of a self-regulating, complex system. When we act against that system, we act against ourselves.[46]

We can also approach oneness through our understanding of networks. Networks emerge spontaneously out of nature and are found in every area of our lives: language, the links between proteins in the cell, the internet, and relationships between people—hence the "six degrees" that apparently separate one person from another.[47] Spinoza's God might be perceived as the network of networks.

Synchronicity is vital to driving networks. From the ticking of clocks, to the flashing of fireflies, things are impacted by tiny changes in other things and brought into line. Christiaan Huygens (1629–1695), the Dutch scientist, was one of the first to observe the phenomenon when his two pendulum clocks hung from the same wooden structure started to oscillate in synchronicity.[48] What Huygens discovered, in Steven Strogatz's words, was a "sympathetic universe" in which things naturally mirror one another and fall into alignment.[49] Huygens, it will be recalled, was a fan of Spinoza's lenses, and the two were acquainted.[50]

We can also see how all things are linked by the way in which we come to know them. We can only understand another human being, for example, by understanding her culture, individual history, biology, chemistry, and psychology. Each of these things exist in relationship to other cultures and histories, the psychology of other humans, the history of humanity, the objects that exist in the world, the chemistry of the entire universe, and so on and so forth. On an experiential level all knowledge and understanding intersects, connects, and is intimately linked. Each

---

46. See Lovelock, *Gaia*.

47. Barabasi, *Linked*, 221. Strogatz, *Sync*, 229–30, 236, 240, 245–46.

48. See Strogatz, *Sync*, 103–08. At 108, Stogatz writes: "The sympathy of clocks taught us that the capacity for sync does not depend on intelligence, or life, or natural selection. It springs from the deepest source of all: the laws of mathematics and physics."

49. See Strogatz, *Sync*, 101.

50. Nadler, *Spinoza*, 183, 221–22.

aspect of existence overlaps and explains physically and conceptually its neighbor whether in space or time.

Spinoza's monism is especially appealing to scientists. Ernst Haeckel (1837–1919), the German biologist (and eugenicist), was heavily influenced by Spinoza. He had begun to use the term "monism" in 1866. In 1899, he published his manifesto, *The Riddle of the Universe*, and in 1906 formed the German Monist League. *The Riddle of the Universe* became an international best-seller. Haeckel held that science had shown that Spinoza was right to claim that mind and matter were but aspects of a single substance. Darwin's theories further allowed all life to be explained as a single totality.[51] In his *Natural Stories of Creation* (1868), Haeckel referred to his natural-scientific worldview as "a monistic religion."[52]

In 1904, Hugo Munsterberg, the psychologist, organized a Congress under the title "Unity of Knowledge." He invited Friedrich Wilhelm Ostwald (1853–1932), the chemist and philosopher, and other men of science, Ludwig Boltzmann, Ernest Rutherford, Edward Leamington Nichols, Paul Langevin, and Henri Poincaré, as speakers.[53]

In May 1911, Ostwald presided over the Internationalist Monist Congress in Hamburg, declaring the start of the "monist century"[54] In 1912, Ernst Mach, Felix Klein, David Hilbert, and Albert Einstein signed a manifesto aimed at the "development of a comprehensive worldview." Several works appeared after these meetings promoting such an ideal. These included Ostwald's *Monism as the Goal of Civilization* (1913), Mathieu Leclerc du Sablon's *L'Unité de la Science* (1919), and Johan Hjorst's *The Unity of Science* (1921).[55] In some ways, these works and Haeckel's can be seen as the twentieth-century equivalents of Kurzweil and other scientific writers on the future. The underlying belief is that science holds the answer, and that answer lies in discovering or reconnecting to unity. The First World War put an end to the monist movement's progress.[56]

Even though the monist movement may have stalled, individual scientists continued to be attracted to Spinoza, particularly Albert Einstein. In 1920, he penned a poem to the philosopher, commencing with the

51. Weir, "Riddles of Monism," 1–2.
52. Weir, "Riddles of Monism," 5.
53. Cat, "Unity of Science."
54. Weir, "Riddles of Monism," 6.
55. Cat, "Unity of Science."
56. Weir, "Riddles of Monism," 7.

words "How much do I love that noble man."[57] Einstein read the *Ethics* and was most attracted to Spinoza's ideas on determinism and the existence of a superior intelligence that reveals itself in nature.[58] In January 1943, he wrote to Willy Aron, a writer of a book on Spinoza, stating that although the "chasm between Jewish theology and Spinozism can never be bridged," he was convinced that Spinoza's thought was "thoroughly imbued with the principles and sentiments that characterize so many Jewish intellectuals" and that he (Einstein) would never have come so close to Spinoza had he not been Jewish.[59] But one does not need to be Jewish to love Spinoza.

Carlo Rovelli, the contemporary scientist, credits the philosopher with seeing that our sense of liberty derives not from observation but from our imagination which presents only a sketchy image of our inner workings. Rovelli accepts with Spinoza that we are our bodies and do not possess free will: "Our free decisions are freely determined by the results of the rich and fleeting interactions between the billions of neurons in our brains: they are free to the extent that the interactions of these neurons allows and determines."[60] Spinoza understood with "marvellous lucidity" that "I cannot do something different from what the whole complex of my neurons has decided."[61]

Panpsychism, the idea that mentality (thought or consciousness) imbues every aspect of the world, is often expressed as a form of monism. In the 1920s, Bertrand Russell in *The Analysis of Matter* (1927) and Arthur Eddington in his Gifford Lectures (1928) put forward such ideas as a way of dealing with the mind-body problem (i.e., that the physical world appears causally closed, leaving no place for mind) and the inability of physicists to give an account of consciousness. The idea that matter is itself conscious has been taken up by contemporary philosophers.[62] Spinoza's idea that the physical world is an expression of the mind of God and that everything can be understood through the attribute of thought

---

57. Jammer, *Einstein and Religion*, 43.

58. Jammer, *Einstein and Religion*, 47, 144. Einstein, however, does not appear to have accepted that God is synonymous with nature. See 148–49.

59. Jammer, *Einstein and Religion*, 43.

60. Rovelli, *Seven Brief Lessons*, 72.

61. Rovelli, *Seven Brief Lessons*, 71.

62. See Schaffer, "Monism"; Roelofs, "Unity of Consciousness"; and Goff, *Consciousness*.

is inherently panpsychist. The rock has a corresponding idea of the rock in the mind of God, which is therefore the rock's mind.

The attraction of Spinoza for scientists, and those of us who respect the scientific method, is easy to appreciate. Spinoza imbues science with meaning. Nature becomes God, and scientific knowledge becomes knowledge of God. The better our science, the more we know God, and the more we know God, the more we flourish and the more connected we feel. Spinoza's views also speak to our contemporary myth of the big bang (although Spinoza would stress that substance is eternal), creation without a personal creator, emerging from a singularity, calling us back to a singularity. Here is our declaration of faith, reinterpreted through Spinoza's thought.

In the beginning the big bang created heaven and earth. The big bang, this scintilla of becoming, contained within it all that there was and all that there has been, and all that there will be to the last moment of time; the chemicals, forces, and energies, the unactualized potential of the myriad stars and galaxies that make up our universe, everything we ever encounter, our families and friends, our loves, lives, and deaths, nature and nurture, every creation and innovation, every thought, mood, and mode, every story in every language, every evil and every good, every conception of God—literally everything. And from that singularity matter took hold, expanding ever outward at time-warp speed, unravelling existence like a carpet, emanating, revealing, disclosing.

Who is not inspired by such a narrative? Its spiritual power reaches beyond questions of who lit the blue touch paper or whether the watchmaker has eyes and awakens in its absolute simplicity a deep sense of wonderment and awe that takes us beyond ourselves to a sense of our inter-connectedness with all things. Our interest in the technological singularity arises from these sentiments. It is also a point around which traditional religious adherents from East and West—theists, atheists, pagans, secularists, humanists, environmentalists, those with a sense of the transcendent or spiritual, poets, and prophets—can gather.

Superficially, oneness also deals a fatal blow to the problem of evil. We have wracked our brains for centuries trying to explain how an all-good God can allow evil to flourish, why the wicked thrive when the righteous suffer. We have not got that far. The best answer is that we cannot understand the mind of God, but that just feels like skirting the issue because the same approach can be applied to every theological question ever asked. The real problem is defining God as good. Richard Dawkins makes the point with characteristic overstatement in his *God Delusion*, where he challenges such a notion. The biblical God, he writes, is

> arguably the most unpleasant character in all fiction: jealous and proud of it; a petty, unjust, unforgiving control-freak; a vindictive, bloodthirsty ethnic cleanser; a misogynistic, homophobic, racist, infanticidal, genocidal, filicidal, pestilential, megalomaniacal, sadomasochistic, capriciously malevolent bully.[63]

For Spinoza's God—the God of necessity, nature, and science—and for those who strictly adhere to the ideal of Kurzweil's singularity or Harari's dataism, there is no problem of evil. God, the singularity, the super-intelligence simply is. To speak of evil is to speak of a will, of intent, of an endgame, a telos. Those concepts make no sense when applied to nature in its totality. The idea of an impersonal totality saves us from needing to philosophize about the problem of evil. God no longer disappoints.

Given God's association with nature and the absence of will or personality, why did Spinoza not simply drop the term "God"? One possibility is that he needed to conceal the true implications of his heresy, but if that was the case, he did not do a good job. It was obvious to all that he was presenting a challenge to traditional religion and traditional conceptions of God.

I suggest that by placing God at the center of his philosophy, Spinoza was not being apologetic, but making a much bigger point. He was showing traditionalists that everything that they needed from God was available without having to rely on any scripture, that God as Nature or Being precedes specific religions and religious conceptions of God. Virtue, love of God, and knowledge of God are all available without tradition. This is a sentiment which has gained much traction. Many feel spiritual, but distanced from traditional religions, believe in God or an absolute power, but not the God of the Bible.

Spinoza revealed to us the God that exists before the Hebrew Bible, before he donned his *Tefillin* (phylacteries) and clothed himself in his *Tallit* (prayer shawl), as described in the Talmud, before he wrapped himself in narrative and myth, prior to his revelation as black fire on white fire.[64] This is the God we encounter prior to the revelation at Sinai, the

63. Dawkins, *God Delusion*, 31.

64. On God's *Tefillin*, see *TB* Berachot 6a. On God's *Tallit*, see *TB* Rosh Hashanah 17b. See also Ps 93:1 and 104:1 for clothing imagery related to God. Midrash Tanchuma Gen 1:1 describes the Torah as written "with letters of black fire on white fire."

God of the All rather than the tribe, the God of philosophical necessity, the underpinning of all knowledge, the unity we intuitively seek, need to know rationally, and desire to love. This is revelatory.

## In Praise of Reason

The second area where Spinoza appeals is in his treatment of reason. Spinoza's insistence on the primacy of reason continues to resonate. We have long known of its value, but all revealed faiths have struggled to reconcile it with the notion of revelation. To illustrate the importance of reason to Judaism, I outline below ideas central to the major Jewish rationalists, including the limits they place on the rational faculty. I will then explore the importance of reason more generally.

Sadia Gaon (882–942), the rationalist philosopher and rabbi, was writing in Baghdad when Islam and Karaism (a religion derived from Judaism, but which rejected the rabbinic tradition) were first making their appearance. In *Kitâb al-Amânât wal-'I'tiqâdât* (*Book of Doctrines and Beliefs*), he writes that the Torah contains "laws of reason" for which the reasons are self-evident and which we would arrive at if left to our own devices. These correspond with what we might think of as natural law. In contrast, the "laws of revelation" are known only through tradition. On them, "reason passes no judgment." Such rules include the laws of *Shabbat*, the festivals, and the dietary laws.[65]

The "laws of reason" are contained in the Torah only to provide a shortcut to that which, in time, we would come to know on our own. Sadia maintains that, by including such laws, the Torah is calling upon us to pursue reason. We also know through reason that grasping truths from our own efforts leads to "a double portion of happiness." It is right, therefore, that we apply reason to understanding the purposes for the commandments contained in the Torah.[66]

Moses Maimonides (1138–1204), as we mentioned, was a major rabbinic authority and the foremost Jewish philosopher of the medieval period. He built on Sadia's ideas. Maimonides's halachic masterpiece, the *Mishneh Torah*, opens its first section with the sentence: "The basic principle of all basic principles and the pillar of all sciences is to know that

---

65. Altman, *Book of Doctrines*, 97.
66. Altman, *Book of Doctrines*, 94.

there is a First Being."[67] Such knowledge can only be attained through reason.

Although for Maimonides, God is beyond human knowledge, we can understand God's actions within the world, the cause and effect which constitutes our experience. In his philosophical work, the *Guide for the Perplexed*, Maimonides considers God's conversation with Moses following the episode of the golden calf. The Hebrews had sinned by worshipping the idol when Moses was on Mount Sinai receiving the Ten Commandments. God accepts Moses's plea to spare the people. Moses then asks God to show him His "glory" (*Kavod*). God responds, "I will make all My goodness pass before you" but Moses should note that "you cannot see My face for no man may see my face and live." God then places Moses into the cleft of a rock, and shields Moses's face as God passes him. The only thing that Moses sees of God is God's "goodness" (Exod 33:12–23).

In Genesis, God declared that everything that he had created "was very good" (Gen 1:31). Maimonides utilizes this reference to explain the word "goodness" as referring to the "whole of creation," the natural world.[68] For Maimonides, the sin of the golden calf acts as an encouragement to "comprehend the nature of all things, their relation to each other, and the way they are governed by God both in reference to the universe as a whole and to each creature in particular."[69]

Knowledge of God's attributes derived from such comprehension is "firmly established." That is, verifiable by objective criteria. Such knowledge comprises "knowledge of His attributes, by which He can be known," how God is manifest in the world.[70] The attributes spoken of here are God's moral attributes, and even these cannot be known fully. God's essential attributes cannot be known at all.

Maimonides's outlook reflects the Aristotelian worldview to which he was introduced through the Muslim philosophers of his age and earlier, Al-Kindi (ninth century), Al-Farabi (tenth century), Avicenna (tenth century), Averroes (twelfth century), and al-Ghazali (twelfth century). As with other Aristotelian philosophers, Maimonides's God is a simple, necessary, and uncaused unity. For Aristotelians, the universe is divided

---

67. Maimonides, *MT*, 1:1.
68. Maimonides, *Guide*, I.LIV.75.
69. Maimonides, *Guide*, I.LIV.75.
70. Maimonides, *Guide*, I.LIV.75.

into pure form and the physical world, composed of matter and form. In this scheme, God is pure intellect, containing no potentiality. Moreover, there is an absolute identity between the thinker, the thought, and the subject of the thought: "All intellect is identical with its action: the intellect in action is not a thing different from its action."[71] What this means is that God's thinking creates (and destroys) reality:

> Everything existing and endowed with a form, is whatever it is through its form, and when that form is destroyed its whole existence terminates and is obliterated. The same is the case as regards the relation between God and all distant causes of existing beings: it is through the existence of God that all things exist, and it is He who maintains their existence by that process which is called emanation.[72]

Carlos Fraenkal explains that for Maimonides, following the episode of the golden calf, God made known to Moses "the form of the created world," that is, the act of God which arises from his self-intellection.[73] The idea that nature arises from God's self-intellection explains why contemplating nature leads to knowledge of God. And so:

> On considering the Divine acts, or the processes of nature we get an insight into the prudence and wisdom of God as displayed in the creation of animals, with the gradual development of the movements of their limbs and the relative positions of the latter, and we perceive also His wisdom and plan in the successive and gradual development of the whole condition of each individual.[74]

Maimonides might have followed this path further and associated God with being in its entirety (including physical being or extension), like Spinoza did later, but he stops short of such a conclusion. Fraenkal suggests that Maimonides was unable to take this step because viewing extension as an attribute of God would undermine the Aristotelian conception of God on which Maimonides's system is based.[75] Maimonides also no doubt would have wanted to avoid any accusation of paganism.

---

71. Maimonides, *Guide*, I.LXVIII.101.
72. Maimonides, *Guide*, I.LXIX.104.
73. Fraenkel, "Maimonides' God," 188.
74. Maimonides, *Guide*, III.XXXII.322.
75. Fraenkel, "Maimonides' God," 188.

Maimonides failure to take the step of associating God with being leaves his philosophy with an inconsistency, as Fraenkel has observed. For Maimonides, God is incorporeal and transcendent (without body and apart from nature) yet connected to all parts of the universe through his providence. Maimonides admits that how this fits together is a "complete mystery." The best he can do is to offer a prayer: "Praised be He whose perfection is above our comprehension."[76]

Maimonides, then, edges toward immanence but draws back. Similarly, at times Maimonides indicates that reason provides access to divine knowledge, but at others is keen to stress reason's limitations. Later, we will discuss Maimonides's negative theology, the idea that we can say nothing positive at all about God's attributes. Such discussions give the impression that Maimonides wishes to promote a spiritual path which values the application of reason while appreciating its constraints. Maimonides takes the same approach to identifying reasons for the commandments (Mitzvot) and the interpretation of the written Torah more generally.

For Maimonides, the commandments are not arbitrary dictates, but expressions of divine wisdom. Maimonides writes, "every one of the six hundred and thirteen precepts serves to inculcate some truth, to remove some erroneous opinion, to establish proper relations in society, to diminish evil, to train in good manners or to warn against bad habits."[77]

Our task is to use our intellectual faculties to try to understand the commandments as best we can. He castigates those "who consider it a grievous thing that causes should be given for any law, and consider it right to assume that the commandments and prohibitions have no rational basis whatever."[78] Maimonides considers those who reject the idea that the commandments have no reasons to be afflicted with a "disease of the soul."[79]

Maimonides, however, stresses that there will be commandments we are unable to understand. In such a situation, we must continue to uphold the law in the belief that it has a rational basis, albeit one which is presently beyond our grasp: "But should he find laws that he does not understand (or does not make sense to him) . . . he should not conclude

76. Maimonides, *Guide*, I.LXXII.119; Frankel, "Maimonides' God," 192–93.

77. Maimonides, *Guide*, III.XXXI.322.

78. Maimonides, *Guide*, III.XXXI.321.

79. Maimonides, *Guide*, III.XXXI.321.

that they are any less important, rather he must keep them and treat them with the utmost respect."[80]

Maimonides is the arch-Jewish rationalist, but time and again he reminds us of the limitation of human understanding, particularly when it comes to divine matters. Reason is better suited to the physical sciences and mathematics than to metaphysics: "This confusion [relating to the application of human reason] prevails mostly in metaphysical subjects, less in problems relating to physics, and is entirely absent from the exact sciences."[81]

There is an intimation here of the idea, popular among traditionalists, that religion and science occupy two "non-overlapping magisteria," an idea popularized by Stephen Jay Gould, the scientist, in his famous *Rock of Ages*. In his book on science and religion, the late Rabbi Jonathan Sacks (1948–2020), a major figure in modern Judaism, distances himself from the term "non-overlapping magisteria." He considers that both science and religion deal with the world in which we live. He also calls for a conversation between these two disciplines rather than compartmentalization.[82] However, in his *Great Partnership*, at least, he remains wedded to the idea that science and religion deal with different things. Science deals with the "what is," that is, the world as we experience it, whereas religion deals with meaning and "what ought to be."[83]

But science and religion do not divide neatly in this way. First, as we have seen, science and the application of reason have long been viewed as leading to knowledge of God, by no less a figure than Maimonides. And this is despite his warning about the limitations of reason when it comes to metaphysics. Science is not therefore just a description of the external world, but how we come to access ultimate meaning. Spinoza's promotion of reason as a source for knowledge of God is in many respects an extension of Maimonides's ideas.

Secondly, even in the seventeenth century, Spinoza demonstrated in his *Ethics* how it was possible to derive a moral code using the scientific method. Since then, philosophers have come up with numerous ethical systems, including utilitarianism and other consequentialist theories, using only the power of reason. Religions may be proficient when it comes

80. Maimonides, *MT*, 8:8.
81. Maimonides, *Guide*, I.XXXI.41.
82. Sacks, *Great Partnership*, 213.
83. Sacks, *Great Partnership*, 214.

to generating meaning, but have not historically been particularly good at instilling values into their adherents which lead them to reach beyond their own group.[84] Reason, as a tool, is well-suited to assist in extending such values beyond the confines of the family or tribe.[85]

Thirdly, science is not just concerned with the "what." Our understanding of how things are inevitably colors and influences our views on how the world ought to be. If we know as a matter of fact that walking in nature makes us calmer and more amiable, then we would be wise to spend more time in nature.[86] If we understand through science the mechanisms that promote or undermine our physical and mental well-being, and how such mechanisms impact our sense of self-worth, community, and relationships, then science earns the right to guide us on how we ought to live. The more science provides coherent ways of explaining the world, the greater potential it will have to opine on what ought to be and to independently generate meaning.

Fourthly, religion has frequently attempted to comment on what there is rather than limit itself on what there ought to be. The Bible depicts death, toil, and pain in childbirth as resulting from Adam and Eve's eating of the fruit of the tree of knowledge (Gen 3:16). The *Mishnah* states that women die in childbirth because they do not observe the laws of family purity, separate tythes when making bread, or fail to kindle the *Shabbat* lights.[87] The idea that death results from sin is embedded in all the Abrahamic faiths. The prophets of old and religious leaders throughout the ages have been prepared to state or speculate on which sins have brought about which calamity, including the coronavirus pandemic.[88]

The real issue is not whether reason and religion are "non-overlapping magisteria," but whether reason can truly speak to every aspect of what it means to be human, whether alone it truly captures all aspects of our humanity.

We will return to the issue of reason's limitations, but for now let us focus on the triumph of reason, because we are at a suitable distance from reason's modern flourishing in the Scientific Revolution of the seventeenth century and the Enlightenment of the eighteenth century to be

84. As evidenced by the millennia of conflicts between religions and different tribes.

85. See Greene, *Moral Tribes*.

86. Florence, *Nature Fix*.

87. Mishnah 2:6.

88. Sokol, "Slammed by COVID-19."

able to see the benefits attained from reason's liberation from the shackles of religion.[89]

In *Enlightenment Now*, Steven Pinker, the psychologist and writer, provides a list of those things on which most people would agree. These include matters of practical well-being, including that "life is better than death. Health is better than sickness. Sustenance is better than hunger."[90] Pinker rightly states that religion provided no means to practically improve any of these things, but science has. In particular, due to advances in science, from the late eighteenth century until 2018, the mortality rate dropped from 1.2 to 0.004 percent.[91] Advancements in agriculture have allowed us to feed more and more people using ever smaller areas of land, and modern commerce has led to a huge increase in global prosperity.[92]

It might be thought that reason and science has suffered a massive setback in the face of coronavirus, which has killed so many, and had such a devastating impact socially and financially. In fact, the opposite is true. What coronavirus has shown is that science holds the key to our salvation. It was science which led the charge in dealing with the pandemic. It is scientific experts who told politicians when we should stay at home and go out. It is doctors who saved lives, and scientists and technologists who worked around the clock on finding cures, vaccines, and tracing apps. The religious leadership either ignored the science, in which case people became ill and died, or took their lead from the scientists. This is not the same as in other plagues. In the fourteenth century, during the black death, religion is all we had. We did not understand the Spanish flu well when it killed millions in the early twentieth century. This does not mean that science has all the answers, but advances in science have improved the way we deal with these calamities.

Through coronavirus, science has also continued to encroach on religion's magisterium, the realm of value and meaning. During the pandemic, we witnessed religious communities gathering for religious and life-cycle events oblivious to the dangers that this posed not only to themselves but to others, while secular doctors and scientists lived out the values that religion claims as its own: selfless devotion, collaboration, care for others, relief from suffering, the value of life over death. Science

89. On the benefits of reason, see Pinker, *Enlightenment Now*, and Rosling, *Factfulness*.

90. Pinker, *Enlightenment Now*, 51.

91. Pinker, *Enlightenment Now*, 57.

92. Pinker, *Enlightenment Now*, 73–78.

and the scientific method have become the guide to working together, forging connection and social improvement.

Pinker is partly right when he writes that "the worldview that guides the moral and spiritual values of a knowledgeable person today is the worldview given to us by science."[93] He is only partly right because those values are reflected in the religions which preceded science, but they have nevertheless required reason to take them where they are today.

Reason is the language in which we can all share, a bedrock on which humanity should rest, a glue that binds. Unless religious morality can speak through the medium of reason, it has meaning only to those believers who are lucky enough to be the recipients of the message to which religion claims to be privy. Reason therefore is the language that religion needs to make itself intelligible to those outside. It is the language which different tribes are forced to speak to get along.

Reason is also the great purifier. It is how we escape our inherited myths and fantasies, rise above them as if in a hot air balloon and peer down. It is the arch-critic, how we stay real, how we stop falling too in love with our own imaginings, and dangerous illusions. When we lose sight of it, we need others with whom we can converse to assist us to regain it. It is one of the greatest treasures that we possess. In a world of fake news, passion politics, religious and ideological extremes, echo chambers, the gut rather than the head, we need reason now more than ever.

In 1782, Naphtali Herz Wessely (1725–1805), an associate of Moses Mendelssohn (1729–1806), the father of the Jewish Enlightenment who we have already encountered, published his *Words of Peace and Truth* (*Divrei Shalom v'Emet*), which encouraged the Jews of Central Europe to embrace Emperor Joseph II's Edict of Toleration, which aimed at promoting secular studies among the Jewish community.

In his tract, Wessely argued that there are two laws: the law of man (*Torat ha-Adam*) and the law of God (*Torat Hashem*). The law of God includes those things "known to Moses through prophesy and must therefore include all ritual." The law of man, in contrast, includes those things "known to the mind." These laws "are not written in a book and most people agree upon them."[94]

Wessely encouraged the Jews to embrace the values of the wider society, incorporating under the category of the law of man a whole host of

93. Pinker, *Enlightenment Now*, 354.
94. Wessely, *Divrei Shalom v'Emet*, 3.

secular subjects such as history and geography, but also ethics. He recommends moral guide books to be written that do not "contradict rationalist principles as enunciated by wise men and scholars of the gentiles."[95] Wessely associated the seven Noachide Laws, the basic principles of morality and monotheism derived by the rabbis from the Noah story, with the law of man.

Wessely insists that the law of man must precede the law of God: "The place where the law of man concludes, there the Divine law begins."[96] Wessely's formulation parallels the thought of German Enlightenment philosophers and educators of his era. Wessely reasoned that a Jew who transgresses the laws of God yet who knows the laws of man remains beneficial to the rest of humanity, whereas he who adheres only to the laws of God benefits neither the Jewish people nor humankind.

Moses Mendelssohn's views on the question of the relationship between natural and revealed law, referred to above, represent a philosophical expression of similar ideas. In his prize essay, *Abhandlung über die Evidenz in Metaphysischen Wissenscahsften* (1764), he wrote that "it is not difficult to show that one can demonstrate the general principles of ethics with geometric rigour and force."[97] The reference to geometry may well be a reference to Spinoza's *Ethics*, with which Mendelssohn would have been familiar, as we have seen. Mendelssohn's trust in reason is maintained in his *Jerusalem*, where he similarly states: "It is true that I recognize no eternal truths other than those that are not only comprehensible to human reason but also demonstrable and verifiable by it."[98]

It is not necessary for someone to adopt whole-heartedly the views of Spinoza or the Enlightenment project to believe in the primacy of reason, to feel its benefits, to sing its praises, to desire its freedom, and to see the advantage of adopting it as the core of the spiritual path.

## Religion as Utility

The third insight of Spinoza I wish to focus on is his view of religion as having practical benefit. We have seen that Spinoza did not reject religion outright but considered that it has utility specifically in ensuring the

95. Wessely, *Divrei Shalom v'Emet*, 13–14.

96. Wessely, *Divrei Shalom v'Emet*, 5–6.

97. Arkush, *Moses Mendelssohn*, 105.

98. Mendelssohn, *Jerusalem*, 94.

obedience of the masses to the dictates of reason. In so doing, Spinoza hammers home what all believers in truth must know. We cannot expect the world to buy into our narrative, to see the world through our eyes, to accept the role of the righteous gentile, when we exult in our preferential role. Spinoza saves us from the danger of setting up our perceived place in the world against the world, from demanding that the world accepts our interpretation of it. But we do not need to abandon our belief in chosenness. On the contrary, we should embrace it. Religion dictates how we should act. It plays a crucial role in the inculcation of ethical values into the heart of its adherents. A religion that does that well is entitled to consider itself chosen.

In 1779, Gotthold Ephraim Lessing, whom we have already met, wrote *Nathan der Weise* (*Nathan the Wise*), a play which tells a story of the travels of Nathan through the orient. Nathan was a wise Jew, which would have been viewed as an anomaly in Lessing's time.

In Act 3, Saladin, the great Sultan, seeks Nathan's opinion on whether Christianity, Islam, or Judaism is the correct religion. Nathan has a dilemma. Any answer other than Islam would land him in huge trouble. Any answer other than Judaism would raise doubts about his piety and integrity. Nathan, being wise, cleverly avoids these snares by relating a parable. It goes:

> In the Orient in ancient times there lived a man who possessed a ring of inestimable worth. Its stone was an opal that emitted a hundred colors, but its real value lay in its ability to make its wearer beloved of God and man. The ring passed from father to most favored son for many generations, until finally its owner was a father with three sons, all equally deserving. Unable to decide which of the three sons was most worthy, the father commissioned a master artisan to make two exact copies of the ring, then gave each son a ring, and each son believed that he alone had inherited the original and true ring. But instead of harmony, the father's plan brought only discord to his heirs. Shortly after the father died, each of the sons claimed to be the sole ruler of the father's house, each basing his claim to authority on the ring given to him by the father. The discord grew even stronger and more hateful when a close examination of the rings failed to disclose any differences.[99]

99. Lessing, "Parable."

The three sons of course are the three Abrahamic religions: Judaism, Christianity, and Islam. The Sultan asks Nathan whether he is going to suggest, based on the story, that Islam, Judaism, and Christianity are of equal worth. The Sultan, and no doubt the audience, expects Nathan to answer in the affirmative, but he does not.

Instead, Nathan explains that the brothers' dispute was eventually brought before a judge. After hearing the history of the original ring and its miraculous powers, the judge ruled that none of them had the authentic ring. The authentic ring "had the power to make its owner beloved of God and man, but each of your rings has brought only hatred and strife. None of you is loved by others; each loves only himself."[100] The judge concluded that the father had either lost the original ring and made three counterfeit rings or, "weary of the tyranny of a single ring," made duplicates. The judge then ordered: "Let each of you demonstrate his belief in the power of his ring by conducting his life in such a manner that he fully merits—as anciently promised—the love of God and man."[101]

The Sultan was impressed with Nathan's story and became Nathan's protector. The parable, placed in Nathan's mouth by Lessing, was not invented by Lessing but is found in earlier sources.[102] It nevertheless highlights an important development in our perception of other religions, and understanding of our own. Nathan was not interested in debating the rights or wrongs of each Abrahamic religion. This disinterest had nothing to do with fear, but because such a debate would be impossible; the question of a religion's authenticity is not something that can be scientifically validated. Instead, each religion is to be judged by its own standards and the way in which it shows itself in the world through its practice. Religion, as a lived tradition, should be judged on how it functions. Lessing, as described above, was an admirer of Spinoza. He might have had Spinoza in mind when he penned this script.

Nathan's parable still has relevance. Religions are appropriately judged by outsiders by the actions of their followers, the societies and communities they build, the spiritual paths they forge, and their contribution to peace, harmony, and human betterment in the context in which they find themselves. The Hebrew Bible is sensitive to how others view those who live by its laws. In Numbers, God threatens to strike the people

100. Lessing, "Parable."
101. Lessing, "Parable."
102. Versions of the tale appear in Boccaccio's *Decameron* and *Gesta Romanorum.*

with pestilence and to cut them off after the tribal heads brought back a negative report of the land of Israel, after being sent by Moses to investigate. Moses pleads with God to hold back the full force of his punishment not because the people deserve mercy, but because "the nations who have heard Your fame will say 'It must be because the LORD was powerless to bring that people into the land He had promised them on oath that He slaughtered them in the wilderness'" (Num 14:15–16). What others think of us matters.

## A Book Like Any Other

Spinoza's views concerning religions' utility described above arise from his rejection of traditional conceptions of revelation. Where, then, does the view that religion have utility leave revelation? Spinoza's views on revelation and the origins of the Bible is the fourth area I wish to focus on.

It has long been a tenet of orthodox Judaism that the Five Books of Moses are the word of God. The *Mishnah* in Sanhedrin states that one who denies *Torah Min ha-Shamayim* (as coming from heaven) has no portion in the world to come.[103] Maimonides's eighth principle of belief is that the Torah is divinely revealed, and that the Torah that Jews have is the same as revealed to Moses, and through him to the children of Israel.[104] In his *Mishneh Torah*, Maimonides further states that it is heretical to state that even a single word of the Torah was added by Moses without divine inspiration.[105]

Within the Jewish orthodox world, these statements were taken literally or almost literally—God dictated every word or almost every word of the Torah to Moses. The corollary of such a view is that the dominant academic position, that the Torah was written and edited by several authors over a long period of time, the final redaction possibly having occurred in the period of Ezra in c. 400 BCE, must be rejected, accommodated, or simply ignored.

In 1957, Rabbi Louis Jacobs (1920–2006), a leader of orthodox Judaism in England, showed his openness to the academic consensus and attempted to reinterpret what was meant by *Torah Min ha-Shamayim* in his book *We Have Reason to Believe*. At first few noticed, but a few years

103. Mishnah Sanhedrin 10:1.

104. Maimonides, *Introduction*, 8th Principle.

105. Maimonides, *MT* Teshuva 3:8; See also *TB* Sanhedrin 99a.

later, Jacobs, who claimed to have been promised the job of principal of Jews' College, an English orthodox educational institution, was accused of heresy. He thereafter broke away from the mainstream Anglo-Orthodox United Synagogue.[106]

The position within certain sections of orthodoxy has changed. I will not attempt here a historical analysis of the evolution of Jewish attitudes to biblical criticism, or where precisely we are now. I merely observe a gentle chipping away at the literal or near-literal approach to *Torah Min ha-Shamayim* within orthodox and neo-orthodox circles, a process of which Spinoza was a forerunner.[107]

As part of this process, orthodox Jews (who I will refer to in this section as "we") were reminded that the version of the Torah that we have is not precisely the same as previous versions. We were told that we do not have an authoritative Masoretic text, but several texts established by the Masoretic schools. We were also reminded of previous authorities who questioned the traditional formulation of *Torah Min ha-Shamayim*, as if somehow this would influence our own assessment of what was being presented as a factual claim.

We were told about the opinion in the Talmud suggesting that the final eight verses of the Torah were written by Joshua rather than Moses,[108] Rabbi Abraham ibn Ezra (c. 1089–1167) who extended this view to the last twelve verses,[109] and Rabbi Yaakov Weinberg (1923–1999) who claimed that Maimonides knew that different variations of the texts existed when he formulated his dogma concerning the divinity of the Torah, but wanted to communicate in a general sense that our Torah is the same as that given to Moses.[110] We also knew that there is nothing in the Torah that refers to the entire Torah being written by Moses.

Even before all this, we were confused about what exactly it is we were meant to believe to have taken place. Let us take the seminal event of the giving of the Torah at Sinai, the theophany. On a plain reading, the Torah contains various accounts, each with its own nuance. Where was Moses during the theophany, up or down the mountain? Was God on

106. Jacobs, *We Have Reason to Believe*, preface.

107. See Shapiro, "Is Modern Orthodoxy Moving?" See also the numerous essays on modern Bible scholarship at www.thetorah.com.

108. *TB* Makkot 11a.

109. Ibn Ezra, Commentary on Deuteronomy 1:2.

110. Shapiro, *Limits of Orthodox Theology*, 116.

the mountain or up in heaven? What did God speak, the first of the Ten Commandments, all of the commandments, the whole Torah?[111]

It is also difficult theologically to get one's head around the idea of a God who dictates, if literal dictation is intended, given that Maimonides urges us to cast off any notion of God's corporality. Not to mention the question of why God would produce a work which looks so very much of its time and place, if God is not bound by time and place, and intended the Torah as a guide for all time?

Being a trial advocate, I imagine receiving a brief to argue the case for *Torah Min ha-Shamayim.* In the common law courts in which I appear, I do not need to prove my case beyond reasonable doubt, but only on the balance of probabilities. That is all very well, but before taking on the case, I would need to understand what it is I am arguing. In this case, I would need clarification on what is meant by Torah, what is meant by heaven, and what is the nature of the God that caused the Torah to come down from that place. I would also only be in position to argue the case if there was consensus on all these points among my clients. Where is that clarification, where is that consensus, and where is the positive evidence on which I am going to rely?

The more one engages in this thought experiment, the more it becomes clear that what was being urged upon us is less belief in a historic event or series of historical events, but an orientation not only toward the teaching, but also the experience described in the text. As I will later argue, part of that experience is comprehending Torah as coming from heaven, as relating to God as dwelling in heaven, as transcendent; that is, engaging with God as other.

Spinoza's claim that the Bible is a book like any other represents an important stage, not so much in the development of modern biblical scholarship, but to the theology of the thinking layperson.[112] His challenge forces his readers to look beyond questions of historical origins, and to confront what it is we want from this book, what it means to us, and how it shapes and will continue to shape us. Spinoza encourages us to appreciate the distinction between history and revelation. Understanding that distinction heralds a new maturity and deepens, rather than weakens, our commitment.

111. See Exod 19:24–25; 20:1; 19:3, 11; 19:25—20:1; and Neh 9:13 explored in detail in Sommer, *Revelation and Authority,* 35–42.

112. For an introduction to the critical approach to the Bible in the seventeenth century, see Morrow, *Three Skeptics and the Bible.*

Central to Spinoza's critique is that the Bible is not a book of philosophy or otherwise based on rationalist principles but something altogether different. Many of us can relate to such a view. Spinoza's position is contrary to the position taken by Maimonides who wants us to view revelation, as far as possible, as corresponding to reason. Maimonides was driven in this regard by a commitment to reason and defending Judaism against those who criticized its teachings as contradicting reason.[113]

In his *Guide*, Maimonides explains that if the Torah appears to conflict with philosophy, this is only because the Torah "speaks in the language of man" so that it can be understood by the masses.[114] In actuality, there is no such conflict. Revelation derives from philosophy, and to be a prophet one is required to first be a philosopher. This entails a process of intensive intellectual training: "He who wishes to attain to human perfection, must . . . first study Logic, next the various branches of Mathematics in their proper order, then Physics, and lastly Metaphysics."[115]

Prophecy in general results from the operation of the Active Intellect (an emanation of God) first through the rational faculty, and then through the imaginative faculty "which becomes perfect and active."[116] However, for Moses, the greatest of the prophets, God's message did not flow through his imaginative faculty at all. Moses simply recorded the unmediated words of God.[117] This depiction of Moses's prophecy as unmediated through the imagination cements the association of reason and revelation. As we have seen, *Halachah* (Jewish Law) deriving from such revelation is conceived by Maimonides as inherently rational and promoting the welfare of the body and the soul.

In his *Theological-Political Treatise*, Spinoza takes issue with Maimonides's claim in the *Guide* that the Torah supports the position that the world is created, rather than eternal.[118] Spinoza observes that Maimonides's approach means that if he had concluded by the application of reason that the world was eternal and not created "he would not hesitate to bend scripture to devise an interpretation that would ultimately render

113. Kraemer, *Maimonides*, 16–18.
114. Maimonides, *Guide*, I.XXVI.35.
115. Maimonides, *Guide*, I.XXXIV.46.
116. Maimonides, *Guide*, II.XLI.235.
117. Maimonides, *Guide*, II.XLV.245.
118. Maimonides, *Guide*, II.XXV.309.

it saying apparently the same thing," regardless of what Scripture actually states.[119]

Spinoza is justifiably critical of Maimonides's position. First, he points out that Maimonides's approach demands reading a biblical text to accord with reason even where its plain meaning suggests something different. Secondly, it means that for Maimonides the Bible's true meaning remains obscure until it is known through reason or reinterpreted to accord with reason. Thirdly, Maimonides's position requires the people to either be philosophers themselves or to rely on philosophers, which would result in new ecclesiastical authorities "which are more likely to be mocked than venerated" by the common people.[120]

In place of the Maimonidean approach, Spinoza introduces a methodology for studying the Bible based on a historical analysis of the text, which requires a consideration of the "nature and properties of the language in which the biblical books were composed and which their authors were accustomed to speak," the arguments that Scripture itself makes without adding any gloss, and the life and characters of its authors.[121]

For my current purposes, I am interested in the impact of Spinoza and similar academic methods on the mind of the believer, rather than the correctness of the specific theories that are being put forward. Spinoza's approach to the Bible has liberated us, although we do not always see it like that. Firstly, it has allowed us to understand more about the text by looking at its context and internal workings. Secondly, it has stripped away our preconceptions and shown us the Torah as seen from the outside, as a "book like any other," to use Spinoza's terminology.

Regardless of our background, after centuries of the application of the historical method, we see a book that appears to us to be very much of its time, although clearly orientated toward a powerful monotheistic message. The creation and flood stories are not unlike creation stories of the ancient Near East.[122] The idea of the covenant is not unlike the suzerain treaties common in days of old.[123] The existence of contradictory texts uninterested in history reflects other narratives of the same

119. Spinoza, *TTP*, 7:19, 113.
120. Spinoza, *TTP*, 7:19, 114.
121. Spinoza, *TTP*, 7:5, 100–101.
122. Azize, *Gilgameš and the World of Assyria*; Sarna, *Understanding Genesis*.
123. Baltzer, *Covenant Formulary*.

period.[124] Laws in the biblical law codes resemble laws in Hamurabi's and other ancient codes.[125] The depiction of God as male and attitudes toward women reflect a particular patriarchal perspective.[126] The use of sacrifices, impurity rights, vows, and curses are all of their time.[127]

Yet, despite all this, the Torah is not like any other book. It holds a meaning for Jews (and others) which is wholly different to that of any other book. It is not something external to us, but is lodged in our hearts, memory, limbs. It exudes from our pores, the words we speak and write, the values we live by, our perceptions of history and the future. Our lives are refracted through it. Spinoza and the critical tradition that followed, have assisted us in framing the real question that we each need to answer. The question is not "Who wrote the Bible?" or "How did the Bible come to be?" but "How is this book different from all other books?" The answer has to address more than content or history. It needs to be about revelation, meaning, and destiny.

Spinoza's critique of Maimonides also highlights the limitations of seeking to square the Torah with what we consider to be rational. If we adopt Spinoza's approach, even partially, any rational critique of the Torah presents no conflict. We do not need to reconcile the biblical account with science, academic theory about the Bible's historical origins, or our current moral values—to twist ourselves into all sorts of contortions—because the Torah is not for him a history, a science, or by itself a moral code.

One approach often taken in modern orthodox Jewish circles is to justify laws or institutions which are morally problematic by claiming that the Torah makes a concession to the social and political realities of the ancient world but aims for gradual ethical improvement. The presumption behind this notion, sometimes referred to as "moral gradualism," is that ancient society was unable to move far from its then-current state, could not undergo radical change toward moral improvement, and so fairy footsteps had to be taken.[128] The gradualist claims that the ideal was always for animal sacrifice or slavery to be abolished, for women to

124. Berman, *Biblical Criticism*, ch. 5.

125. Kugel, *How to Read the Bible*, 270–72; Sonsino, "Characteristics of Biblical Law."

126. Ross, *Expanding the Palace of Torah*.

127. On curses, see Anderson, "Social Function of Curses in the Hebrew Bible."

128. Harris, *Faith Without Fear*, 109.

be more equal to men, for whatever we now consider to be morally desirable to have been intended all along.

This approach owes much to Maimonides's *Guide*. He wrote that it is "impossible to go suddenly from one extreme to the other: it is therefore according to the nature of man impossible for him suddenly to discontinue everything to which he has been accustomed."[129] The late Rabbi Nahum Rabinovich (1928–2020) relies on Maimonides to explain why slavery could not be outlawed in the Bible. He writes:

> In the ancient world, it was almost impossible to sustain a proper economy without vast amounts of human labour, and that human labour was usually recruited for the most part from slaves. The leading thinkers among the nations could not conceive of a successful society without abundant bonded servants; as a matter of economics, it was simply impossible.[130]

The idea is superficially attractive. It suggests advancement, human progress, and moral evolution, but it is also flawed. To start with, is it really the case that slavery could not have been abandoned in the ancient world? While it is true that all cultures had it, there were those such as the Stoics who encouraged the humane treatment of slaves stressing that human value is based on moral worth not external status.[131] Manumission of slaves (albeit with strings attached) was also possible in ancient Greece and Rome, and some former slaves became philosophers.[132] Surely the Jews, a slave nation who knew how awful slavery is, were in an excellent position to establish a new society in a new land from the off without slavery?

Secondly, there is virtually nothing in the biblical text to indicate a push in the direction of abolitionism with respect to slavery in general. Exodus 21:21 provides laws to protect the Hebrew slave who can serve only six years and must then have an option to go free. Leviticus

---

129. Maimonides, *Guide*, III.XXXII.322. Maimonides might have been inspired to take a gradualist approach through his encounter with Islam. The Koran initially recommends that alcohol not be consumed (II:219), then prohibits its drinking during prayer (IV:43), then finally prohibits it altogether (V:90–92).

130. Rabinovitch, "Way of Torah," 9.

131. Seneca, *Moral Letters*, 47, referred to in Wiedemann, *Greek and Roman Slavery*, 224,

132. E.g., Phaedon of Elis, who was close to Socrates and provided Plato with a title for one of his works. Wiedemann, *Greek and Roman Slavery*, 234. See also Zelnick-Abramovitz, "Not Wholly Free," 335–44.

25:44–46 warns Israelites not to rule harshly over one another, but the "children of the sojourners who dwell among you" may be bought, sold, inherited, and kept forever.

Thirdly, if the true end of the Bible is to lead us in a specific direction, why is the ultimate destiny so well hidden, even from Judaism's scholars? Maimonides applied his idea of moral gradualism to idolatry and animal sacrifice, but he does not apply the same idea to slavery, which he accepted, or to his views of women or gentiles.[133] On slavery, he writes that, as a matter of law, non-Jewish slaves can be treated harshly, although "the quality of benevolence and the paths of wisdom demand of a human being to be merciful and to strive for justice." In practice, therefore, one should be kind to ones' non-Jewish slave, but this is not a legal obligation.[134] Maimonides also does not say that the Bible is leading us in the direction of abolitionism.

There is a discussion in the Babylonian Talmud about whether one is permitted to free a non-Jewish slave. Rabbi Ishmael held that it is permissible, but Rabbi Akiva forbade it.[135] Maimonides follows the view of Rabbi Akiva.[136] Why could Maimonides not see what we would accept as the more moral outcome? Why did Rabbi Akiva oppose Rabbi Yishmael, if the Torah's purpose is to lead us to greater morality? The problem with moral gradualism is that we do not seem to be able to see where we are heading until we are there.

Indeed, there are religious texts which go out of their way to justify an outlook which today is viewed as reprehensible. The Torah describes how Noah planted a vineyard and became drunk after exiting from the ark. His sons discovered him naked and covered him with a blanket. In the morning, he awoke and cursed his son Ham saying: "Cursed be Canaan; the lowest of slaves shall he be to his brothers" (Gen 9:22–27). The Midrash Rabbah plays on Ham's name. It says that, on account of Noah's curse, *yatsa cham mefucham*, "Ham came out black-skinned."[137] The Midrash associates blackness with Ham and slavery. The precise nature of

133. Maimonides generally saw women as being biologically unequal to men, and gentiles as being unequal to Jews for historical-social reasons. See Kasher, "Intellects of Women and Gentiles." His views on these matters are unsurprising given the period in which he lived.

134. Maimonides, *MT* Hilchot Avadim 9:7.

135. *TB* Sotah 3a.

136. Maimonides, *MT* Hilchot Avadim 9:6.

137. Midrash Rabbah Genesis 36:7.

Ham's sin is the subject of speculation in the Midrash, but whatever he did it was obviously something really bad.

This Midrash has no bearing on Jewish law, but such associations form a troubling backdrop to modern justifications for slavery. Gomes Eanes da Zurara, a medieval chronicler, observed: "And here you must note that these blacks, though they were Moors like the others, were nonetheless slaves [*servos*] of these by ancient custom, which I believe to be the curse which after the flood [of Noah] threw on his son [Cain]."[138] In 1857, James A. Sloan, a Presbyterian minister, similarly wrote that "Ham deserved death for his unfilial and impious conduct. But the Great Lawgiver saw fit, in his good pleasure, not to destroy him . . . All Ham's posterity are either black or dark colored, and thus bear upon their countenance the mark of inferiority which God put upon the progenitor."[139]

If the views in the biblical treatment of slavery were intended to be a staging post toward a more enlightened view, one would expect views like those in the Midrash to have been unanimously abandoned in the modern period, but this is not the case. The Netziv, Rabbi Naftali Zvi Yehudah Berlin (1816–1893), writes in his *Ha'emek Davar* about the slave class whose members are born to be slaves "from birth, from the womb, and from conception." This class does not include *Shem* and *Yaphet* (Noah's other sons) whose "inner spirit longs to be free" but only, one must infer, the sons of Ham.[140]

The Bible may well have represented a radical development in the evolution of morality in its day and contributed to our moral intuitions more generally, but at some point in early modernity, reason and our moral intuitions overtook the values contained in the ancient scriptures, and religion has been playing catch up ever since. It is reason which caused us to question animal sacrifice, led to the emancipation of slaves, and many of the freedoms we now enjoy.

It took feminism to inspire Jews to look for feminist readings of the Torah. It took abolitionist tendencies to inspire biblical abolitionism. It took environmentalism to inspire biblical environmentalism. It takes a sea change in attitudes to sexuality and gender to inspire a new approach to homosexuality and gender. Religious readings of the text are

138. Crónica 85, ch. 16, quoted in Schorsch, *Jews and Blacks*, 147.

139. Sloan, *Great Question Answered*, 75, 78–80, quoted in Goldenberg, *Curse of Ham*, 176,

140. Berlin, *Ha'emek Davar*, 9:25. On slavery in Judaism generally, see Shmalo, "Orthodox Approaches to Biblical Slavery," 1–20.

not influencing wider society, wider society is influencing religious readings of the texts.

The Bible's role now is not to teach everything about ethics but to
provide an alternative voice and set of values, a vantage from which to assess whence we have come from and where we are heading. To recognize
this is to set God free from the text.

What Spinoza and the modern scholarship which followed has also
shown us is that the Bible is not in fact a book of reason after all. That is
not to say that there are not rational elements in it, but the Torah reaches
beyond reason. Spinoza sees biblical prophecy as a work of imagination.
In one sense, imagination is error-free because imagination is not expected to be true. For Spinoza, error arises when we confuse imagination
with reason. So long as we understand the difference between imagination and reason and that imagination cannot safely make truth claims
regarding theological matters, the exercise of the imaginative faculty can
help us to act morally and is a virtue.[141]

The insights presented to us by Spinoza, and the critical tradition
of which he is a part, stand on the foundations of reason and rational
inquiry, but force us to embrace imagination and the experiential, which
lead us to traverse the purely scientific. As argued, the appearance of the
Bible as a book like any other requires us to explain why it is not a book
like any other by giving credence to our experience of it as something
wholly unlike anything else. The recognition that the Torah is not a work
of philosophy but reaches beyond reason brings us face to face with the
wordless and mystical. Spinoza's rational non-dualism also draws us to a
place beyond our common experience. We will need soon to reach beyond Spinoza, but for now hold these thoughts.

## The Individual as Psychological Being

A further insight bequeathed to us by Spinoza is that we are psychological
beings open to rational investigation, and that a proper understanding of
our psychology is required for self-flourishing. As stated above, such an
understanding anticipates modern psychology and contemporary therapeutic approaches to well-being. I want to explore Spinoza's therapeutic
system further, as it continues to provide useful insights.

141. Spinoza, *Ethics*, II.XVII.132.

Descartes postulated that our mind is separate from our body, but Spinoza held that the mind and body are "one and the same individual, which is conceived now under the attribute of thought, now under the attribute of extension."[142] The body is the object of the mind.[143] Our bodies and minds are intimately connected, two ways of speaking about the same thing. We must therefore take care of our bodies:

> It is, I say, the part of a wise man to refresh and recreate himself with moderate and agreeable food and drink, as also with the perfume and beauty of plants, with dress, music, athletic sports, theatre, and other things of the same kind, which each can use without any injury to the rest.[144]

We have already seen how Spinoza distinguishes between internal and external causes. When external things affect us, we are passive. When an internal thing affects us, we act through our natures and are active. We act through our natures when we have more adequate ideas of how these affects work, that is, when we understand our psychology and what makes us tick. Such self-knowledge involves the application of pure reason, which Spinoza associates with love of God: "He who clearly and distinctly understands his emotions loves God, and loves him in proportion as he understands [himself and] his emotions."[145] This is no easy task.[146]

Spinoza describes how passions (which he also calls affects) arise and continue in the mind until a stronger passion stops them in their tracks.[147] The three primary passions are pleasure (or joy), pain (or sadness), and desire.[148] Passions can arise externally or be generated internally. It is virtually impossible for us to act by internal forces alone: "Hence it follows, that man is necessarily always liable to passions, that he follows the common order of nature, obeys it and accommodates himself to it as much as the nature of things demands."[149]

Although Spinoza does not believe that our actions are uncaused, by improving the adequacy of our ideas we can act more in accordance

---

142. Spinoza, *Ethics*, II.XXI.134.

143. Spinoza, *Ethics*, II.XXI.134.

144. Spinoza, *Ethics*, IV.XLV.Schol 2.259. See similar advice on the maintenance of the body in Maimonides, *MT* Hilchot Deot 4:1–10.

145. Spinoza, *Ethics*, V.XV.300.

146. Marshall, *Spiritual Automaton*, 20–21.

147. Spinoza, *Ethics*, IV.VII.233.

148. Spinoza, *Ethics*, III.XI.Schol.171.

149. Spinoza, *Ethics*, IV.IV.Coroll.232.

with our internal causes than our external ones. He writes that a thing is called free which "exists solely from the necessity of its nature and is determined to action by itself alone."[150] One who is led by his rational desires has more freedom than one led by external passions.[151]

Spinoza describes how our passions are generated in ways to which we can all relate. He writes that we often associate two unrelated passions by virtue of having experienced them together at some point.[152] We also tend to associate people, places, or events with the painful or pleasurable experiences encountered when first experiencing them. This is liable to impact our attitude to those things. Similarly, we run toward that which we imagine will bring us joy and flee from that which will bring us sadness.[153] We associate with people who we believe are like us.[154] We act to attain validation or to avoid rebuke.[155]

Spinoza recommends keeping our passions in check by adopting "maxims for life" or "guiding precepts" and forming positive habits:

> The best thing we can do, therefore, as long as we do not have a perfect knowledge of our emotions, is to conceive a right theory of life or certain guiding precepts, to fix them in the memory, and apply them to particular cases of frequent occurrence, that our minds may be deeply impressed by them, and that they may always be at hand.[156]

One such maxim or precept is that hate should be conquered by love.[157] Spinoza also recommends that we distinguish our emotions from the thought of the external causes to which they are attached.[158]

The psychological/therapeutic approach promoted by Spinoza resonates with our contemporary interest in well-being, including physical exercise, mindfulness, positive psychology, and emotional intelligence. There is also a parallel with modern therapies, such as Cognitive Behavioral Therapy, which arose from the approaches of Albert Ellis in the

---

150. Spinoza, *Ethics*, I.Definition.7.73.

151. Marshall, *Spiritual Automaton*, 145.

152. Spinoza, *Ethics*, III.XIV–XV.174–75, L.197.

153. Spinoza, *Ethics*, III.XXV.180.

154. Spinoza, *Ethics*, III.XXVII.182.

155. Spinoza, *Ethics*, III.XXIX.183.

156. Spinoza, *Ethics*, V.X.Schol.297–98.

157. Spinoza, *Ethics*, V.X.Schol.298. See Marshall, *Spiritual Automaton*, 157, 191.

158. Spinoza, *Ethics*, V.II.292.

1950s and Aaron T. Beck in the 1960s, which asks us to treat our thoughts as separate from external events and uses techniques aimed at changing the narratives we tell about ourselves and others.

The science and practice of well-being has in many ways become a new religion, at once universal, life affirming, therapeutic, easy to understand, and free from the baggage of the traditional faiths. Spinoza's association of self-knowledge with love of God reflects our contemporary spiritual orientation which starts from care of the self. This is as true for religious people as much as secularists.[159] At some level, we are all Spinozists now.[160]

159. A pioneer of the psychological/therapeutic approach within twentieth-century Jewish ultra-orthodoxy was Rabbi Dr Abraham J. Twerski. His brother, Rabbi Michel Twerski, teaches the Three Principles, espoused by Sydney Banks, which have a distinctly monistic flavor. The three principles are Mind (the energy and intelligence of all life), Thought (the creative element of the universe and source of reality), and Consciousness (pure awareness).

160. Hence the space for works explicating Spinoza's practical philosophy for the general reading public such as *Think Least of Death*, by Steven Nadler, which came out when I was finalizing this book.

# 5

# The Darker Side

SPINOZA'S CONCEPTIONS OF GOD, reason, the self, and politics purport to be based on mathematical principles, but they do not in fact reach the level of mathematical truth. The later Enlightenment sought to divide the world between reason and myth. Reason was viewed as good, myth as bad. However, as Horkheimer and Adorno noted in the *Dialectic of Enlightenment*, based on their work during the Second World War, the Enlightenment itself constituted a new myth about myths, our natures, and origins: "The myths which fell victim to the Enlightenment were themselves its products."[1] The Enlightenment myth shared with the ancient myths the idea that man is the center of the universe, that his task is to preserve himself and dominate, and that fate predominates.[2] Spinoza's ideas, which foreshadow those of the European Enlightenment, constitute yet another myth about origins and existence. His narrative, like everyone else's, is designed to explain the world in a way which is most advantageous and attractive to him.

Here is also the place for us to acknowledge that, despite Spinoza's attractiveness, there is a dark side to his ideas, which epitomize problems with the technological worldview on which much of our contemporary thinking is based. Spinoza's philosophy pointed the way toward the Enlightenment, and the unshakable belief in reason and scientific advancement, but humans are not purely rational, and the world does not operate solely on rational principles. Chaos is everywhere at work and will not bow to reason, contrary to what Spinoza, and those who followed on

1. Horkheimer, *Dialectic*, 5.
2. Horkheimer, *Dialectic*, 6–8.

93

similar paths, would have us believe. A world built purely on reason cuts us off from our humanity. A world molded by mathematics and technology risks creating a virtual reality which will narrow rather than expand our capacities and horizons.

Spinoza's God, as the God of reason, suffers from similar shortcomings, despite its grandeur and unifying potential. It is overly mechanical and threatens individuality and difference.[3] For Spinoza, humans are modes of the totality, waves on the surface of the sea of infinity, and already subsumed within the All. A God of everything, without will or care, risks obliterating distinction and reducing existence to the nothingness from which it came. We are as naught before such a substance, powerless to act freely, frozen in eternity. We might be drawn instinctively to Spinoza's God, but can we live with it, when our freedom and humanity is at stake? The same question can be asked about the technological singularity we are apparently heading toward.

In this chapter, I will argue that we must retreat from Spinoza's God in the very knowledge of its existence. It is a truth stripped bare, a leafless tree in winter. We need rain and sun, nutrients, new buds, fresh leaves, flowers, and fruit. Spinoza, the heretic, touched the bedrock, but we need to build on it. Soon, we will need to depart from Spinoza and turn to Heidegger, the hater, and other revealer of profound truths, but first we need to expand on the dangers inherent in Spinoza's rationalist immanentist philosophy.

## Humans Are Not Facts

Spinoza's philosophy is dominated by an almost-religious belief that all being is reducible to cause and effect and driven only by the drive to be, *Conatus*. For Spinoza, imagination is at worst aberrant and at best a utility required to keep the masses obedient to the natural laws of reason and the state. On this approach, the human being is an object to be known

---

3. Ernst Haeckel, the biologist and admirer of Spinoza, mentioned above, certainly found nothing in Spinoza to contradict his promotion of eugenics, the inhumane desire to level humanity in the name of efficiency. In Haeckel, Darwinian theories of evolution combined with Spinozian pantheism to allow him to promote a mechanistic view of the world in which life arose without divine will, and to champion the idea of a single substance. Haeckel wrote that in Spinoza's "pantheistic system the notion of the world (the universe, or the cosmos) is identical with the all-pervading notion of God . . . it is the purest and most rational monism" Haeckel, *Riddle of the Universe*, 219, quoted in Armond, "Cosmic Men," 43.

scientifically and to be manipulated technically for practical purposes. Imagination allows us to live cooperatively by constructing narratives, but it is reason which grants us access to the universal. There is a contemporary scientific mindset which operates on similar assumptions.[4]

In his short book *Being Human*, Rowan Williams, the former Archbishop of Canterbury, challenges the modern tendency to view human beings as facts, as objects which stand besides other objects. Williams reminds us that

> what makes me *this* person rather than another, is not simply a set of facts. Or rather it's the enormous fact of my being here rather than elsewhere, being in these relations with those around me, being a child of these children, the friend of x, the not-so-intimate friend of y. I stand in the middle of a network of relations, the point where the lines cross.[5]

Our experience involves not just brute facts, but a complex network of associations, a hierarchy of care and concerns, imagination, memory, feeling, depth. We are not just a bundle of descriptors. We are more than the sum of our parts and capable of reaching beyond the confines of our personalities and circumstances to achieve incredible things. Williams quotes Vladimir Lossky (1903–1858), the Russian theologian, who describes humans as uniquely capable of "overstepping" their natures while still containing them. Lossky held that it is that ability to overstep which points to our being more than "one unique instance of its kind."[6]

Raymond Tallis, the neuroscientist and philosopher, also describes human overreaching, but here in the context of perceiving external objects:

> Our perception yields objects that transcend our awareness; we are explicitly aware that the object is more than our

---

4. Although this is the prevalent view, there are some who argue for a less one-dimensional Spinoza who acknowledges the importance of the imagination within the human realm. See Garver, *Cunning of Imagination*. Susan James similarly shows Spinoza's recognition of the importance of the imagination in constructing narratives, She also warns against exaggerating the "dysfunctional character of imagination," as Spinoza sees it. She writes: "Despite its deficiencies, it provides us with a largely efficacious grasp of the world and ourselves, and underpins many sensible habits and decisions about what to do and how to live." James, "Narrative," 255.

5. Williams, *Being Human*, 31.

6. Lossky, "Theological Notion of the Human Person," quoted in Williams, *Being Human*, 30.

perceptions—it is not exhausted by our perceptions—and that it is other than ourself. This transcendent object, which is seen as something only partly revealed, is related to a transcendent self that is other than it. There is no room for this kind of thing in a causally hard-wired universe of material objects, which would include material organisms and material organs in those organisms, such as the brain.[7]

Tallis later describes how our inner workings differ from those of animals. He writes: "Unlike the physiological emotions of animals, our feelings are forever articulating themselves, making sense of themselves, narrating themselves, appealing to moral and other expectations, rights and wrongs, and possibilities and impossibilities."[8]

Spinoza is sensitive to how perceptions operate and how feelings manifest themselves, but his response is to seek to box, analyze, and ultimately control such perceptions and emotions, which he blames on the imagination, external forces, and inadequate ideas. By so doing, he devalues aspects of what it means to be human.

## For the Other

Spinoza's philosophy is also totalizing. We are part of a single substance. Our sense of individuality and our sense of the other is a figment of our imaginations. As described, a crowd might be as much of an individual as an individual person.[9] There is no separateness. Ethics involves shutting out the external world and acting only from internal causes. A focus on externality leads to inadequate ideas. The outside is foreign, because in truth there is no such thing as the outside. There is only God. For Spinoza, living ethically means living rationally, which means treating others well because it is more beneficial for us to live in peace and security with our neighbors than in a state of war. This is a purely pragmatic philosophy. There is no objective good, no sense of the other as anything containing depth, as containing the possibility to "overstep" herself, as a world unto himself, as someone who makes moral demands on us. This is a shortcoming. Relationship is a fundamental aspect of who we are.

---

7. Tallis, *Aping Mankind*, 109.

8. Tallis, *Aping Mankind*, 235.

9. Spinoza, *Ethics*, III.PXVII.176.

Emanuel Levinas (1906–1995), the Jewish-French philosopher, provides a corrective to Spinoza's philosophy. Levinas's ethics is built on what he considers to be the primordial encounter with the other. Soon after we are born, we appreciate that there are others besides ourselves, who exist independently from us, who are unknowable, yet who make demands on us by virtue of their very existence: "The strangeness of the Other, his irreducibility to the I, to my thoughts and my possessions, is precisely accomplished as a calling into question of my spontaneity, as ethics."[10]

Levinas considered that Spinoza's idea of God as the absolute keeps humans enclosed as if in a fortress, preventing openness to the new or other.[11] For Levinas, without independence, there can be no autonomy and without autonomy there can be no ethical possibility: "Thought and freedom come to us from separation and from the consideration of the Other [*Autrui*]—this thesis is at the antipodes of Spinozism."[12]

Levinas saw individuals as being constantly drawn inward, as stuck to their own lives: we are "riveted to ourselves, enclosed in a tight circle that smothers."[13] The means to escape is through encounter with beings independent of us, the other, or otherness, alterity.[14] The other is a condition of our ability to be a rational human being. Without such other or others, there can be no adequate ethics. For Levinas, God is the ultimate other. In contrast to Spinoza, Levinas's God is not the God of everything, but a transcendent God, separate from us, calling us to live a life of holiness. Levinas believed that without such God, we are entrapped within ourselves.

Contrary to Spinoza, Levinas suggests that we can only perceive God because we are separated from him and that there is something in the nature of God which prevents totalization: "To have the idea of Infinity it is necessary to exist as separated . . . If totality can not be constituted it is because Infinity does not permit itself to be integrated. It is not the insufficiency of the I that prevents totalization, but the Infinity of the Other."[15]

---

10. Levinas, *Totality and Infinity*, sec. 1, 43.

11. See Cohen, *Out of Control*, 24.

12. Levinas, *Totality and Infinity*, sec. 1, 105; Cohen, *Out of Control*, 31.

13. Levinas, *Nausea*, 66, quoted in Cohen, *Out of Control*, 36.

14. Cohen, *Out of Control*, 37.

15. Levinas, *Totality and Infinity*, sec. 1, 79–80.

## Feeling

Spinoza's ethics are also devoid of emotion. The only true emotion for Spinoza is love of God, but this love is a purely intellectual love that involves adequate knowledge, rather than a reciprocal relationship of care and attachment: "He who loves God, cannot desire that God should love him in return."[16]

Spinoza might retort that his approach avoids overly sentimentalizing our moral judgments and promotes practical problem-solving without excessive passion. The danger, however, is that it desensitizes us to the evils we encounter and allows little room for care, empathy, the need to listen, or gratitude, and other qualities which characterize and enhance human existence.

Here again, Levinas's ethics present a challenge to Spinoza's. They are full of empathy and longing. Levinas writes:

> The tenderness of skin is the very gap between approach and approached, a disparity, a non-intentionality, a non-teleology . . . Proximity, immediacy, is to enjoy and to suffer by the other. But I can enjoy and suffer by the other only because I am-for-the-other, am signification, because the contact with skin is still a proximity of a face, a responsibility, an obsession with the other, being-one-for-the-other.[17]

Love for the other emerges from and leads back to love of self in a virtuous cycle: "It is the passivity of being-for-another, which is possible only in the form of giving the very bread I eat. But for this one has to first enjoy one's bread, not in order to have the merit of giving it, but in order to give it with one's heart, to give oneself in giving it."[18] Similarly, while Levinas accepts with Spinoza that evil has no intrinsic meaning, he held that the existence of evil requires us to find meaning, to feel the pain of those who undergo its torments, and to act to alleviate its effects.[19]

It might be countered that Spinoza's ethics are not as coolly rational as made out. Spinoza's proposition that we are all part of a single substance, an aspect of God, linked by cause and effect, implies that boundaries are illusory, mere social conventions, a result of inadequate ideas.

16. Spinoza, *Ethics*, V.XIX.301.

17. Levinas, *Otherwise than Being*, 90, quoted in Cohen, *Out of Control*, 53.

18. Levinas, *Otherwise than Being*, 72, quoted in Cohen, *Out of Control*, 54.

19. Cohen, *Out of Control*, 100.

This notion should give rise to its own ethical imperative. Given our essential interconnectedness, we are all responsible for each other.

It is difficult to overlook, however, that Spinoza's *Ethics* does not take this direction. It is not built on ethical responsibility or any attempt to encounter the other as other, but on purely practical considerations. Our lives are better if we act rationally, and this involves acting ethically. Spinoza's oneness is not about interconnectedness, which implies relationship and responsibility, but sameness, the eternal uniformity of substance in which all difference is subsumed.

## Life of the Community

Some have also pointed to the danger of Spinoza's ideas to the life of the community, and political life, associating his thought with totalitarianism.[20] Their views are relevant to the dangers inherent in the ideas of immanence and totality more generally, which is central to this book.

It will be recalled that Spinoza disparages the multitude who are incapable of thinking or acting rationally. For him, the highest authority is the state to which we relinquish all freedom through a social contract. The state has power and is therefore just, because justice and power operate in tandem. Spinoza's biggest fear is not power, but anarchy, and the resultant chaos. The state must therefore aim primarily at peace and security, which are the necessary conditions of the life of philosophy and science.

Jean-Luc Nancy, the French thinker, attacks the idea of immanence applied to the political arena. He contends that such immanence "would instantly suppress community, or communication." There would be only "the continuous identity of atoms." He continues: "Collective enterprises dominated by a will to absolute immanence have as their truth the truth of death. Immanence, communal fusion, contains no other logic than that of suicide of the community that is governed by it."[21] The idea of individuals as atoms well captures Spinoza's view of the individual as a soulless particle, now coalescing, now roaming free, subservient to the laws of physics.

---

20. Others, however, have taken a contrary view. Those who have valorized Spinoza's political thought for its democratizing influence have included Michael Hardt and Antonio Negri. See Gratton, "Spinoza and the Biopolitical Roots of Modernity," 91.

21. Nancy, *Inoperative Community*, 12.

Richard Cohen is also critical of Spinoza's politics. He adopts Levinas's criticism of Spinoza, claiming that it "unmasks its alliance with the politics of totalitarianism."[22] In response to those who claim that Spinoza promoted democracy, Cohen shows through a close reading of chapter 16 of the *Theological Political Treatise* that Spinoza's real interest is not democracy as the rule of the many, but a democratic handing over of individual power to the state. Democracy for Spinoza is most often the absolute submission of the people to the will of the sovereign.[23]

Peter Gratton also points out Spinoza's undemocratic tendencies. He links Spinoza's view of the state to his views of God and Nature. The state, like nature (and God), is univocal. It speaks with one voice. It speaks with one mind. There is nothing outside of it, no platonic notion of the good to aspire toward, no overarching telos or goal. Just as all beings are manifestations of a single substance, so each citizen is a manifestation of the state. Within the state, there is no freedom apart from private freedom in the form of freedom of thought. All action is required to be directed by reason, and because the masses are incapable of acting rationally, the state must use its power, and the power of fear, to direct them.[24]

There is something deeply disturbing about a political system which assumes ignorance, and which is willing to subjugate people to ideas recognized as false for their own apparent ultimate good. Such an idea justifies false propaganda and fake news.

## Oneness and Utopia

Monism when made programmatic also has much in common with utopias which demand a shared vision, and often have potentially destructive consequences.

22. Cohen, *Out of Control*, 24.

23. Cohen, *Out of Control*, 147.

24. Gratton, "Spinoza and the Biopolitical Roots of Modernity," 94–95. Gratton sees Spinoza's negative depiction of women as epitomizing this attitude: "It is the unreasonable women who threaten the fraternity of men and their politics of friendship." Gratton, "Spinoza and the Biopolitical Roots of Modernity," 100. Spinoza is also not alone in seeing the masses as undifferentiated and incapable. Nietzsche, Tocqueville, Mill, Le Bon, Caneti, and Freud thought similarly. See Kwek, "Power and the Multitude," 156.

Aurel Kolnai (1900–1973) describes the desire for utopia as a "hankering after some tensionless union of value and being."[25] Roger Scruton (1944–2020) similarly describes utopia as aiming at a state "in which everything is ordered according to a single will," the reconciliation of differences, the overcoming of conflict, and the soldering together of humankind in "a metaphysical unity."

He writes that utopias "tell the story of the fall of man, but in reverse: the prelapsarian innocence and unity lie at the *end* of things, and not necessarily at the beginning—although there is also a tendency to describe the end as a recovery of the original harmony."[26] He holds such goals to be unachievable, and claims that the attempt to implement them leads only to disaster.[27] Spinoza's thought is similarly both a looking forward and reconnection not so much to an original harmony, but to an underlying monistic reality.

Experience so far supports Scruton's position. Utopias tend to disappoint or to implode as the individualistic drive reasserts itself. Witness the rise and fall of communist and authoritarian states. The average duration of communes in the United States between 1640 and 1940 is four years.[28] The reason for the failures of such societies will not always be about rebellion against uniformity. However, the human instinct to exert individuality cannot be ignored. Change in the Kibbutz movement also resulted in part from discontent with collective property and collective living, and the reemergence of pre-cultural individualist values.[29]

In his controversial book, Yoram Hazony, a Bible scholar, promotes nationalism based on a critique of the idea of empires. He writes that "wherever the principle of the unity of unfamiliar humanity is imbedded in the heart of the state, it necessarily gives birth to conquest, to the subjugation of distant peoples, and to the destruction of their way of life so that the 'realm of peace,' as the empire understands it, can be extended."[30] Empires level, subsume all into their embrace, cannot tolerate outsiders:

25. Kolnai, *Utopian Mind*, 70.

26. Scruton, *Uses of Pessimism*, 65.

27. Scruton, *Uses of Pessimism*, 72–73. Scruton sees post-humanists as aiming at such utopian ideal. At 230–31, toward the end of his book, he takes fire at the post-humanists, such as Ray Kurzweil, who he claims are not so much engaged in "predicting" the future as "escaping" it.

28. Spiro, "Utopia and Its Discontents," 557.

29. Spiro, "Utopia and Its Discontents," 560–667.

30. Hazony, *Virtue of Nationalism*, 95.

"the principle of the unity of humanity does not permit any consistent comity toward outsiders."[31]

Hazony further remarks that the regime of peace and prosperity imposed by empires is characterized by a concern with abstract categories, perceived as being universal, but which are in fact "detached from the circumstances and interests, traditions and aspirations of the particular clan or tribe to which they are now to be applied."[32] For Hazony, humans are first and foremost members of clans and tribes, not empires or global humanity. It is these units which should be most respected.

Hazony overlooks the level of diversity tolerated by some empires and has his own political agenda, which includes wanting to take aim at institutions like the EU and UN, but his observations reflect the risks inherent in any theory or movement which wants to draw the universe into its circle. Spinoza's philosophy has the potential to be used in that way.

In *A Radical Jew*, Daniel Boyarin sees the Christian apostle Paul as "motivated by a Hellenistic desire for the one, which among other things produced an ideal of the human essence, beyond difference and hierarchy."[33] While Boyarin considers Paul's impulse as laudable, he observes that, in terms of ethnicity, "his system required that all human cultural specificities—first and foremost, that of the Jews—be eradicated, whether or not the people in question were willing." He sees rabbinic Judaism as a reaction against such levelling.[34] Boyarin, however, is also aware of the dangers of ethnocentrism, resulting from particularism, and wishes to avoid that too.[35] Boyarin's critique of Paul is relevant to all systems drawn to oneness whether philosophical, theological, political, or technological. Boyarin reminds us that the answer in each case is not to swing completely in the other direction, but to find an area of middle ground.

## Overstepping Boundaries

Moving away from the political arena, a further challenge to philosophies which promote boundlessness is where to draw lines. If we are all one,

31. Hazony, *Virtue of Nationalism*, 95.

32. Hazony, *Virtue of Nationalism*, 96.

33. Boyarin, *Radical Jew*, 7.

34. Boyarin, *Radical Jew*, 8.

35. Boyarin, *Radical Jew*, 228–60.

where does my space begin and yours end? What is it which establishes my connection to one community or family more strongly than to another? Boundaries and rules become problematic in such a context. Lines become porous or blurred. No wonder, then, that mysticism is sometimes accompanied by antinomianism, a breaking of rules.

In *Waking Up*, Sam Harris, the popular intellectual, describes various obstacles to the spiritual path, including spiritual teachers who go awry and the evolution of dangerous cults. He thinks that these are features of the terrain. Spirituality lends itself to fakery. One cannot fake being a good chef or gymnast, "but one can fake being an enlightened adept."[36] Harris also blames the need we have for certainty, to be directed like children, to relinquish decision making, which makes us vulnerable.[37]

However, there is also often an aspect of the spiritual teaching itself which leads to acceptable boundaries being crossed. Harris cites the case of the Tibetan Lama, Chogyam Trungpa Rinpoche, who caused controversy due to his alleged inappropriate behavior.[38] Trungpa taught that "[morality] or discipline is not a matter of binding oneself to a fixed set of laws or patterns . . . [a bodhisattva] has opened himself completely and so does not discriminate between this and that. He just acts in accordance with what is."[39]

Harris does not say so, but there is something in the mystic quest for oneness, and the attendant desire for nullification of self, which undermines conventional morality. A loss of the sense of self is a freedom as well as a danger to others. Rules and codes of behavior are directed to embodied individuals who experience guilt, respect, shame, who feel the eyes of the world upon them. When the boundaries of self are removed, rules and codes of behavior are often transgressed. In contrast, a sense of self allows for flourishing, keeps us grounded, and protects us from trespassing into the space inhabited by others.

36. Harris, *Waking Up*, 154.
37. Harris, *Waking Up*, 158.
38. Harris, *Waking Up*, 158.
39. Trungpa, *Cutting through Spiritual Materialism*, 173–74, quoted in Harris, *Waking Up*, 162.

### Resisting the Singularity

The above critique of Spinoza is equally applicable to the notion of the singularity, as I am using that term; namely, the end point of AI's ambitions, the goal of "technique." Technique, as explained in our introduction by reference to Jacques Ellul, is the "totality of methods" which aspires to "absolute efficiency." Technique, like Spinoza's God, asserts its power absolutely. Technique operates without emotion under the laws of cause and effect and recognizes no value beyond the system, which retains absolute power. Nothing can escape from its orbit, and it is to the system that our own power and freedom is given up as we embrace the passivity which the system demands. The ultimate result of the singularity is the still sameness of Spinoza's God, absolute clarity, an infinite glass lake. Boundaries are eradicated, as we are absorbed into a death without the possibility of resurrection.

What risks being lost within the singularity are the human qualities of care, concern, the interplay of forces which comprise life, imagination, memory, past, future, imperfection, uncertainty, randomness, the heart, the head, the hand, goodness, and relationship. The singularity, as a concept, as a reality, should be resisted. This is what our humanity dictates. Such resistance, however, should not involve an all-out assault on technique or the philosophical ideas which gave rise to it and propel it forward, but a movement between perspectives, a dialogue between the immanent and transcendent, a recovery of our humanity and sense of renewal. Our critique of Spinoza and the singularity is not an end, but a beginning.

This is now the point where we need to introduce Heidegger, our second major philosopher. His philosophy directly engaged the scientific and rational and the world of technology, which was emerging during his lifetime. His ideas offer a counterpoint to Spinoza's thought. They also preempt many of the points made above, and many of those referred to in the previous chapter were influenced by him. Vladimir Lossky (1903–1858), the Russian theologian, appears to have been influenced by Heidegger.[40] The same is true of Raymond Tallis.[41] Levinas was a student of Husserl and Heidegger, and introduced phenomenology into France, but later sought to leave "the climate" of Heidegger's work, particularly after Heidegger's association with national socialism and his appointment as

---

40. An observation made also by Konacheva, "Vision of God," 312–36.

41. See for example Tallis, *Aping Mankind*, 235, 352.

rector of Freiburg University in 1933.[42] Many of Levinas's ideas, however, are essentially Heideggerian.[43]

## Heidegger's World

To understand Heidegger, it is necessary to take a slight step back in history. The Romantics of the late eighteenth and early nineteenth centuries, who we have already mentioned, were the first to appreciate our myopia. They reacted against the Enlightenment, denied that reason is the answer to our problems, and refused to accept that the future was our only goal. Emotion, passion, individualism, the past, nature, the aesthetic appreciation of the world, are all vital to who we are. In England, those who took up this challenge included William Wordsworth (1770–1850), Samuel Taylor Coleridge (17772–1834), John Keats (1795–1821), Lord Byron (1788–1824), Percy Bysshe Shelley (1792–1822), and William Blake (1757–1827).

Between roughly 1797 to 1802, a movement referred to as Jena Romanticism emerged in Germany with a similar aim. Poets and writers associated with this movement included Friedrich Wilhelm Joseph Schelling (1775–1854), Friedrich Schleiermacher (1768–1834), and Friedrich von Hardenberg (Novalis) (1772–1801).[44] Friedrich Nietzsche (1844–1900) sought to distance himself from this earlier romantic tradition, but his philosophy evinces a romantic power all the same. He was a destroyer of accepted truth, a promoter of passion, a believer in the power of the human will to overcome. Like the Romantics, Nietzsche showed us the paths closed by reason, in his case, by returning to and revitalizing Greek classicism. His life story too follows the romantic trajectory; he was a lonely romantic genius who tragically fell mad. Nietzsche died in August 1900, when Heidegger was just ten years old.

Heidegger was born in Messkirch, a town in Baden, Southwest Germany, on September 26, 1889.[45] He was attracted to Nietzsche as a young

42. Drabinski and Nelson, introduction to *Between Levinas and Heidegger*, 2.

43. See collection of essays in Drabinski and Nelson, *Between Levinas and Heidegger*.

44. Others associated with this movement included Wilhelm Heinrich Wackenroder (1773–1798), Karl Wilhelm Friedrich Schlegel (1772–1829), August Wilhelm Schlegel (1767–1845), and Ludwig Tieck (1773–1853).

45. For a brief intellectual biography of Heidegger see Dreyfus, *Companion to Heidegger*, 1–14.

scholar, lecturing on him in the years 1936 to 1940. Aspects of Nietzsche's approach that would have suited Heidegger include a critique of reason, a sense of the poetic, and a return to the past. Like Nietzsche, Heidegger had a Christian upbringing, entering a Jesuit school as a novice in 1909. Heidegger left two weeks later due to ill health. His studies at Freiburg University took in theology, mathematics, and then philosophy. In 1913, he received his doctorate in philosophy from the university and in 1925 became a lecturer there.

By 1919, he had rejected Catholicism. In the same year, he started lecturing in "phenomenology" while acting as an assistant to Edmund Husserl. Husserl is considered to be the father of phenomenology. Phenomenology is the attempt to describe experiences or things as they appear to us, not how they actually are (if that is even possible), and not how we arrive at such ideas through metaphysics or theoretical speculation. It is therefore less interested in ethics or logic than other branches of philosophy. Crucial to phenomenology is the meaning that things have to us. Phenomenology studies conscious experience as experienced from the subjective or first-person point of view.

From this short description, one can see already how different this idea is from Spinoza's rationalism. Spinoza wants to know how one thing relates to another in terms of cause and effect. Spinoza takes an interest in phenomenology but only to identify what it is about our experiences which is so misleading. Salvation comes from comprehending the mathematical ordering of existence, God. For Heidegger, reason is just one aspect of being. Phenomenology, our experience of the world, is what really counts. It is this experience in which we place value, through which we encounter the world and the things we care about, and where we can find fulfillment.

Heidegger shared with the Romantics the task of breaking down the subject/object dichotomy beloved of Descartes and Enlightenment thinking. But what marked out Heidegger's thinking from the earlier German Romanticism was a shift in perspective which can be seen in the role attributed to art, including poetry. For the Romantics, the role of art was to rupture our subjective view of the world so that we can reach beyond the seemingly objective to an imagined absolute which underlies it.[46] This was Spinoza's task also. In contrast, post-Romantics, such as Heidegger, saw the world as an interplay of disclosure and hiddenness

46. Corby, "Making Nothing Happen," 119–20.

and art as an attempt to reveal or disclose the world in all its complexity.[47] Heidegger did not often refer to God, but speaks of gods, viewing them as something other than us, which call to us as if from a beyond. The point is that we encounter *Dasein* or being in a spirit of relationship. In this respect, Heidegger is a transcendentalist.

There is something uncannily Jewish about Heidegger's way of thinking. Judaism is a religion of the world, of lived experience. God is encountered in history, through ritual, through law, through real-life tests and challenges. Reason is just one means to generate meaning. Heidegger's ideas also have a poetic, other-worldly, mystical quality, covering themes which overlap with the Jewish mystical tradition. Some have suggested that such ideas filtered through to Heidegger through Christian Kabbalists and mystics with whom Heidegger and the Romantics who influenced him were interested.[48] Husserl, Heidegger's teacher, had a Jewish background, as did many of those attracted to or influenced by phenomenology.[49] In 1924, a year after he was appointed associate professor of philosophy at the University of Freiburg, Heidegger embarked on his love affair with his Jewish student, Hannah Arendt. Heidegger had been married since 1917 to Elfride Petri.

Although Heidegger may have liked individual Jews, he hated the Jewish people and what he understood them to represent, as we mentioned in the first chapter. In 1927, Heidegger published his masterpiece, *Being and Time (Sein und Zeit)*. In 1928, he became a professor, succeeding Husserl, and in 1933 was elected as rector of Freiburg University after joining the National Socialist Party. He resigned as rector in 1934 but did not give up his membership of the National Socialist Party.

After the fall of the Third Reich, he was banned from university teaching, but was reinstated in 1951. He died in 1976 and was buried in his hometown of Messkirch. Heidegger's body of works is immense, and the content of his writing dense, and often impenetrable. As a Jew, it is hard to separate Heidegger the philosopher from the Nazi sympathizer and the writer of the *Black Notebooks*, but there is something oddly alluring about this thinker. Between the jargon, the convoluted sentences, the complexity and pretension, there is a sense of a door of perception

47. Corby, "Making Nothing Happen," 126–28.

48. Wolfson, *Heidegger and Kabbalah*, 4, 9. See also Zarader, *Unthought Debt*.

49. See Wolin, *Heidegger's Children*.

swinging open, a casting of light on my Jewish tradition, on Spinoza, on technology, and on how we might live.

## Dasein

Heidegger's project in *Being and Time* is to understand *Dasein*, a word I have used a few times now, translating it as "being." *Dasein* is the place where our experiences happen, the underlying structure of human existence, the way that we arrive at our goals and meanings—our intentions. In using the term *Dasein*, Heidegger, as explained, wanted like the Romantics to collapse subject/object dualism. By *Dasein*, Heidegger does not mean our subjective view of things, nor does he mean how things are objectively. *Dasein* is instead the space in which we operate and the meanings and values which emerge from our experiences within it, the way we make sense of the world. It is described by Heidegger as something independent of us, but also intimate with us.

*Dasein* is hard to grasp because we are immersed in it all the time and because our contemporary worldview is dominated by the scientific way of looking at things. Science seeks to isolate objects. It cares about their properties and behaviors, not about their place within the realm of being. Heidegger attempts to rewind history to a time before the scientific worldview became dominant. What he finds is a way of encountering the world as a totality. Objects were not seen scientifically or technologically but experienced in their interconnectedness with other objects and us. We are not beings set apart from the world.[50]

Heidegger's analysis, like Spinoza's, constitutes a critique of Descartes. Descartes sought to divide the world between the human knower and the known object, but Heidegger wants us to see that we are always in fact engaged with objects. *Dasein* implies "Being-in the-world" or "Being-with-others." We are not mere observers, but active participants. Seeing the world as *Dasein* is to see the world primordially, in the way that it is experienced before we isolate aspects of being or apply scientific categories.[51]

A scientific understanding of the world provides only a partial view of what matters to us. Concern is a feature of *Dasein*: "*Dasein* is a being that does not simply occur among other beings. Rather it is ontically

50. For a brief outline of *Dasein*, see Mulhall, *Heidegger and Being and Time*, 60–88.
51. Heidegger, *Being and Time*, 10.

distinguished by the fact that in its being this being is concerned *about* its very being."[52] *Dasein* is not reducible to mere definitional characterizations—what we do or what we like. It is constantly searching, struggling to understand itself, and never at rest. It is therefore also the realm of human potential.

*Dasein* by its nature contains the possibility of things to take on multiple meanings: "*Dasein* always understands itself in terms of its existence, in terms of its possibility to be itself or not to be itself. *Dasein* has either chosen these possibilities itself, stumbled upon them, or in each instance already grown up in them."[53] It is how existence manifests itself in all its multiplicity and possibility.

*Dasein* is also always my own. It has the character of *Jemeinigkeit*, "always-being-my-own-being": "*Dasein* is my own, to be always in this or that way. It has somehow always already decided in which way *Dasein* is always my own. The being which is concerned in its being about its being is related to its being as its ownmost possibility."[54] We all experience a particular space, so in that sense, it is not just our own, but we each encounter it in a deeply personal way. *Dasein* therefore expresses us each individually, reflecting our concerns and shaping our becoming.

Juxtaposing Heidegger's views to Spinoza's highlights what is missing from the latter. Spinoza failed to properly account for our lived experience. He does not recognize that cause and effect are not the only determinants to the living of a good life. The contrast between Spinoza and Heidegger is most evident in a comparison between *Dasein* and Spinoza's *Conatus*. *Conatus*, as "every thing, as far as in it lies, strives to persevere in its existence," applies to everything in the world.[55] *Dasein*, in contrast, relates to human beings, and is broader in scope than *Conatus*. Humans do not just want to survive, but to flourish by owning and shaping their existence. That requires a striving toward authenticity. Although Heidegger recognizes that we can never fully escape our embeddedness, we can choose and commit to those paths which are open to us. The inertia of Spinoza is thus transformed by Heidegger into an active striving toward living in all its modalities. For Heidegger, we experience the

52. Heidegger, *Being and Time*, 12.
53. Heidegger, *Being and Time*, 12.
54. Heidegger, *Being and Time*, 42.
55. Spinoza, *Ethics*, III.VI.169.

world as care and openness to meaning. For Spinoza, we know the world through reason and should be suspicious of words like "meaning."

Moreover, *Dasein* does not bemoan the temporal, as does Spinoza, but identifies this as a central component of *Dasein*. As we saw earlier, the present does not exist here and now in isolation from the past and future. It contains the past and the future and is shaped by them. The present is also something I can make my own. Spinoza urges us to view things from the standpoint of eternity, and to eschew the transitory. Heidegger reveals our temporal humanity.

The point that emerges from Heidegger is that the individual is part of the network of being. She is not reducible to pure cause and effect, cannot be known in isolation, and resists categorization.

## Heidegger and Ethics

Many, including Levinas, have criticized Heidegger's thinking as lacking an ethics.[56] As we have seen from his views on Spinoza, Levinas was particularly sensitive to any thinking which sought to totalize, to reduce everything to a single continuum. Levinas considered Heidegger's thought to be totalizing in the sense that his concern was the interconnectedness of being and thought that this explained his sympathies for national socialism.[57] Levinas also thought that Heidegger was more interested in an intellectual understanding of *Dasein* than commitment and more interested in freedom over ethics.[58] Levinas saw the problem as ontology (the study of being) itself, which considers being as the primordial experience: "We therefore are also radically opposed to Heidegger who subordinates the relation with the Other to ontology . . . rather than seeing in justice and injustice a primordial access to the Other beyond all ontology."[59]

In place of seeing others as mere participants in being, Levinas posited ethics as first philosophy, the sense that there are others beyond and independent of us: The other affects us "as other, independent of us:

56. In addition to Levinas, others who criticize Heidegger for this reason include Edith Wyschogrod, Herman Philipse, and Werner Marx. The criticisms include that Heidegger's thought is relativistic, formally empty, and indifferent to the other. Atkins, *Ethical and Theological Appropriation*, loc. 1867–914.

57. Drabinski and Nelson, introduction to *Between Levinas and Heidegger*, 3.

58. Levinas, *Totality and Infinity*, 45–46; Atkins, *Ethical and Theological Appropriation*, loc. 1848.

59. Levinas, *Totality and Infinity*, 89.

behind every relation we could sustain with him, an absolute upsurge."[60]
It is the "relation of a being to a being" which is primordial. Levinas was
keen to explain that this is not a relationship between a subject and object, but a more profound connection in which the other can never truly
be known.[61]

However, as Zohar Atkins points out, Levinas overlooks Heidegger's
recognition that any total understanding of being is impossible and his
call for an existential orientation toward being which is open, awe-filled,
and poetic.[62] Atkins further explains that a careful analysis of Heidegger's
work shows that *Being and Time* can be read as an ethics of "care."[63] Heidegger himself stated that "*Dasein*, ontologically understood, is care"[64]
While "care" here should not be associated with care in the sense we
generally understand that word, but with "will" or "wish," it is also not
associated with egocentrism but with an openness to the world.[65] In the
*Fundamental Concept of Metaphysics*, Heidegger refers to "individuation," which he sees as "that *solitariness* in which each human being first
of all enters into a nearness to what is essential in all things, a nearness
to world."[66]

Atkins sees Heidegger's idea of care, as capable of being framed
positively, as an ethical idea: "It suggests that our being is elementally
ethical, and that in every moment, we are engaged—even when we do
not consciously know it—in projects whose stakes are ethical."[67] On
this reading, Levinas can be viewed as building on Heidegger's system,
making manifest that which lies hidden. Atkins also seeks to build on
Heidegger's approach by encouraging listening and gratitude for existence as core ways of responding to the world.[68] I accept with Atkins that
Heidegger's thought lends itself to an expansive ethics, even if he did not

60. Levinas, *Totality and Infinity*, 89.

61. Drabinski and Nelson, introduction to *Between Levinas and Heidegger*, 4.

62. Atkins, *Ethical and Theological Appropriation*, loc. 479–87.

63. Atkins, *Ethical and Theological Appropriation*, loc. 2014–46.

64. Heidegger, *Being and Time*, 57.

65. Atkins, *Ethical and Theological Appropriation*, loc. 2055–63.

66. Heidegger, *Fundamental Concept of Metaphysics*, 8, quoted in Atkins, *Ethical and Theological Appropriation*, loc. 2071. See also loc. 2086.

67. Atkins, *Ethical and Theological Appropriation*, loc. 2086.

68. Atkins, *Ethical and Theological Appropriation*, loc. 83, 3849: "thinking is most basically a posture of listening." See also ch. 6 on gratitude.

fully develop that potential. I consider such development to be a project worth pursuing.

## The Technological Worldview

Heidegger's views are also of import because they directly engage with technology. We have seen how, in *Being and Time*, Heidegger wishes to reach back to a time before the scientific mindset. In his later writings, he takes aim at technology directly. He identifies a societal orientation which he calls "Enframing" (*Gestell*). Gestell drives us to place entities into a specific frame of reference and set them to work, so that we can extract value from them.[69]

The scientific method contributes to such Enframing by setting up a "ground-plan" which views the subject of study as being subject to strict laws. In an attempt to identify the laws, theories are put forward and tested by experiment. A community of researchers applies the laws identified and attempts to expand upon them in a feedback loop which, in a 1938 lecture, Heidegger calls "industry" (*Betreib*).[70]

Heidegger demonstrates the process of Enframing by reference to the River Rhine. Under the guise of Enframing, the river is not a natural feature but a source of waterpower or a tourist attraction. It has public utility, as a source of energy, a cash generator, a generator of memory. It is subject to our control: "In the context of the interlocking processes pertaining to the orderly disposition of electrical energy, even the Rhine itself appears to be something at our command."[71] In the past, objects were experienced as encounter, but in the technological age, we seek to exert power over and squeeze value from all things.

In around 1934, Heidegger presented a lecture course on the Rhine Hymn, *Der Rhein*, and another work, written by Johann Christian Friedrich Hölderlin (1770–1843), the poet and philosopher. The Rhine Hymn portrays the Rhine as a demigod. Heidegger relates this to his concept of *Dasein*: "The river is not a body of water that only flows past by the place of human beings. Rather, its flowing as landforming first creates the

69. Heidegger, *Question concerning Technology*, 38. See also Richardson, *Heidegger*, 326–28.

70. The Age of the World Picture discussed in Richardson, *Heidegger*, 329–30.

71. Heidegger, *Question concerning Technology*, quoted in Ihde, *Heidegger's Technologies*, 77.

possibility of the grounding of the dwelling of human beings. The river is not just by way of comparison, but is as itself a founder and poet."[72] The River Rhine, therefore, is not an object to be exploited, but a being which exudes meaning. The contrast between this conception of the river and its technological Enframing is startling.

According to Heidegger, the immediate damage from the technological stance is not the disasters that result from technology, but the damage to our psyches: "The threat to man does not come firstly from the potentially lethal machines and apparatus of technology. The authentic threat has already attacked man in his essence."[73] Technology colors how we view every endeavor. For example, we view plants, not as a manifestation of being, but through the established disciplines of biology, botany, and horticulture. The technological worldview hides being from us: "[Enframing] drives out every other possibility of revealing."[74]

The damage does not stop at blocking our understanding of the world around us. It distorts the view of ourselves. We see ourselves as entities which Enframe and as resources to be Enframed. At the same time, we lack the control that technology aims at because we do not freely choose to Enframe the world. The orientation is forced upon us. The system feeds on itself and threatens to engulf us: "The racing of technology might install itself everywhere."[75] Heidegger is not suggesting that science and technological methods do not lead to truth, but only that the truth they reveal is partial.

Heidegger was no doubt reacting to the technological advancements of his age, perhaps reflecting on the industrialization of war and killing on a vast and previously unimaginable scale which he observed. His observations continue to make sense in our times when we can see technology's ambitions even more clearly. We are racing to establish the world on a technological footing. We want to control the processes, the outcomes, smooth out existence, mitigate risks, obliterate inefficiency, turn chaos into order. When we define ourselves by this task, we risk diminishing our humanity.

For Heidegger, the solution is not to seek to turn back the clock, but to change our orientation, to reconnect to *Dasein*, to create space for

72. Quoted in Davis, "Need Delimited," 236.

73. Heidegger, *Question concerning Technology*, 38.

74. Heidegger, *Question concerning Technology*, 38.

75. Heidegger, *Question concerning Technology*, 38. See also Richardson, *Heidegger*, 333.

randomness and an openness to meaning, to allow a return to "the gods," to myth and otherness.

The views of Jacques Ellul, mentioned in the first chapter, have also proved prescient. He was writing at a similar time to Heidegger. In the *Technological Society* (1954), he claimed that the technologies that we create to solve real-world problems end up reshaping the human ends at which they were initially aimed to serve. Ellul saw philosophy and technology as being under the enthrall of technological culture.[76]

Ellul claimed that prior to the eighteenth century, technology proceeded by way of an unconscious imitation of nature. From that point, reason and conscious effort toward efficiency became the driving forces. He writes that in technique "a rational process is present which tends to bring mechanics to bear on all that is spontaneous or irrational . . . Every intervention of technique is, in effect, a reduction of facts, forces, phenomena, means and instruments to the schema of logic."[77] Ellul further observes that morality plays no role in technique: "It tends on the whole to create a completely independent technical morality."[78] Technology is a self-determining organism without any external restraint.[79] It obeys only "intrinsic imperatives."[80] The absence of freedom characterizes both Heidegger's and Ellul's view of technology. This assessment of technology is relevant to both Spinoza and the singularity.

## Taking Stock

This chapter has been about the dangers of Spinoza's thought, but its intention is not to undermine Spinoza completely. Spinoza offers us a spirituality free from religious superstition, which has as its center a non-dualist, immanent, God, a focus on scientific reason, an appreciation for religion's role in educating the public in virtue, and an understanding of the individual in psychological terms.

Spinoza continues to have much in his favor. Reason has proved itself and must remain the foundation for any system. Spinoza's thought has shown religion to itself and taken us beyond its mythic categories.

76. Ellul, *Technological Society*, xxv.

77. Ellul, *Technological Society*, 79.

78. Ellul, *Technological Society*, 97.

79. Ellul, *Technological Society*, 125.

80. Ellul, *Technological Society*, 153.

Spinoza also formulated a conception of God which accords with our scientific tendencies, and inner sensibilities. With his obsession with oneness, which draws us to its center, he encourages us to formulate a rational mysticism. There is no reason to abandon his thought in its entirety.

However, Spinoza's philosophy has a darker side, which emerges especially from an assessment of Heidegger's philosophy and others influenced by him. There is more to humanity than reason. We experience the world through *Dasein*, whose nature contains the potentiality of things to take on multiple meanings. We do not exist as types but as individuals embedded in a world of possibility and individual relationships. We are not the same.

Spinoza stresses the All, but the world in which we inhabit is one of relationship and care. We experience good and evil as independent aspects. It is dangerous to pretend that they are mere illusions. Heidegger stresses the need for transcendence, to reach beyond ourselves.

Moreover, Spinoza, the great proponent of non-dualism, adopts an extreme dualist position when it comes to reason and imagination. Reason is all good and imagination all bad when unaware of its own limitations. On the prevalent reading of Spinoza, there is no middle way. The enemies of Spinoza's rational non-dualism are irrational belief, myth, and superstition, the fruits of imagination.[81] Narratives, like those in the Bible, serve to keep the masses in check, but are founded on falsehood. All falsehood, explains Spinoza, comes from the imagination.

For him, life should be an endless process of mathematical comprehension and rational problem-solving. There is no room for story, other than a utility to keep those of frail mind and uncontrollable passions under control. According to Spinoza, given the danger of myth and the irrational beliefs that it spawns, it is right that it be kept under control by the state. We can of course think what we like and express ourselves privately in whichever way takes our fancy, but ultimately our fates are decided by nature alone and the dictates of the political leaders of the day.

81. Deleuze describes Spinoza as belonging to a great tradition for which "the practical task of philosophy consists in denouncing all myths, all mystification, all 'superstitions,' whatever their origin." Deleuze continues "Like Lucretius, [Spinoza] sets the image of a positive Nature against the uncertainty of gods: what is opposed to Nature is not Culture, nor the state of reason, nor even the civil state, but only the superstition that threatens all human endeavor." Deleuze, *Expressions in Philosophy*, 270.

While there are problems with all this, we must acknowledge too the dangers of an overactive imagination. We live in a postmodern world which has given vent to the tendencies unleashed by those who have rebelled against reason. Objective truth is shunned. Fake news proliferates. Extremes prevail. Political stability crumbles. Nationalisms rear their ugly heads. We lose our ability to distinguish between the fantasies of our mind and scientific realities.

But this assessment is only half true. In fact, what we have is a bifurcation. Scientific thinking has not died or been replaced, but the world is split so that some domains are controlled purely by the technological and others totally by the mythical. The world is divided into two worldviews which we are unable to combine productively in a way which both gives meaning and propels us forward.

As indicated in my introduction, we need to find balance—a coming together of the different aspects of *Dasein*—so that none takes precedent over the other. The achievement of balance is not an exercise in thinking, but a discipline, a journey outward and a return. Religion can be a vehicle for the promotion of rational religion, as Spinoza observed, but it is also a source of narrative, meaning, and vision- revelation, an unconcealment in the Heideggerian sense. We need to leave behind Spinoza's rationalism and to introduce a new voice arising from the imagination, the poetic, and the mystical.

In the chapters that follow, I will set out a theology of the future based on the observations of Spinoza and Heidegger. These thinkers split the atom of our approaches to living, pulled apart the fruit, by holding up certain truths. I want to form their insights into an approach to religion which seeks to unite technology and myth so that we can live with a sense of one without being obliterated by it.

More specifically, I would like to utilize aspects of Spinoza's and Heidegger's philosophies to think about revelation and the place of imagination in discovering religious truth. I would also like to trace the process by which the God of everything revealed himself also as the other, the God of no thing and becoming. In so doing, I will explore, through the biblical narratives, the emergence of the individual as something distinct from God and world, and capable of independent creative understanding and relationship. These are capacities worth preserving in our technological world.

# 6

# Revelation for Non-Dualists

IF WE TAKE SPINOZA'S monism seriously, we cannot deny the divinity of the Torah. The Torah arises from and is dependent on God, passing, as we shall see, through the single infinite continuum of physicality, in the physical form of its transmission and reception, and the single infinite continuum of thinking, in its ideas and exposition. The Torah in this context is not just the Torah written on scrolls with black ink on white parchment, but its expression in the mouths of the Jewish people, its recipients and elucidators, and its living embodiment. It exists not just as thought, but as extension, emblazoning itself on the life of a particular people and human history in general.[1]

But we can still ask if everything is God, what makes something more godlike than something else? As Spinoza wrote, "Natural knowledge has as much right to be called divine as any other kind of knowledge, since it is in the nature of God, so far as we share in it, and God's decrees, that may be said to dictate it to us."[2] Spinoza continues to explain that unlike knowledge derived from reason, divine knowledge "extends beyond its limits."[3] The statement could be taken to indicate an acceptance by Spinoza that biblical wisdom reaches beyond reason, but Spinoza, it will be recalled, considers biblical prophecy to be a product of imagination from

---

1. Rabbi Levi Ben Gershon (Ralbag) (1288–1344) comments on Moses's request to remove his name from God's book if the people are not granted forgiveness after the sin of the golden calf. Ralbag explains that existence, which arises from God, is referred to as a "book." Just as a book gives expression to what is internal to the writer, so reality expresses the mind of God. See Levi Ben Gershon, *Biur ha-Milot*, Exod 32:32. I am grateful to Professor Daniel Rynhold for this reference.

2. Spinoza, *TTP*, 1:2.13–14.

3. Spinoza, *TTP*, 1:2.14.

which all errors spring. In Spinoza's philosophy, perfection and reality are the same thing and equate to clear thinking.[4] The more rational an idea, the more godlike it is.

In this chapter, I want to champion the place of imagination, to give reign to its expansiveness in order to formulate a conception of revelation which combines Spinoza's monism with Heideggerian phenomenology, the world as we experience it. By doing this, I hope to keep the truths of both these thinkers in play. Spinoza taught us to see God in the unchangeable totality, that reason is supreme, and imagination distorts. Heidegger's methodology creates space for imagination, creativity, value, and change. These tendencies form the nucleus of the biblical revelation: the God of earth, of which we are a part, which is immanent and close, and the God of heaven, which is transcendent, distinct, and receptive.

The first perspective is the universal and rational, it summons us to think beyond distinction, to connect; it desires to draw everything within its matrix. The second perspective, transcendence, opens up the possibility of imagination, as we strain across the canyon of existence to reach the God we can never know.

## The Nature of Revelation

As noted earlier, in his *Ethics*, Spinoza described three types of knowledge: imagination, reason, and intuition.[5] Imagination is the way that we connect things that we come into contact with to form what we consider to be universal notions, but which in fact involve confused ideas derived from the senses or by linking things that we have heard or seen to earlier memories. He provides numerous examples of how imagination confuses. When we look at the sun, we imagine that it is a short distance from us, even when reason tells us it is very far away.[6] If we see Peter, Paul, and Simeon at different times of day, we will associate each with that time of day.[7] Imagination also depends on our particular background. A soldier who sees horse prints in the sand will immediately move from thinking about the horse to the thought of a horseman, and then to the thought of

---

4. Spinoza, *Ethics*, II.D6.114.

5. Spinoza, *Ethics*, II.XL.Schol 2.145–46.

6. Spinoza, *Ethics*, XXV.141.

7. Spinoza, *Ethics*, II.XLIV.147–48.

war. A farmer, on the other hand, will move from the thought of a horse to the thought of a plough and then to a field.[8]

The imagination, therefore, involves the reflection of our passive experiences onto external reality. We imagine the things that we think will serve us: "The mind, as far as it can, strives to imagine those things which augment or assist the power of action of the body."[9]

Spinoza also thinks that we often lead the lives and follow the outlooks we do depending on the imagined connections that we make between aspects of the world. Imagination has value because it expresses something about the relationship between bodies, and only really becomes dangerous, as stated earlier, when we take the imagined non-existent things as real. Nevertheless, knowledge derived from imagination is far weaker than that derived through intuition and reason.

Spinoza's second category of knowledge is reason, the way we form "common notions" and "adequate ideas" about things. Spinoza's third category of knowledge is intuition. It is not a form of inspiration or "gut feeling," but knowledge we become familiar with over time to such an extent that we stop being fully cognizant of why it is correct; for example, mental arithmetic which we use habitually without thought. It is reason sped-up.[10]

We have explained above that Spinoza considers biblical prophecy as deriving from imagination: "Prophecy does not require a more perfect mind but a more vivid imagination."[11] However, Spinoza does seem to suggest that a revelation not filtered through the imagination is possible. He does not explain how such a revelation comes about and considers it to be very rare, so rare in fact that, according to Spinoza, Jesus is the only person to have achieved this.[12]

We saw above that for Maimonides only Moses's prophecy was unmediated by imagination.[13] Spinoza has replaced Moses with Jesus, and by so doing has adopted the notion of the superiority of the New Testament

8. Spinoza, *Ethics*, II.XVIII.132–33.
9. Spinoza, *Ethics*, III.XIX.Dem.178.
10. Spinoza, *Ethics*, II.XL.Schol 2.145–46.
11. Spinoza, *TTP*, 1:20.20.
12. Spinoza, *TTP*, 1:20.20.
13. Maimonides, *Guide*, III.XXVII.312.

over the Old Testament prevalent among Christians.[14] Spinoza, however, does not adopt a traditional Christian position.

For him, Jesus was not a man of miracles, but a teacher of the practical implications of natural law.[15] Spinoza writes that he does "not believe that anyone has reached such a degree of perfection above others except Christ."[16] But Jesus's perfection consists in his expression of his human nature. He "understood things truly and adequately," that is, rationally. Since Jesus was not speaking just to the Jews but to the human race, his mind needed to be "adapted to the views and general doctrines of the human race, that is, to the principles that are universal and true."[17]

In some respects, Spinoza and Maimonides are engaged in the same exercise: an attempt to identify the rational aspects of revelation. Maimonides takes a maximalist approach. The entirety of revelation is rational, although it is not always easy for us to see this. In contrast, Spinoza takes a minimalist approach. He considers revelation to be most rational when its laws correspond to natural law. Overall, however, revelation derives from imagination, except when it comes to those teachings of Jesus which offer non-legal practical guidance. Spinoza and Maimonides both also warn of the dangers of imagination and seek to enlist it in the service of reason.

As indicated, I see the benefit of adopting Spinoza's approach to revelation as primarily an expression of the imagination. The mechanism by which the Torah came to be is shrouded in mystery, but there can be no doubt that our own encounter with it owes very little to reason. From the moment the words lift from the parchment, they take on a life of their own. Our mind sets to work on them, constructing images, ruminating on its dictates. Emotions arise and spiral. The past makes itself felt. The future calls. The universe is sifted through it, like sand through a sieve. Paths open up and clearings appear. Our personalities, outlooks, and experiences are brought to bear. The quality of the experience is unlike anything else. But how did we come to this encounter?

We started from the immanent God of everything, the rational universality of Spinoza, and moved gradually, as the Torah unfolds, to a

---

14. Steven Nadler denies that Spinoza's views on Christianity's superiority to Judaism are antisemitic or motivated to ingratiate himself with the Christians of his time. See Nadler, *Book Forged in Hell*, 157n45.

15. Nadler, *Book Forged in Hell*, 173–75.

16. Spinoza, *TTP*, 1:18.19.

17. Spinoza, *TTP*, 4:10.63–64.

conception of God as transcendent. The primordial separation which led to the immanent and transcendent perspectives allowed creation to unfold and gave rise to the possibility of revelation. As we progress through history, we do not lose sight of either immanence or transcendence but hold tightly to both in a lived paradox. The combination of these two perspectives, heaven and earth, creates balance, yin and yang, and helps us to avoid the extremes, frees us from our idolatries. It also provides a compelling way to retain a sense of oneness, the singularity already present and always beckoning, while preserving human uniqueness and the force of ethical obligation.

## Emanation

The Jewish mystical tradition has long grappled with the question of how there can be a world separated from God if God is infinite and there is no place where he is not. For Isaac Luria (1534–1572), one of the Kabbalah greats, God created the world by first withdrawing into himself through the process of *Zimzum* to create a circular space or void. He then infused that void with divine light pipetted through ten channels, vessels, or emanations (*Sefirot*), each representing a different quality (Crown, Wisdom, Understanding, Kindness, Might [or Judgment], Beauty, Splendor, Victory, Foundation, and Sovereignty). These channels are sometimes described as being made of glass. At some point, the divine light became too much for the glass vessels to hold and they shattered sending glass and divine light in all directions. The divine light is good. The glass vessels are referred to as the "husks" (*Klipot*). They are the source of evil in the world, in that they are deficient in divine light. After this cataclysm, the good and bad became mixed. But even in the face of such ideas, Kabbalists have not relinquished their belief in oneness. The myth of *Zimzum* and the shattering of the vessels becomes a worldview, an approach to living, but the mystic remains suspended in paradox.[18]

Spinoza, like the Kabbalists, has some explaining to do. If we are part of God, why do we experience the world as separated and distinct? One answer is that when Spinoza writes that "whatever is, is in God," he means not that we are part of God in some physical sense but that we depend on the conception of God; God provides the ontological

18. For a brief account of this process, see Dan, *Kabbalah*, 73–81.

underpinning or causal ground for our being.[19] God's existence allows us
to exist. Furthermore, because God's essence involves all possibilities, all
possibilities must necessarily come to be. As explained by Beth Lord, "All
possible being is necessarily actualised, because God's essence is the actu-
alisation of all possible being."[20] God therefore causes us in the sense that
we are modes caused by the self-actualization of substance. Lord writes,
"[We are] the infinite and changeable expressions of God as extension,
and God as thinking."[21]

Part I, Propositions XXI–XXV of the *Ethics* are particularly difficult.
Lord presents an explanation in her guide to the *Ethics* which has some resemblance to the notion of emanations within the kabbalistic tradition.[22]
She explains that because God is infinite, the attributes, such as extension
and thought, must also have this characteristic, and so must the modes
that derive from them (the "immediate modes"). Infinite understanding
follows from the notion of infinite thought. Infinite motion and rest follow from the notion of infinite extension. From each of these immediate
modes comes "mediate infinite modes." In a letter, Spinoza refers to these
as the "face of the whole universe."[23] These infinite mediate modes "vary
in infinite ways, yet always remain the same." Lord encourages us to think
of the infinite mediate modes as a "single, infinite continuum of physicality and a single infinite continuum of thinking."[24]

"Finite modes," explains Lord, exist in the level below the immediate
modes, and the mediate infinite modes. These are the "surface features
of these infinite continua." Finite modes of extension are the temporary,
changeable expressions of the infinite continuum of physicality. The finite
modes of thinking are the temporary expressions of the infinite continuum of thinking. The "finite modes are the waves on the ocean, which
come into existence, last a certain amount of time and then fall back into
the infinite continuum from which they came. The waves are determined
to be what they are by the 'depth' of the ocean that causes them."[25] There
are parallel streams of causality within the attributes of extension and the

19. Spinoza, *Ethics*, I.XV.83–84.
20. Lord, *Ethics*, 36.
21. Lord, *Ethics*, 38.
22. Lord, *Ethics*, 38–42.
23. *Letter 64*, quoted in Lord, *Ethics*, 39–40.
24. Lord, *Ethics*, 40.
25. Lord, *Ethics*, 41–42.

attribute of mind, which allows us to trust that our thoughts reflect the physical realm of causality.[26]

We have seen that for Spinoza, science is the way we come to understand the laws of causality that give rise to the attributes of thought and extension. Physical laws deal with the nature of the relationship between physical bodies. The laws of logic deal with the nature of the relationship between thoughts. Knowledge of these laws brings us to the knowledge and love of God.[27]

We have here a theory of emanations, a staged series which by degrees arrives at the world of separation which comprises our daily experience. Spinoza draws no parallels between his analysis and Kabbalah, but it is possible to treat Spinoza's project as a rational mysticism which parallels the more speculative mysticism of Isaac Luria just described. On one level, the Kabbalists (most notably Luria) and Spinoza are addressing the same experience; namely, that the world is divided and distinct, separate from God. While some Kabbalists might take *Zimzum* literally, others view it as an analogy. God is one, but phenomenologically, we do not feel part of God. God is beyond our grasp, something that we reach toward. The idea of emanation, and the anterior notion of *Zimzum*, are true in the sense that they encapsulate how we come to feel distinct within the world yet connected at some level with infinity.

Kabbalah has its own history and esoteric tradition distinct from the Hebrew Bible, but the project in which the two are engaged are not dissimilar when looked at through a non-dualist lens. They both describe the fissure, the birth of transcendence out of oneness, the emergence of consciousness, the separation of one thing from another, the division between matter and anti-matter. An aspect of the Kabbalah's interpretive task is to identify the primordial unity shining forth from between the lines of the biblical text.

The Torah speaks of an age that predates the common era by thousands of years, but its character substantially reflects what is now termed, following the philosopher Karl Jaspers, the "axial age," which runs from about 800 BCE to 200 BCE. This is the period in which the intellectual and religious systems which shaped human society and culture came to fruition. It is the age of the ancient Greek philosophers, the Buddha, and great Hindu, Buddhist, Jain, and Zoroastrian sages. It is the age also of

26. Lord, *Ethics*, 53–57.
27. Spinoza, *Ethics*, V.XXIII.309–10.

Confucianism and Daoism, and the Hebrew prophets and scribes, who according to modern scholarship put together the Bible.

According to Charles Taylor, what characterizes this period is a change of attitude toward the social order, the cosmos, and the human good. The individual human was seen as a member of society which could be organized toward a common goal. The cosmos was no longer subject to blind fate. Gods were perceived no longer purely as manifestations of nature but came to be viewed as distinct from the world. The world also held out the possibility of human purpose beyond mere survival. Human flourishing came to be associated with more than health, wealth, and prosperity.[28] The axial age, then, saw the emergence of self-reflection and individual consciousness. It was the point at which we bit into the fruit of the tree of knowledge, the moment when dualism was born.

Francis Oakley, in his discussion of the history of monarchy, describes the monistic world that predated the axial age. He writes that the idea of kingship

> emerged from an "archaic" mentality that appears to have been thoroughly monistic, to have perceived no impermeable barrier between the human and divine, to have intuited the divine as immanent in the cyclic rhythms of the natural world and civil society as somehow enmeshed in these natural processes, and to have viewed its primary function, therefore, as a fundamentally religious one, involving the preservation of the cosmic order and the "harmonious integration" of human beings with the natural world.[29]

Karen Armstrong also notes that "the ancient religions had believed that the deities, human beings, and all natural phenomenon had been composed of the same divine substance; there was no ontological gap between humanity and the gods." She considers that before the axial age, the "divine dimension had somehow retreated from the world" and become alien.[30]

On this reading, monotheism breaks onto the historical scene, either rupturing the immanentist idea that God or gods and the world are one or reintroducing God to the world, albeit one which is not entirely

28. Taylor, *Secular Age*, 151.
29. Oakley, *Kingship*, 50–57.
30. Armstrong, *Buddha*, 53–54.

associated with the world. But oneness does not just precede monotheism historically. It comes before it conceptionally and intuitively.

We are first and foremost part of a totality, the universal. Following the switch described, the human person stands as something apart from God and other humans. This separation provides the ability to gain perspective, a place to look out upon the world, and a place outside from which we reflect on ourselves. History, identity, future, potential, change, are all now possible. Imagination, the capacity so distrusted by Spinoza, is set free. We encounter this world as *Dasein*, non-intellectually, non-scientifically, returning to the universal only after discovering reason. The Torah traces and speaks to this transformation, the move from monism to monotheism and back, the dialectic.

The Torah commences, "In the beginning God created heaven and earth" (Gen 1:1). This is fissure, the split between the divine realm (heaven) and the human realm (earth). Creation, or rather our experience of it, takes place within this divide. The theme of separation is repeated throughout the Genesis story: "God saw that the light was good, and God *separated* the light from the darkness" (Gen 1:4). God later "*separated* the lower waters and the upper waters" (Gen 1:8). God created lights in the heavens "to *separate* night and day" (Gen 1:14). And God set the lights in the expanse of the sky to rule over night and day and "*separated* light from darkness" (Gen 1:18). Time and seasons, the days and years, become distinguishable.

The idea of separation continues to feature in the story of the creation of the first humans. Adam and Eve are created distinct from one another. They are eventually cast from the presence of God when exiled from the garden of Eden after the sin. But to live apart from other human beings is not an option. The task is to enter into relationships. A man is commanded to separate from his parents and to cleave to his wife so that they can become "one flesh" (Gen 1:24). Brothers are supposed to show empathy for one another despite their differences. These are acts aimed at reunification, a call to regain a sense of the singularity.

The world of separation, however, is a world of chaos and uncertainty. Within a few paragraphs from the start of creation, Cain has killed his brother Abel out of jealousy (Gen 4:5). Individuals are no longer in equal relationship to each other or to God. Families, tribes, and nations, struggle to find common accord.

The Torah not only narrates our coming to be as distinct consciousnesses within world, the formation of *Dasein*, as Heidegger might describe it, but in some senses seeks to bring it about. It promotes a world of difference, I and Thou, the permitted and forbidden, a world of potential conflict. This new state is not easy. It lacks the comfort, security, and simplicity of non-dualism, but it generates meaning and provides a framework for moral action. We are shown the face of the other, and by the very nature of the experience called upon to respond rationally, ethically, emotionally, and poetically, and in that response the world reveals itself to us.

Richard Friedman in his book *The Hidden Face of God*, describes how in the Bible God undergoes a process of withdrawal. In Genesis, God creates and talks directly to Adam and Eve. He forbids them to eat of the tree of life and casts them from the garden of Eden. Ten generations later, God engages with Noah. He commands him to build the ark. A further ten generations later, God appears to Abraham, Isaac, and Jacob. Later, Moses encounters God in a burning bush and leads the people out of Egypt. The people are given the Ten Commandments at Sinai, but God speaking is a fearful experience and direct revelation to the nation stops. Friedman views the experience at Sinai as the high point of God's interaction with the Israelites. After it, God becomes increasingly absent. His interventions become less spectacular, less frequent. And while God spoke to Moses "face to face," from this point on, God communicates mainly through visions, angels, dreams, and human intermediaries (Num 12:6–8).[31]

God continues to accompany the Israelites after Sinai, but not in the direct manner he had accompanied them until now. He now leads them by "a pillar of cloud by day" and "a pillar of fire by night." Cloud obscures. Moses's face, the face which has seen God, too is now obscured. He wears a veil or mask to hide the divine radiance which mysteriously shines from him following his encounter with the divine (Exod 34:29–35).[32]

In God's final speech to Moses before his death, found toward the end of Deuteronomy, the last book of the Five Books of Moses, God explains that in the future "I shall hide my face from them" (Deut 32:20).[33] Moses dies in Deuteronomy 34 shortly after this declaration. The Five Books of Moses, therefore, end with a statement concerning God's disappearance.

31. Friedman, *Hidden Face of God*, 16–17.

32. Friedman, *Hidden Face of God*, 17–18.

33. Friedman, *Hidden Face of God*, 18–19.

The process of God's disappearance continues throughout the books of the prophets. The last public miracle is Elijah's face-off with the prophets of Baal, the Canaanite deity, at Mount Carmel, the worship of which is sanctioned by King Ahab and Queen Jezebel. Elijah challenges the prophets to a test by requiring offerings to be made to God and Baal, but without the use of fire. Baal produces no fire, but God does. The fire consumes the offering, wood, stones, and soil.[34] The last two-hundred years of the Bible took place without large-scale miracles.[35]

The switch from direct divine intervention to a more naturalistic historical account is also evident in the book of Joshua set in the period of conquest of the Holy Land. God intervenes heavily in the early victories of the fall of Jericho (ch. 6), and Ai (chs. 7–8), but it is Israel, who later fights, chases, and captures five kings without God's assistance (ch. 10). Israel acts alone too in the later southern and northern campaigns (chs. 10–11; 1 Kgs 18).[36]

It is possible to describe the process of God's appearance and withdrawal in Spinozistic terms, albeit in a way that Spinoza never did. We might say that the God of the Bible emerges from the God of nature (or being) thereby establishing the possibility of relationship, yet no sooner has the biblical God made his presence known, he starts to recede. This withdrawal creates space, allows the possibility of human flourishing, makes way for the exercise of reason and imagination. Spinoza is blind to God's withdrawal and does not see its importance. Instead, he displays an almost idolatrous worship of reason, which led him to view the Bible as a work of flawed imagination, aimed purely at obedience. In fact, the space opened-up by God's disappearance is the key to revelation.

Revelation involves paradoxically both the hiding of God and his "unconcealment," to use a Heideggerian term. Revelation hides God, which is the sum of all knowledge, the singularity which leaves no room for difference, and reveals that which is hidden, not by demanding obedience to the dictates of reason, but by creating spaces, possibilities for imagination to explore. It invites humankind to step beyond God, to leap between nodes like a spark, to co-create. Reason knows only cause and effect, numbers, systems, the abstract. Revelation deals with experience, the particular, the nation, meaning. It narrows the focus, shines a light on

34. Friedman, *Hidden Face of God*, 22–23.

35. Friedman, *Hidden Face of God*, 25.

36. Levan, "Wars of Joshua," 37–50.

small things to show their enormity, and by so doing reveals us to ourselves. Information is valuable because it expresses limited possibilities as opposed to the infinity of every possibility. As Levinas stated, "Without separation there would not have been truth; there would have been only being."[37] Revelation is the imparting of information. In monistic terms, we can see this process as God's eternal folding and unfolding, the infinite knowing and unknowing of itself.

## Unconcealment

There are different types of truth. There is truth as correspondence, encapsulated by statements which objectively describe the world "out there," such as Manchester United won the English football premier league in a particular year. Heidegger says about this type of truth that "the 'locus' of truth is the proposition [Aussage] (judgement)," and "The essence of truth lies in the 'agreement' of the judgement with its object."[38] This kind of truth requires (1) a proposition about what is; and (2) facts that accord with that proposition. Heidegger claims that Aristotle initiated the idea of truth as "agreement" and blames him for the mistaken belief that we encounter it before any other kind of truth, i.e., that it is "primordial."[39] By setting us on this course, Aristotle caused us to lose sight of the fact that *Dasein*, our being in the world, precedes our rational cognizance of the world.

Heidegger wants to introduce us to a different type of truth, involving not correspondence but knowing and self-knowing.[40] This more original truth stands behind our apparent concern with truth as correspondence.

Heidegger asks us to imagine a person with his back to a picture hanging crookedly on a wall. The person says, "the picture on the wall is hanging crookedly." The person then turns round and sees that the picture is indeed hanging crookedly. For Heidegger, the truth here is not so much the correspondence between the statement that the picture is

---

37. Levinas, *Totality and Infinity*, 1.60. See also 1.63: "The great force of the idea of creation such as was contributed by monotheism is that this creation is *ex nihilo* . . . because the separated and created being is thereby not simply issued forth from the father, but is absolutely other than him."

38. Heidegger, *Being and Time*, 206.

39. Heidegger, *Being and Time*, 206.

40. Heidegger, *Being and Time*, 208.

hanging crookedly and actuality, but the person's turning toward the wall to determine the position of the picture.

The act of demonstration, which occurs when the person turns round to face the picture, brings the person in touch with the object of his interest and unconceals that object: "The being [i.e., the picture] that one has in mind shows itself as it is in itself, that is, it shows that it, in its selfsameness, is just as it is discovered or pointed out in the statement."[41]

But Heidegger reaches back further. In order for statements to uncover how things are, those things must already be open to view. Heidegger contends that there is a primordial conception of truth which precedes truth as agreement or correspondence, and that is the act of letting "beings be seen in their unconcealment (discoveredness), taking them out of their concealment."[42]

He later explains that "discovering is a way of being of being-in-the-world. Taking care whether in circumspection or in looking in a leisurely way, discovers innerworldly beings. The latter become what is discovered."[43] The impression is that our lives are a process of discovering, coming to know things by considering or contemplating them. Things resonate within us when we are attuned to them and this tells us about ourselves, our inner worlds. The process leading to unconcealment involves care—concern with the things that come to our attention, and in which we take an interest as individuals or communities.

Behind the idea that things need to be uncovered is the recognition that they are usually hidden from our sight, despite being before our eyes. Why do we miss things? Why do we not see things as they are? We will look in some detail at the answers given by Heidegger in later chapters, but the short answer is that we are distracted, too immersed in the day-to-day to see what lies before us. We flee from things that unconceal, such as death and anxiety, and embrace that which conceals, such as worldly distractions and the opinions of the "they" (others) who we blithely repeat and blindly follow.[44] Unconcealment becomes possible when things go wrong, when objects break, when the seamless fabric of experience becomes torn. In Jewish terms, we might say that revelation is the light

---

41. Heidegger, *Being and Time*, 209.
42. Heidegger, *Being and Time*, 210.
43. Heidegger, *Being and Time*, 210.
44. Heidegger, *Being and Time*, 212–13.

that shines through the tear caused by God's withdrawal, made possible by the break in the totality of oneness.

Heidegger's conception of truth as unconcealment allows us to recover something essential about revelation. Revelation is that which reveals. It is not a description of what happened in a specific time or place, but the opening of gateways to wisdom, insights, worlds of meaning and ways of living that would otherwise be closed. The experience of such revelation is what allows us to call it divine.

## Imagination Reinstated

Imagination plays a crucial role in the ongoing process of unconcealment. Like Spinoza, for Heidegger the imagination is not a faculty of the soul. It is also not the faculty of apperception as formulated by Kant which provides the possibility of knowledge through the synthesis of intuition and thinking. Instead, as described by Elliot Wolfson, imagination is the "clearing, the between of Da-sein."[45] Wolfson quotes Heidegger. Imagination is "the axis in the turning point of the event, the self-opening center of the counterplay between call and belonging, within which [being] is constituted as a formed image and beings are imagined to be really present at hand."[46]

Imagination, therefore, has to do with who we are in the world. It manifests a sense of belonging and call to the beyond. In kabbalistic terms, it is that which forms the void (*Chalal Panui*), following God's *Zimzum*, the dissolution of monism in favor of transcendence. Furthermore, it is imagination which leads us to envisage that beings are really "present at hand," that is, distinct objects of theoretical apprehension, subjects known only from scientific analysis, when in fact they are not just that at all. Heidegger here is turning Spinoza on his head. Imagination is not the enemy of reason, but the phenomena which gives rise to scientific thinking in the first place. It is also the illusion that such thinking reflects what we commonly refer to as "reality."[47]

Just as scientific thinking is less "real" than we believe, our dreams are more "real" than we believe. We consider dreams to be the most

---

45. Wolfson, *Heidegger*, 117.

46. Heidegger, *Contributions*, 191–92, quoted in Wolfson, *Heidegger*, 117.

47. See Wolfson, *Heidegger*, 117–18.

extreme invention of the imagination, but for Heidegger, they are not fantasy, but a form of unconcealment. Wolfson explains:

> The shadow-like and fading nature of the dream does not convey that the dream is nothing, but rather that it is the appearing of the non-apparent, that is, the appearing of what abstains from appearing, the presenting of what prevails as absent, not because it is a presence that is not present—the nothing measured according to the metrics of being—but because it is present as non-present, the nonbeing that belongs to the being of the human being.[48]

Dreams allow the impossible, contradiction, opposites to exist side by side. They reveal aspects of existence, while at the same time obscuring them. Dreams also distort time; hours and years pass in an instantaneous moment. The imagination "vacillates between infinity and finitude."[49] Past, present, and future join and separate.

When we consider these views, we come to appreciate how Spinoza's denigration of imagination narrows the possibility for revelation. On the other hand, imagination is all too easily mistaken for truth in the manner of correspondence. In its role as a creator of myth, a tool for the formation of allegiances, and creator of frameworks for unquestioning obedience, imagination's potential to cause destruction is immense.

In a footnote to *Halachic Man*, Rabbi Joseph B. Soloveitchik (1903–1993), the scion of Jewish modern orthodoxy, denounces

> the self-evident falsity of . . . the entire Romantic aspiration to escape from the domain of knowledge, the rebellion against the authority of objective, scientific cognition which has found its expression in . . . the phenomenological, existential and antiscientific school of Heidegger and his coterie, and from the midst of which there arose in various forms the sanctification of vitality and intuition . . . [which] have brought complete chaos and human depravity to the world. And let the events of the present era be proof![50]

The warning is apt but does not undermine the importance of imagination to the process of revealing the hidden. Imagination is also not the opposite of objective scientific cognition. Reason comes to fruition

---

48. Wolfson, *Heidegger*, 118.

49. Wolfson, *Heidegger*, 119.

50. Soloveitchik, *Halakhic Man*, 141n4.

through imagination and operates as a check on it. Imagination as the power of revelation has allowed reason to flourish. As an initial aspiration, we can embrace Maimonides's ideal of the prophet philosopher, who has managed to perfect both the imaginative and rational faculties:

> Prophecy is, in truth and reality, an emanation sent forth by the Divine Being through the medium of the Active Intellect, in the first instance to man's rational faculty, and then to his imaginative faculty ... A man who satisfies these conditions ... will only include that which is real knowledge, and his thought will only be directed to such general principles as would tend to improve the social relations between man and man.[51]

But we might also look to the mystics who go further than Maimonides in embracing imagination. For them, reason can get in the way. Rabbi Naftali Zvi Hurwitz of Ropshitz (1760–1827), the Galician Hasidic Rebbe, discusses why the Torah contains both laws which can be explained rationally and laws which cannot. He writes that in fact all laws should be performed without applying any intellect. Laws that can be explained rationally simply provide an entry point, but reason can only reach so far: "Only one who performs [all commandments] in the same way that he performs commandments without reasons achieves complete faith, which has no measurement or boundary, because faith cannot be grasped intellectually."[52]

During the same period, the Hasidic Master, Rebbe Nahman of Bratslov (1772–1810), recommended carrying out "acts of madness" in order to reach beyond the intellect, for example rolling in mud and refuse: "At that point [the practitioner] attains insights that transcend his intellect."[53] Faith resides in the imaginative faculty:

> When prophecy "spreads out," then the imaginative faculty is purified and rectified. As the verse states, "By the hand of the prophets shall I be imagined" (Hos 12:11). Because essentially, when the imaginative faculty is rectified, the true faith of holiness is rectified, and false faiths are nullified. This is because the essence of faith depends upon the imaginative faculty.[54]

51. Maimonides, *Guide*, II.36.225–26.
52. Hurwitz, *Zera Kodesh*, Parshat B'Chukotai, 260. My translation.
53. *Tiku Emunah*, secs. 10–14, quoted in Mark, *Mysticism and Madness*, 19.
54. *Likutei Moharan* I 7, quoted in Mark, *Mysticism and Madness*, 23.

Revelation and divine service therefore entail applying imagination and reaching beyond reason, although wisdom dictates that reason must never be abandoned or set aside for long. So far, we have discussed only the mechanism of revelation, the importance of imagination, the path from the God of being to the God of the Bible, and his withdrawal. We have said little about the content of revelation, the character of *Dasein* it gives rise to, what has been unconcealed, and how we might live in the encounter. These issues will be addressed in the following chapters.

# 7

# God as Being, Becoming, and Nothing

## The Dynamic God

WE HAVE SEEN THAT the Bible opens up a space separate from God. God is no longer associated only with being but is now relatable also as the Other; the Other from which we emerge and who slowly recedes. The Bible gives God a face, a garment, and it is only through the garment that we have something to relate to. Psalm 93:1 reads, "The LORD is king, He is *robed* in grandeur; the LORD is *robed*, He is *girded* with strength."[1] God reveals himself through his clothes, through nature, through wisdom, through Torah.[2]

But clothes do not tell the full story. They reveal only a contour, they merely hint at the character of the occupant which in this case has no corporeality, no body to cover. The Bible does not state, but we know, that the God which it describes is not the God clothed in its descriptions. These descriptions reflect the mere phenomenology of our lived experience: the God that calls to us, that has an outstretched hand, that hears or does not hear our cries, that hides his face.

The God revealed through the Torah is active, in the colloquial sense, within the world, in contrast to Spinoza's God which is active only in the sense that it is the only thing which truly is. God is fixed, unmoving in his infinitude. The world (*Ha'aretz*) recalls the Hebrew word for

1. See also Ps 104:1.
2. The *Zohar* 2:94a:6 associates strength (*Oz*) here with the Torah.

running (*Ratz*). It is continuously in motion, literally and metaphorically. The earth rotates around an axis, circles a sun, is a point of rotation for the moon, a dot in a spiral galaxy. And when we peer down using satellites or from spaceships, we see water running, streams, rivers, seas, streams of tears and confusion, a beehive of activity, directionless, busy, confused, a chaos within order and order within chaos. Existence is not stable. Life is unpredictable, probabilistic, uncertain.

God shudders and moves. In the Bible, Ezekiel saw a vision of heavenly creatures accompanied by something which "looked like burning coals" that "kept moving about among the creatures," and the creatures "darted this way and that (*Ratzu v'Shov*) like lightning" (Ezek 3:13–14; my translation). Back in Exodus, God had already described himself as *Ehyeh Asher Eheyh*, a God not just of being but of becoming through an infinite knowing of itself (Exod 3:14).

Our perceptions constantly shift, move in cycles of exile and return, backward and forward, and with each new movement, new worlds reveal themselves, insights are born. God appears now as other, now as all, now as nothing.

Jacob is on his way to Bet El after fleeing the anger of his brother, Esau. He has a dream:

> A ladder was fixed upon the earth and its top reached to the heavens, and angels of God were going up and down. And God was standing over [or beside] [the ladder] [or Jacob] and [God] said, "I am the Lord, the God of your father Abraham and the God of Isaac: the ground on which you are lying I will give to you and to your offspring." (Gen 28:12–13; my translation)

The story conveys a theology. God is both immanent and transcendent. The ladder is set in God's midst. Powers and perceptions move back and forth along its rungs between heaven and earth, as immanence turns into transcendence, and transcendence into immanence.[3] The God atop the ladder is the transcendent God. The God at the base of the ladder is the immanent God manifested in the history of a particular people, a particular family, the God of Abraham, the God of Isaac, a God clothed in narrative experienced in different ways by different people through each

---

3. This is my Midrashic interpretation. Maimonides describes God as standing both on and above the ladder. For Maimonides, "the phrase 'stood upon it' indicates the permanence and constancy of God, and does not imply the idea of physical position." See Maimonides, *Guide*, I.XV. On other creative interpretations of Jacob's ladder see Robinson, "On or Above the Ladder?"

encounter. The notion of the dynamic God allows us to move beyond the God of being but also to escape our particularism. We are urged to comprehend and feel the unity of the universe while also viewing ourselves as distinct, in a position of relationship, morally activated.

This dual or shifting perspective between immanence and transcendence is a defining feature of Habad Hasidism. Naftali Loewenthal describes the interplay between the rational and mystical in Shneur Zalman's *Tanya*, Habad's founding text. This involves two modes of contemplation. The first, termed the Higher Unity, "leads to the awareness that space and time are really abnegated from existence in the face of His Being and Essence." The second mode of contemplation is the Lower Unity. In this mode "the contemplative sees the world and relates to it as world; at the same time he perceives that it is an expression of the Divine."[4]

The Torah holds out the possibility of transcendence, but also leads us to a path of self-realization, to the insight demanded by Spinoza that our imagination has the capacity to lead us astray, just as it reveals. As the biblical narrative unfolds, and the ethical and legal instructions take their effect, we come to understand that nothing is God.

The atheist will take such a statement as confirmation that there is no God, but this is not what is intended. Nothing is God implies two things, which I consider to be fundamental to the postmodern spiritual path. The first is that no thing is God. Anything that we can point to, any person, political stance, ideology, creed, or dogma, that one holds up as the answer to all our problems, a panacea for all our ills, including any positive description of God, is liable to mislead. Nothing is God is a statement about the limits of knowledge, about entities which are unsuitable as a focus for veneration and worship. Convictions can be strong, but they must be provisional and lightly held.

The second aspect of the statement is related to the first and has to do with what we call reality and its underpinning: nothingness. Nothingness is a concept known to the Jewish mystics, Master Eckhart (1260–1328), the German Christian mystic and theologian, Franz Rosenzweig, the Jewish philosopher, and Heidegger, but one whose unconcealment arises from contemplation of the written Torah itself. Nothingness underlies everything. Its presence is felt by the world of objects, and the possibility of their none existence, and it is this possibility which generates meaning. Nothingness calls to us from both the here and now and the beyond.

---

4. Loewenthal, *Hasidism Beyond Modernity*, 133, commenting on *Tanya*, II.7.

I will deal first with the idea that no thing is God, and then consider the concept of nothingness, before explaining how this might impact our everyday consciousness.

## No Thing Is God

Contrary to what Spinoza asserts, the Hebrew Bible is not a work requiring pure obedience. It certainly contains numerous laws and warns of dire consequences if these are not followed, but it also contains ideas which force us to confront the abuses of power. At times it almost encourages disobedience, even against God, and presents anarchic possibilities. It might even be suggested that, in some respects, the Torah contains within its core the seed of its own destruction and remaking. Below, I identify seven ideas within the biblical tradition which highlight its anarchic potential. I want to suggest that these ideas prevent stagnation and fixity of power and thought, but instead expand the space for human action and fill the space left by God's contraction.

## Iconoclasm

The first idea is iconoclasm, the injunction to remove oneself from idolatry and to destroy idolatrous images. Biblical Judaism is obsessed with idolatry. The first and second of the Ten Commandments adjure: "you shall have no other gods before me," and "you shall not make idols" (Exod 20:1–14; Deut 5:6–18). Commands against idolatry then comprise 20 percent of the Ten Commandments. Idolatry was also a constant temptation for the Israelites throughout their early history, and it was the misuse of an image (i.e., the worship of a golden calf) that almost ended the Jewish project at inception (Exod 32:1–4).

For the rabbis, worshiping idols is one of the worst things that any person can do. It is one of the three things for which Jews must lay down their lives (along with bloodshed and sexual immorality).[5] Actions which further idolatry (such as selling items which may be used to worship idols) are heavily proscribed by legislation.[6]

---

5. *TB* Pesachim 25a–b; Sanhedrin 74a–b; *Shulchan Aruch*, Yoreh De'ah 157. For a discussion on the parameters of this law, see Blau, "Idolatry and Martyrdom."

6. See *Shulchan Aruch*, Yoreh De'ah 139:15; 151:1–4. See also 142:12; 145:1–8 (building or plants forbidden when made/planted for idolatrous purposes or turned

Idolatry is not of course about figurines of stone or clay, but about ascribing any intrinsic value to anything other than God.[7] The anarchic potential of such an idea is immense for it means that, by the command of the Creator, no human being, no authority, no power, can assert any power over you.

Pierre Joseph Proudhon (1809–1865), the French anarchist, politician, and philosopher, sees the appropriation by human beings of the commanding voice behind the Ten Commandments as the root of all tyranny. He writes in his aptly named *Away with Authority* as follows:

> One of the most solemn moments in the evolution of the authority principle was when the Ten Commandments were handed down. The voice of an angel commands the people prostrate at the foot of Mount Sinai:
> Thou shalt . . .
> All legislation has borrowed this style and all, when speaking to man, employ the sovereign formula . . . whatever the law, from whatever mouth it emanates, it is sacred once it has been uttered by that fateful trump which, is in our day, the majority:
> Thou shall not gather together.
> Though shall not publish.
> Though shall not read.
> Though shall respect thy representatives and functionaries.[8]

He continues to play on a religious theme, turning to the biblical command to love God enunciated by Jews in the *Shema* (Deut 6:4–9):

> And you shall love the government, thy Lord and thy God with all thy . . . Because the government knows better than thee what thou art, what thou deserves, what is appropriate for thee, and it has the power to punish those who offend against its commandments, as well as to reward, even to the fourth generation, those whom it favors.
> O personality of man! Can it be that you have been wallowing in such abjection for the past sixty centuries! You claim to be

into an object of idolatry); and 146:14–15 (idolatrous items should be sought out and destroyed). An interesting modern discussion on the application of such laws arose as a result of orthodox Jewish women wearing wigs made of human hair that had been dedicated to a Hindu temple. See Brill, *Judaism and Other Religions*, 222–24.

7. See Hefter, "Idolatry."

8. Proudhon, *Away with Authority*, quoted in *Ni Dieu Ni Maître*, 96–97.

blessed and sacred, but you are only the tireless, free prostitute of your servants, your monks, and your henchmen.[9]

Proudhon might have observed, based on such observations, that tyranny is what happens when humans play God.

## Kingly Power

The second idea is the limit imposed on the monarch and other earthly rulers. Rabbinic commentators and modern scholars remain divided on whether the Torah holds an ideal of kingly rule or sees it as a terrible idea which ultimately failed.[10] In Deuteronomy, the Torah permits the appointment of a king, albeit with limitations. The king cannot amass wives, horses, or wealth, and is subject to the law (Deut 17:14–20).

But in the First Book of Samuel the tone is openly hostile: "This will be the manner of the king that shall reign over you: he will take your sons, and appoint them unto him, for his chariots, and to be his horsemen; and they shall run before his chariots." The speech continues with a warning that the king will take your daughters, take your fields, take your produce, take your servants: "And ye shall cry out in that day because of your king whom ye shall have chosen; and the Lord will not answer you in that day" (1 Sam 8:11–13).

Proudhon is fixated with the same theme:

> To be governed is to be watched over, inspected, spied upon, directed, legislated for, regulated, penned in, indoctrinated, preached at, monitored, assessed, censured and commanded by beings who boast neither the entitlement, the expertise, nor the virtue.[11]

While the period of the Kings brought some stability after the period of the Judges, in many ways it was a disaster. We see infighting, corruption, idolatry, and the splitting of the kingdom into two parts: Judah and Israel. Ten tribes eventually disappeared.

A discussion in the later Babylonian Talmud describes a debate in which the biblical and prophetic depictions of kingship are discussed:

---

9. Proudhon, *Away with Authority*, quoted in *Ni Dieu Ni Maître*, 96–97.

10. See Kimelman, "Abravanel," 195–216.

11. Proudhon, *Away with Authority* quoted in *Ni Dieu Ni Maître*, 97.

> R. Nehorai says. [The appointment of the King] is to Israel's dis-
> credit, as it says "... for they have not rejected you but they have
> rejected me, that I should not be king over them" [1 Sam 8:7].
> Said R. Judah: But is it not a command of the Torah that they
> should request a king, for it says "you shall surely place a king
> over you?" [Deut 17:15].[12]

We find a similar difference of opinion in the medieval period. By this
time, Plato had come up with his ideal of the philosopher king, which he
viewed as a better alternative to the anarchy of democracy. His ideas were
known and reflected upon by Jewish scholars in the medieval period.
Some saw royal rule as ideal.[13] Others thought monarchical rule was a
bad idea.[14] And others took an intermediate position.[15] Isaac Abravanel
(1437–1508) was one of those opposed to the idea of kingship. Abravanel
was treasurer to King Alfonso of Spain and lived through the inquisition
and expulsion (which he tried to stop), and so knew about the problems
of monarchical rule. He wrote, "Leadership of kings is bad, harmful and
extremely dangerous."[16]

The point, however, is that even those who support monarchical
rule recognize that the king is subject to the dictates of God and laws
of the Torah, like all other citizens. The king is commanded to have a
Scroll of the Law (*Sefer Torah*) with him at all times, as a reminder of his
obligations (Deut 17:18–20).[17] The rabbis also required the king to read
the Torah publicly once every seven years.[18]

This is different to the model of kingship practiced in Egypt and
Mesopotamia at the time of the Bible. Ancient kings were gods or

12. *TB* Sanhedrin 20b.

13. For example, Maimonides, Menahem ha-Meiri (1249–1315), and Nissim of
Gerondi (1320–1376).

14. For example, Sadia Gaon, Avraham ibn Ezra (1089–1167), and Obadiah ben
Jacob Sforno (1475–1550).

15. For example, Gersonides (1288–1344), Nachmanides (1194–1270), and
Bachya ben Asher (1255–1340). See Kimelman, "Abravanel," 199–200.

16. Abravanel, *Commentary on Deuteronomy 17*, quoted in Kimelman, "Abravanel," 202.

17. The king in fact requires two scrolls: one to be placed in his treasury, the other
to be taken with him. *TB* Sanhedrin 21b, R. Shlomo Yitzchaki (1040–1105) (Rashi).

18. The obligation is derived from the ceremony of *Hakhel*. See Deut 31:10–12;
Mishnah Sotah 7:8.

god-like. The Bible requires the king to be subject to God's law and a servant of the people in which sovereignty properly resides.[19]

## Empire

The third idea with anarchic potential is biblical anti-imperialism. In ancient times, any self-respecting tribe or larger grouping would desire to become an empire, to exert its authority far beyond its own ancestral borders. In the twenty-fourth century BCE, Sargon the Great conquered the city-states of Sumer and Akkad to become the ruler of Mesopotamia, and declared himself "king of the universe."[20] Hazony sees such imperial ambitions as a universal aspiration at the time. He contrasts such an outlook with anarchism. He writes that "an anarchic or feudal order is built upon relations of mutual loyalty among familiar individuals," whereas empires encourage allegiance to "a great abstraction" rooted in the premise that "great masses of humanity" depend on the imperial state to provide "universal peace and prosperity."[21]

The Hebrew Bible certainly has little positive to say about empires. In *Radical Then, Radical Now*, Jonathan Sacks observes how the negative view of empires is conveyed in the life stories of Abraham and Moses, who move away from the great empires of their birth, that is Ur and Egypt, respectively, in order to find their calling. Egypt, Assyria, Babylon are all portrayed as abusive of others and self-destructive.[22] The Jews become a people at Sinai before they get a land, and when they do get a land, it is circumscribed by boundaries. Conquering neighboring lands is not a religious ideal.[23] The imperial impulse, then, is to be kept at bay. Judaism, like anarchism, distrusts power and the powerful, which empires symbolize.

Hazony, looking at all this politically, claims that the Hebrew Bible proposes a third type of political order as an alternative to imperialism or anarchy. This alternative is "the distinctive Israelite institution of the national state, which seeks to transcend the dilemma of empire and anarchy

19. Sacks, *Future Tense*, 61–62.

20. Mieroop, *Cuneiform Texts*, 70.

21. Hazony, *Virtue of Nationalism*, 91–93.

22. Sacks, *Radical Then, Radical Now*, 77–108.

23. On conquering land as an ideal, see Neusner, *Comparing Religions through Law*, 193–99.

by retaining what is most vital in each, while discarding what makes each of them most dangerous."[24] The Israelite nation state is an abstraction, like an empire, because it comprises more than a clan or family, but resembles the anarchic order because it has a distinctive character "having its own language, laws, and religious traditions, its own past history of failure and achievement."[25] This allows for different nations to pursue their own purposes and to develop their own "vision of human life."[26] We might add a theological gloss here. Inherent in the idea of the Israelite nation is a coming together of the universal and particular, the abstract (empire) and the poetic (family), the God of the All and the God of a particular nation encountered through a particular worldview, *Dasein*.

## The Individual

The fourth idea is the importance of the individual. At the start of Genesis, we are told that each human being is created in the image of God (*b'Zelem Elokim*) (Gen 1:26–27, 5:2–3).[27] The Israelites are further commanded to become a kingdom of priests (*Mamlechet Cohanim*) and holy nation (*Goi Kadosh*). Jonathan Sacks argues that a kingdom of priests relates to literacy. In ancient times, only the scribes could write. In contrast, the Torah espouses the idea of a "society of universal literacy" which in turn makes possible "a society as a covenant of equal citizens freely bound to one another and to God."[28] All human beings are part of the chain of discovery and transmission and should have access to knowledge. All individuals count.

The notion of the autonomous individual independent of society in its modern guise has its roots in the seventeenth and eighteenth centuries, but the Bible represents an important stage in the process, as we will see in more detail later.[29] Once the individual was recognized as a moral

24. Hazony, *Virtue of Nationalism*, 100.

25. Hazony, *Virtue of Nationalism*, 101–2.

26. Hazony, *Virtue of Nationalism*, 102.

27. See also Mishnah Avot 3:13.

28. Sacks, *Dignity of Difference*, 135. The Bible here does not distinguish between men and women, although until the modern period women were not taught Torah to the same extent as men. This is changing.

29. Modern Judaism absorbed Enlightenment ideas of the individual and combined them with traditional outlooks. See Bor, "Enlightenment Values," 48–63; and Bor, "Moral Education."

category, the right of that individual to forge her own life and speak out against power would inevitably also have to be recognized, which leads to the next idea.

## Challenging God

The fifth idea is challenging God. Although the Torah demands loyalty, God is not beyond questioning. When God is about to destroy Sodom, he seeks Abraham's advice. Abraham demands to know why the righteous must perish with the wicked (Gen 18:16–33). Later, after the episode of the golden calf, Moses pleads with God not to destroy the people (Exod 32:11–14). Abraham loses his battle. Moses wins his.

In Numbers, we read how some men who had become ritually impure prior to Passover appealed to Moses and Aaron, Moses's brother, for another opportunity to bring the Passover sacrifice. God agreed and instituted a second Passover (*Pesach Sheni*) to accommodate such situations (Num 9:1–13). Later, in the same book, the daughters of Zelophehad (Mahlah, Noah, Hoglah, Milcah, and Tirzah) "came forward," demanding "before Moses, Eleazar the priest, the chieftains, and the whole assembly" that a woman whose father dies without leaving a son should be able to inherit her father's land. God agreed (Num 27:1–11). In both these last two stories, the language used by the complainants is almost the same, essentially: "Why is it we are being held aback?"[30] As a result of their efforts, these individuals were granted rights.

A religion that finds value in challenging God, albeit not in every case, prevents God's image from ever settling, breaks the bonds of fate, and creates space for otherness, dialogue, movement.[31]

---

30. Compare the language at Num 9:7 (*Lama Nigara*) and Num 27:4 (*Lama Yigora*).

31. It is interesting that given this tradition, Abraham does not challenge God when commanded to sacrifice his son, Isaac, in the *Akedah* (Gen 22:2). Korach's challenge to Moses and Aaron on the grounds of equality at Numbers 16 was also viewed as inappropriate. Challenging God, it would seem, is not always a fitting response. A difference between Sodom and the *Akedah* is that Abraham was invited to comment in the former case, while the Akedah involved a command. The issue also with Sodom was the indiscriminate nature of the punishment. This was not a factor in the *Akedah*. The fact that many Jews prefer to focus on Abraham's questioning stance in the Sodom story over his obedience in the *Akedah* shows how biblical texts take on a life of their own in the minds of those who live them. These days, questioning resonates more strongly than faith.

## Breaking the Tablets

The sixth idea is that the law must sometimes yield to a greater truth. There are times when it must be smashed and broken. This idea is suggested by Moses's breaking of the first set of tablets containing the Ten Commandments when he sees the Israelites circling the golden calf on his descent from Sinai (Exod 33:12–23). It is often assumed that Moses broke the tablets out of anger and that his action was a grave error.

However, the biblical text does not blame Moses. When recounting the episode later in Deuteronomy, Moses states matter-of-factly that "I grasped the two tablets and threw them from my hands, and smashed them before your eyes" (Deut 9:17). The Talmud even praises Moses for his actions: "well done that you shattered [them]."[32]

Among the explanations for Moses actions is a suggestion that the law needed to be broken to teach the people that nothing, other than God, has intrinsic holiness. The principle applies to all things, even the tablets of the law. Rabbi Meir Simcha HaCohen of Dvinsk (1843–1926) suggests just this in his *Meshech Chochmah* where he adds that the Torah is dependent on God alone. It is only the weak of mind who require it to take on form.[33] Moses, then, smashed the tablets to prevent the law becoming deified.[34] However, the broken tablets were kept in the ark of the covenant.[35] Broken, suspended, or obsolete laws retain their sanctity.

## Messiah

The seventh idea is the Judaic notion of the messiah, the belief that at some point in the future, history will be overhauled and tyranny will be conquered and replaced with a utopia of sorts. As we have seen there are numerous different ideas about what the messianic world will look like, but the most important feature of Jewish conceptions of the messianic

32. *TB* Yevamot 62a.

33. HaCohen, *Meshech Chochma*, Exod 32:19.

34. In *TB* Eruvin 13a, R. Yishmael forbids the writing of a Torah scroll using ink containing iron sulphate (*kankatom*) which made it indelible. Others applied the prohibition only to the section dealing with a wife suspected of unfaithfulness (*Sotah*) who was made to drink water in which the section was dissolved (Num 5:12–31). R. Yishmael's view suggests phenomenologically, like the breaking of the commandments, a connection between the sacred text and the possibility of erasure.

35. *TB* Menachot 99a.

age for our purposes is that it has not yet come. Utopia is always in the future. The perfect political system, the absolute justice and equality we yearn for, the end of all ills, is always one step away. The messianic ideal is always present *in potentia*, but never quite reached.

The rabbinic tradition in many respects neutralized the radical possibilities of the ideas that we have looked at above. When pressed under the thumb of the mighty Roman Empire, it would be suicide to espouse radical ideas about individualism and power or attempt to speak truth to power. Some Jews did not let this deter them. There were zealots, or *Sicarri*, as Josephus calls them, who sought to oppose Roman rule by whatever means. Although a handful of rabbis supported the revolt against Rome, most notably Rabbi Akiva, the general rabbinic attitude toward Rome, and later ruling powers, became one of enmity mixed with begrudging acceptance.[36] The effect of this pragmatism was to narrow the scope of religious concerns to the communal and religious practice. Provided the state allowed the practice of *Halachah* (Jewish law) and was not too oppressive, it could be respected. When the state threatened religious practice, there would be more grounds for opposition.[37]

In the modern period, radical Jewish ideas once again gained resonance. By the late eighteenth and into the nineteenth century, many Jews were attracted to the anti-establishment and radical movements of the time. The inter-war period in Germany is particularly interesting in this context, because one sees a direct conflict between the older generation, who felt a sense of loyalty to the German Kaiser and the First World War effort, and the new generation who tended to see war as futile and wanted change in the form of socialism, anarchism, zionism, or combinations of all of three.

As Jews grappled with the issues of the day, some turned toward Jewish tradition to find concepts that would lend support to their political views. Jews interested in anarchism in this period included Gustav Landauer (1870–1919), the political theorist, Walter Benjamin (1892–1940), the writer, Martin Buber (1878–1965), the philosopher, and Gerschom Scholem (1897–1982), the professor of mysticism.[38] This interest is also

---

36. On Jewish attitudes to Rome from the twelfth to fifth centuries, see Goodman, *Rome and Jerusalem*, 501–11.

37. Rakeffet-Rothkoff, "Law of the Land," 16.

38. See Loëwy, *Redemption and Utopia*.

found among religious thinkers, including Abraham Isaac Kook who we have already mentioned.[39]

Gershom Scholem is the father of the academic study of Jewish mysticism, but his relationship to Jewish mysticism was not purely academic. He discovered his Jewish roots as a youth in Germany, before moving to British Mandate Palestine when he was twenty-six. There he became a librarian and eventually professor of Jewish Mysticism at the Hebrew University. He was, at one time, a political anarchist, and fascinated by the idea of the messiah, and what he saw as the central role of the individual to mend the broken sefiriotic system within the Lurianic Kabbalah, described earlier.[40]

In his ground-breaking *Major Trends in Jewish Mysticism*, Scholem describes the breaking of the vessels and explains that, for Luria, the task of repairing the system and putting the world to rights (*Tikkun*) depends on free individual action directed toward a common goal. It "raise[s] every Jew to the rank of a protagonist in the great process of restitution."[41] The notion of the messiah is essential to this enterprise. "The world of *Tikkun*," he wrote, is the world of "messianic action."[42] Scholem was also taken with the idea of the breaking of the tablets mentioned above.

In one of his essays, Scholem refers to a kabbalistic idea linking the first set of tablets to the Tree of Life in the Genesis story and the second set of tablets to the Tree of Knowledge. The second set, the one that we have, comprises the historical Torah and represents limitation and law. The first set, which was broken, denotes freedom, the combination of good and evil into a unity, and the state of nature: "A revelation of the Torah bestowed upon a world in keeping with the original state of man . . . in which there [i]s no need to hold the powers of uncleanness and death in check by prohibitions." Scholem suggests that the second set of tablets represents the Torah of *Galut*, exile, while the first set constitutes the Torah of revelation—the pristine past and hoped-for future.[43]

We might amend this exposition slightly. The first set of tablets might be seen as marking the original state of humanity and associated with Spinoza's God, the universal, oneness. On this view, the second set

39. See Shapira, *Jewish Religious Anarchism*.

40. On his life see Prochnik, *Stranger in a Strange Land*; Engel, *Gershom Scholem*.

41. Scholem, *Major Trends*, 284; Engel, *Gershom Scholem*, 78.

42. Scholem, *Major Trends*, 274; Engel, *Gershom Scholem*, 79.

43. Scholem, *Kabballah and Its Symbolism*, 68–70; Prochnik, *Stranger in a Strange Land*, 287–88.

of tablets marks emergence from that state, a breaking of that worldview. The second tablets speak to a world of relationship, *Dasein*, community, the mission of a particular people. The first and second set of tablets do not though simply mark a historical development. They are orientations which are forever present, both of which are required. The temptation always is to settle on one or the other, but fixity marks the path toward idolatry. What is required is movement, a *Ratzu v'Shov* to use Ezekiel's terminology, constant, effortful, conscious, directed, a letting go and appropriation, breaking and mending, an exile and return.

## Nothingness

The idea that no thing is God bulldozes everything in its path, including Spinoza's idea of God as being and the descriptions of God in the Hebrew Bible. Each of these conceptions are subject to challenge, fold in on themselves when exposed to critique, until nothing is left other than a wordless silence.

As we have seen, Maimonides saw the episode in Exodus 33 as expressing the idea of God's unknowability: "No one can see my face and live." This is at the root of his negative theology which holds that any positive description of God falls short. For Maimonides, even the description that God "exists" is inadequate because that word means something different in relation to God than it means to us.[44]

He writes:

> All we understand is the fact that He exists, that He is a Being to whom none of His creatures is similar, who has nothing in common with them, who does not include plurality, who is never too feeble to produce other beings, and whose relation to the universe is that of a steersman to a boat; and even this is not a real relation, a real simile, but serves only to convey to us the idea that God rules the universe; that is, that He gives it duration, and preserves its necessary arrangement.[45]

The same approach applies to all other qualities. When we say God has power, we mean God does not have or lack power in the way that we have

44. Maimonides, *Guide*, I.LVI.80.
45. Maimonides, *Guide*, I.LVIII.82.

or lack power. When we say God has wisdom, we mean that God does not have or lack wisdom in the way that we do.[46]

In this discussion, Maimonides further insists that all people must understand that God is incorporeal because "without incorporeality there is no unity, for a corporeal thing is in the first case not simple, but composed of matter and form which are two separate things by definition, and secondly, as it has extension it is also divisible."[47]

Every quality must therefore be imagined and then destroyed, intellectualized out of existence. Negative theology can be understood as a process of taking a box containing every image and description of God and removing each item until what we are left with is the box. A further stage is to remove the box itself.

It is at this point that language breaks down. Our minds cannot cope:

> In the contemplation of His essence, our comprehension and knowledge prove insufficient; in the examination of His works, how they necessarily result from His will, our knowledge proves to be ignorance, and in the endeavor to extol Him in words, all our efforts in speech are mere weakness and failure![48]

Our response is a silence born of humility and, for Maimonides, this would be the only appropriate response if tradition had not instructed us to speak the words we speak, and the actions we live by. Kenneth Seeskin draws a parallel here between Maimonides and Levinas. Like Maimonides, the latter describes the inundation of thought when contemplating the infinite.[49]

Spinoza's God of being might take us in a similarly mystical direction. Being has no independent existence but is a part of the infinite substance we call God. In one sense, Spinoza's God is corporeal (God is Nature), but the nature we experience has no independent reality outside of God. Maimonides appears to have no issue in treating the world as real, but as we have seen, like Spinoza, holds the world to be ontologically identical with God. For both these thinkers, reality is not what it seems.

Modern physics too has led us away from the concrete world we once took for granted to a view of reality as shimmering forces and

46. See Seeskin, "No One Can See," 48–61.

47. Maimonides, *Guide*, I.XXXV.50.

48. Maimonides, *Guide*, I.LVIII.83.

49. Seeskin, "No One Can See," 52.

information exchanges given shape by our perceptions and experiences. Carlo Rovelli describes reality as "this network of relations, of reciprocal information, which weaves the world. We slice up the reality surrounding us into objects. But reality is not made up of discrete objects. It is a variable flux."[50]

In discussing Maimonides's conception of God's incorporeality, Marc Shapiro notes that the idea that God was incorporeal was not always unanimously accepted by Jews, Christians, or Muslims.[51] Of the Jewish corporealists, Moses ben Hasdai Taku (thirteenth century), a Tosafist, took a particularly extreme position holding it blasphemous to deny that God literally sits on his throne.[52] The gulf between corporealists and incorporealists might have been bridgeable if both had appreciated that matter is far more ethereal than we once believed.

Meister Eckhart (1260–1328) was a German theologian and mystic. He was heavily influenced in his thinking by Maimonides but sought to bring the world into much closer alignment with God than it was in Maimonides's system. For Eckhart, "God is simultaneously the most transcendent and most immanent entity."[53]

Eckhart considered there to be no true differentiation between God and the created universe: "Someone might perhaps think that Existence is the name of the four letters itself [*YHVH*], because the term 'existence' (*esse*) has literally four letters and many hidden properties and perfections."[54] His catchphrase was *Deus est esse* (God is Being).[55] This is not unlike Spinoza's later *Deus sive Natura*.

Like Maimonides, and the later Spinoza, Eckhart held that God was in a state of constant self-knowing. Marjus Enders explains that for Eckhart, God's "self-relationship" or "self-communication" is the "antecedent to every objective existent."[56] For objects to be, they must overcome the negativity (non-being) which precedes them. God precedes that

50. Rovelli, *Reality Is Not What It Seems*, 224.

51. Shapiro, *Limits of Orthodox Theology*, 47.

52. Shapiro, *Limits of Orthodox Theology*, 55.

53. Schwartz, "Meister Eckhart and Maimonides," 399.

54. Eckhart, *Expositio libri Exodi* 164, LW II, 144, 9–12, quoted in Schwartz, "Meister Eckhart and Maimonides," 405.

55. Progues generalis to the Opus tripartitum quoted in Enders, "Meister Eckhart's Understanding of God," 369. The catchphrase is often referred to as "the teaching of the transcendentals."

56. Enders, "Meister Eckhart's Understanding of God," 369.

non-being. He is the force which counters what is not to create space for being. Eckhart held that God's name, *Ehyeh Asher Ehyeh*, revealed at Exodus 4:14, is pure self-affirmation, what Eckhart calls the "negation of the negation" because it abolishes all limitations.[57] It is the nothingness which precedes non-being.

Several Kabbalists expressed God's essence as nothingness, referring to God as *Ein Sof*, the without (*ein*), end (*sof*). The word *ein* is related to the Hebrew word *Ayin*, nothing. The Kabbalist Asher ben David (thirteenth century) explained: "The inner power is called *Ayin* because neither thought nor reflection grasps it. Concerning this, Job said, 'Wisdom emerges out of *Ayin*.'"[58] Joseph Gikatilla (1248–1305), another Kabbalist, similarly describes *Ayin* as "the depth of the primordial being." He writes, "No one can understand anything about it . . . It is negated of every conception."[59] A gloss on the foundational kabbalistic work, the Book of Formation (*Sefer Yetsirah*) (c. fourth century), by the Castilian Kabbalist, Moses Shem Tov de León (1240–1305), describes *Ayin* as that which precedes the One, the point of wisdom.[60]

Meister Eckart's negation and the Kabbalists' *Ayin* both reach toward understanding God at a point prior to there even being a possibility of a relationship with him, whether of immanence or transcendence; a God without distinction before being and non-being, prior even to the appellation of God as One.[61]

The idea that God is something prior to transcendence or immanence is suggested by the biblical description of God as being of heaven and earth. Heaven, like earth, is created. Heaven is not outside creation, and the God of heaven therefore must also relate to creation.[62] An interest

57. Eckhart, *In Exodum*, n73, LW II, 77, 9–12, quoted in Enders, "Meister Eckhart's Understanding of God," 366–69.

58. Matt, "Concept of Nothingness," 44. This is a play on Job 28:12. The original reads "where [*me-ayin*] is wisdom to be found?" Asher ben David reworks this to read *mei* (from) *ayin* (nothingness) wisdom is to be found. In other words, wisdom comes from nothingness.

59. Matt, "Concept of Nothingness," 44.

60. Wolfson, *Heidegger*, 109.

61. Wolfson writes of *Ayin* that instead of viewing it as a substance or "hypersubstance," "it is preferable to grasp it as a semiotic marker of the being that symbolizes the interrelatedness of all beings in the same way that the Buddhist doctrine of co-arising contests the reification of substance as an enduring essence." Wolfson, *Heidegger*, 110.

62. Scarborough, *Comparative Theories*, 29. The heavens are created in the first verse of the Bible.

in nothingness marks a reaching toward the God beneath the emanated qualities of immanence and transcendence.

Nothingness becomes an important concept in Rosenzweig, who takes issue with the conception of a single nothingness within German Idealism. For Rosenzweig, such a conception prevents an understanding of difference. In fact, a different nothing, or potential not to be, applies to each element in the world. In humans such potential manifests itself in the fear of death. Death is not one thing, but each person's death is unique, a nothing which transforms this particular subject into that particular object. To speak about a single nothing is to deny death, and the individual nothingness on which knowledge of particulars depends. One should not then speak of the nothing which discloses "the essence of pure being" but of "a nothing" which is "indissoluble and always-enduring for a particular being."[63] Heidegger espoused a similar idea about the individual nature of death.

Nothingness (das nichts) is also an important concept for Heidegger. Heidegger sees nothingness not as privation, but as the possibility for revelation. In "What Is Metaphysics?," Heidegger explains, "Only on the ground of wonder—the revelation of the nothing—does the 'why?' loom before us. Only because the 'why' is possible as such can we inquire into grounds, and ground them."[64]

Wolfson explains that for Heidegger, being depends on nothingness, and nothingness depends on being. Heidegger saw nothingness's dependency on being as the "ultimate truth": "Even nothingness itself is not present without being."[65] What Heidegger appears to mean is that just as being sits alongside the possibility of its non-being and derives from it, so too can nothingness exist only when there is a possibility of it being something. It is being's derivation from non-being and the possibility of its return to non-being which gives being its character and the possibility of meaning.

For Heidegger, everything that we encounter appears to be made possible by the separation, including in time and space, between us and those things we observe and a separation between the object we are

---

63. Rosenzweig, Star of Redemption, 22:20, quoted and discussed in Pollock, Franz Rosenzweig, 148–49. Rosenzweig's conception of nothingness was inspired in part by Hermann Cohen's (1842–1919) discussion of mathematics. Pollock, Franz Rosenzweig, 151.

64. Heidegger, "What Is Metaphysics?," 109.

65. Heidegger, "Elucidations," 170, quoted in Wolfson, Heidegger, 97.

observing and other objects. We and all the things we observe are limited by our and their circumstances. The existence of those limits is what allows us and the things we observe to exist as separate entities, and it is the possibility that we and the things we observe might or might not exist, and how we and they might exist which generates meaning.

Heidegger also discusses nothingness when dealing with fear and anxiety. Heidegger explains that fear depends on something concrete, whereas anxiety comes from nowhere: "In what anxiety is about, the 'it is nothing and nowhere' becomes manifest."[66] Anxiety is not about a particular situation, but about the world as a whole. What crowds in upon us is "everything objectively present as a sum."[67] Heidegger further observes that when our anxiety subsides, we frequently say, "It was really nothing."[68] We associate the world with nothing and nothing with the world, but that nothing is in fact something. It is that which stands behind the world and discloses it. Anxiety is in fact grounded in the "primordial 'something' [*Etwas*] of the world."[69]

Nothingness is the divine clearing, a space for revelation, free from fixed conceptions of God. Nothingness, experienced often as anxiety, brings us face to face with the unknowable and ineffable. It demands our humility.

The Mexican philosopher Héctor Sevilla Godínez beautifully captures the humility that accompanies the contemplation of nothing:

> Nothingness cannot be profoundly known; only supposed, inferred, imagined; conceived in an indirect manner. Not controlled by intellect. Nothingness supposes something greater than the human capacity of understanding it. It is not feasible to know that which overcomes our understanding, which is why Nothingness, among all things, is what mostly escapes our manner of describing ourselves in the world.[70]

Godínez further observes that

> there does not exist anything that nothingness does not possess; everything that is, is in Nothingness. The movement of the stars, the heavens, and even the clouds themselves, is enabled by the

66. Heidegger, *Being and Time*, 181.
67. Heidegger, *Being and Time*, 181.
68. Heidegger, *Being and Time*, 181.
69. Heidegger, *Being and Time*, 181.
70. Godínez, "Being of Nothingness," 148.

corporeal limits of their own entities. There, where the limits are, is also the presence of Nothingness.[71]

Godínez sees no need for God when encountering nothingness, but it is God that allows us to move beyond nothingness back to the world of separation, to engage human concern. God and nothingness are not accidental co-relatives. The Bible unconceals their relatedness.

The book of Ecclesiastes contains the well-known phrase: "Utter futility [*Hevel Havalim*]!—said Koheleth—Utter futility [*Hevel Havalim*]! All is futile! [*Havel*]" (Eccl 1:2). Kohelet, the writer of Ecclesiastes, had tried everything that the world had to offer—money, women, wisdom—and found them all to be lacking. *Hevel* is translated as futility, but can mean impermanence, fleetingness, steam, or breath. The word *Hevel* is repeated thirty-eight times in the work.

Hevel is a biblical character. In Genesis 4:1–8, Cain slew his brother Hevel (Abel) because he was jealous that Hevel's offering from the herd was accepted by God over Cain's offering of produce. We mentioned this episode in an earlier chapter. Hevel was the first person in the Bible to die. Hevel it might be said understood Hevel, the impermanence of things, and therefore clung to them less than did his brother.[72]

The book of Ecclesiastes is sometimes seen as downbeat. There is nothing new under the sun. Every pleasure is fleeting. All life is temporary. But the book in fact promotes a faithful stoicism. Impermanence allows one to face life head on, to find contentment in the now, to see beyond all distraction, and serve God in the knowledge that only he is "the sum of the matter, when all is said and done: Revere God and observe His commandments! For this applies to all mankind" (Eccl 12:13).

Heidegger's treatment of nothingness comes into play here. Nothingness allows us to see what is important. *Hevel* is what remains when all the frivolities of the world are stripped bare, when all descriptions of God are negated. *Hevel* is breath. It points to God as nothingness, the element missing from God as being. God is the master (*Bal*) who created the material world (*Tevel*) from breath or nothingness (*Hevel*). God resides in nothingness. But it is difficult to live in a world dominated by the sense of *Hevel*. We need affirmation, the negation of nothingness. *Cain*, the affirmation, conquers *Hevel*. From that tragic destruction, society emerged.

71. Godínez, "Being of Nothingness," 149.

72. Dor-Shav, "Ecclesiastes."

The Hasidic leader, Naftali Zvi Hurwitz of Ropshitz stated in the name of his teacher, Menachem Mendel of Riminov, that it is possible that the only thing revealed on Sinai was the Hebrew Letter *Aleph* of the word *Anochi* (the Hebrew word for "I am"), the first word of the first commandment.[73] The implication is that *Aleph*, a vowel and symbol for the number one, in its weightlessness, contains all meaning. The line between physicality and nothingness is very slight indeed.[74]

The idea of God as nothingness protects us against associating God too closely with the material world of our senses. It denies the existence of fixed essences and instead instills an awareness that everything we know and encounter is enveloped by non-being, that all our certainties are made of air because we ourselves are made of air, generating meanings which mutate and disappear. Nothingness, however, also captures the notion of infinite possibility, which is the essence of the biblical description of God as becoming.

The Japanese philosopher Kitaro Nishida (1870–1845) embraced the notion of *satori* or *mu*, nothingness, emptiness, or void as learned through the Zen tradition. This is an ineffable, non-dual realty, a sense of the beyond arrived at through experience rather than intellectualization.[75] Nishida wrote that

> the Western thinker must resign to two idols over all; the idolatry of the argumentative reason and the idolatry of the clear reason, united to the individualist will. We cling to the first, in philosophy, for fear of the alleged irrationality of the emotive-narrative-imaginative world. We cling to the second, in theology, for fear of the pantheisms. However, as a consequence of both idolatries, we remain captive in the jail that we ourselves have edified: that of a rationalist and dualist thought. It is imperative to go through a treatment of both deformities and the emptying of idols.[76]

73. Hurwitz, *Zera Kodesh*, Shavuot, 96.

74. In *TB* Eruvin 13a, Rabbi Yishmael warns Rabbi Meir, the scribe, to be careful lest he omit a single letter when writing a scroll lest he destroy the entire world. Rashi provides the example of the sentence: *Hashem Elokechem Emet* (the Lord Your God is Truth) (Jer 10:10). Without an *Aleph*, the Hebrew word for truth (*Emet*), which starts with an *Aleph*, would spell *Met*, the Hebrew word for death, which would imply that God is dead. Here again, the *Aleph* makes all the difference.

75. Wilkinson, *Nishida and Western Philosophy*, 7–13.

76. Nishida, *Pensar desde la Nada*, 134, quoted in Godínez, "Being of Nothingness," 159.

I take from Nishida that we need to be wary of both Spinoza's rational monism and Heidegger's emotive-narrative-imaginative world. God is above and beneath both. The emptying of idols is also a continuous process and not a one-time event. As part of the emptying, we must also empty the call to empty idols. Rosenzweig reminds us also that each of our nothings are experienced differently.

To be free is to remain open to all possibility, to resist certainty, to be reminded that every ideology is capable of leading to tyranny, every truth will be overturned, every tower of Babel falls, and every hero turns to dust. Every god and every concept of God, however abstract, however exulted, in the end of the day comes to our minds through speculation, and must therefore be an exercise of imagination, which is imperfect. We must therefore engage constantly in defeating our own idolatries and those of others, breaking all idols, so that all that remains is wide open sky. It is this effort which allows for self-flourishing.

# 8

# Authenticity

## The Turn Inward

MODERNITY IS CHARACTERIZED BY the turn inward, the shift away from a corporate identity, in which individuals defined themselves by the roles they play in society—a mother, a son, an artisan—toward the "I." Reason's trajectory closely aligns with the rise of the individual. Larry Siedentop traces the origins of Western liberalism to a moment of rebellion against the power of Rome. At that time, reason was viewed as the exclusive preserve of the elites who governed the masses from a distance. Judaism, claims Siedentop, championed the notion of a remote God who governed by law, inaccessible to human reason, but Christianity reclaimed reason and Paul universalized the Jewish message, inviting individuals to "seek a deeper self, an inner union with God."[1]

Through this process, rationality lost its aristocratic connotations, and individual human conscience moved to the fore. As Tertullian, the Church Father, wrote, "It is a basic human right that everyone should be free to worship according to his own convictions. No one is either harmed or helped by another man's religion."[2] This inward journey led to Augustine's *Confessions*, one of the first autobiographies. It presented a life for the first time told from the inside and focused on feelings as much

---

1. Siedentop, *Inventing the Individual*, 60.
2. Tertullian, *Ad Scapulam*, quoted in Siedentop, *Inventing the Individual*, 78.

as thoughts. Yet, reason remained venerated as religions' handmaiden in the monastery and through religious debate and disputation.

In making these arguments, Siedentop overlooks the evolution of the individual within the Hebrew Bible. We have already described the emergence of the biblical God out of oneness, God's gradual apparent retreat, and the emerging power of human agency. Richard Friedman who, as we saw, charted God's withdrawal in the Hebrew Bible, shows how this is matched by the rise of the individual.[3] At the start of creation, God's will is paramount—"let there be light," "let the earth sprout vegetation"—but once humans are formed, other wills come into being (Gen 1:3, 11). Adam and Eve, by an assertion of will, fail in the one command they were given by eating of the forbidden fruit. But this expression of will led them to knowledge; "their eyes were opened." They knew that they were naked (Gen 3:7).

God decries Adam and Eve's misstep, but a simple question coaxes them to exercise their reason: "Where are you?" (Gen 3:9). God is not interested in Adam and Eve's geographical location, but he was testing their ability to self-reflect. Adam and Eve are undeveloped characters. They exercise will but are childlike.

Ten generations later, the Hebrew Bible narrates the story of Noah who is commanded to build an ark, to take a moral stand. Like Adam, Noah is given just one commandment whose performance has cosmic significance. The difference between the two stories is not only that Noah succeeded where Adam and Eve failed, but that Noah's personality is far more developed than Adam's or Eve's. Ten generations later, we meet Abraham, whose personality is more developed than that of Noah, Adam or Eve. The divine commands given to this patriarch are more personal and demanding than those given to his predecessors. God commands him to go from his land, birthplace, and father's house to the land which "I will show you" (Gen 12:1). As we have seen, he confronts God about his plans to destroy the city of Sodom. He is later commanded to sacrifice Isaac, his son, whom he loves (Gen 22:2). The lives of Isaac and Jacob are also described in detail. We are given insight into Jacob's internal working through the description of the trick on his brother to obtain the birth-right, the mystical vision of angels ascending and descending, and the night-long fight with the angel by the Yabok river in which the angel wounded Jacob's thigh. The story ends with the angel declaring that "you

3. Friedman, *Hidden Face of God*, 38–49.

have fought with God and man and have prevailed" (Gen 32:28). This is no literal battle, but an existential moment, a coming into being of an individual independent of God.

Although technology aspires to assist us as individuals, it also threatens the existence of the individual. It draws us into its web, connects us, feeds off us, confirms us to ourselves, amplifies certain ideas over others, directs us how to think, and seeks to know us intimately so that it can manipulate our choices. A singularity or superintelligence will go further in its levelling by obliterating freedom altogether, and rendering care, compassion, and the search for meaning meaningless or irrelevant. A reminder of our existential origins brings us back to ourselves.

## Joseph

Of all the stories in Genesis, the one which most encapsulates the development of the individual is the story of Joseph. The story about him is the longest narrative section in the Hebrew Bible (Gen 37–50).[4] It is a story of maturation, self-discovery, and transformation, leading to social impact. It is also the story of all of us, lost in our own dreams and illusions about the way we are perceived or deserve to be perceived. But above all it is a story about revelation, seeing in a way which allows us to understand ourselves and the face of the other. It is a call to return to who we are, to attain *Teshuva* (a return to our origins). Remarkably, it is also a story where God appears only slantly, without direct intervention, not absent but threaded through Joseph's prayers and dreams, weaved into life's events and happenings. The Joseph story invites interpretation, the application of imagination.[5]

We meet Joseph as a youth of seventeen, the youngest of Jacob's children, an assistant shepherd to his brothers. Joseph saw himself as the link between his brothers and his father, a way of keeping his brothers in check. He brought his father bad reports about his brothers. Jacob loved Joseph more than his other sons because he was the "child of his old age"

4. Kugel, *In Potiphar's House*, 13.

5. The story has often been associated with biblical notions of "wisdom" and the biblical sage who knows how to live well and control his passions, and who sees God's divine plan within disjointed history. Kugel, *In Potiphar's House*, 14. Given the rich potential of this narrative to elucidate the idea of seeing the face of the other, it is surprising that more was not made of it by Emmanuel Levinas. See Ben-Pazi, "Joseph," 166–82.

(Gen 37:3). Jacob marked him out by making for him an ornamental tunic or, in the popular imagination, a coat of many colors. Neither Jacob nor Joseph had any sense that Joseph's position, his actions, or the way he was treated by his father would attract hate and jealousy. They imagined, like we all do, that while others' slights cut us to the core, the things we do or say affect only us.

There is a Jewish tradition that Joseph's coat represented the tunic worn later by the high priest in the temple.[6] The high priest's role was to embody the people of Israel, to be a unifying presence. Tradition holds that the high priest's tunic, like Joseph's coat, was made of the normally forbidden mixture of wool and linen (*Shatnez*).[7] Wool is reminiscent of the offering of Cain, the shepherd. Whereas linen, which comes from flax, represents Hevel, the farmer.[8] The composition of Joseph's coat symbolizes the coming together of brothers, threatened by each other's existence. Joseph, like the high priest, had a potential unifying role, but this was not initially perceived.[9] Instead, his early years were marked by division.

Joseph's brothers supposed that because of Jacob's special love for Joseph, they were unloved, but this was untrue. For his part, Joseph imagined that because he was so loved, he was superior to his brothers and untouchable. This was equally untrue. He also wrongly imagined that his dreams ought to be his brother's dreams. He told them how he dreamed that their sheaves bowed to his, and how the sun, moon, and eleven stars bowed down to him (Gen 37:5–11). We judge him to be naive, but this is a mistake that we all make. We want others to buy into our narratives of ourselves and feel sad and alienated when they do not. We clothe ourselves in our ornamental tunics, the dress of our professions, the mask we show to the outside world, and then convince ourselves and others that this is who we are.

6. *TB* Arakhin 16a. R. Anani taught that "the [priestly] coat atones for bloodshed, as it is written, 'And they dipped [Yosef's] coat in blood.'" My translation.

7. See Exod 27:6 and 27:15. The law of *Shatnez* is found in Lev 19:19 and Deut 22:11. According to talmudic law, *Shatnez* is permitted in the fringes (*Tzizit*) commanded by biblical law to be attached to four-cornered garments as a holy reminder. See *TB* Yevamot 4a.

8. See Commentary of Rabbi Bahya ben Asher (1255–1340) on Lev 19:19, which makes this connection.

9. The role of unification can be viewed also in mystical terms.

The brothers were beset by their own insecurities. They hated their brother, their flesh and blood, the insider who was also the outsider chosen by their father to watch over them. Their father was blind to what was going on. Jacob sent Joseph into the fields to check up on the "peace" of his brothers (Gen 37:14). The brothers were not at peace. Indeed, the very person who shattered their sense of self-worth was the person being sent to check on them. A stranger asks Joseph what he was looking for (Gen 37:15–16). The answer reflects what we are all looking for, brothers (and sisters), people we can connect with, who can validate our existence, but external validation is hard to find and fragile.

The brothers plot to kill Joseph, but were persuaded by Reuben to throw him in a pit (Gen 37:21–22). They strip him of his coat and dip it in blood. Their father infers that Joseph has been killed by a wild animal, a reasonable conclusion, but one that is wrong (Gen 37:31–34). Like Joseph and his other sons, Jacob is misled by what he sees. He sees what he wants to see. The ornamental coat, now blooded, continues to lie. The brothers had sold Joseph to a caravan of merchants traveling to Egypt and he ends up in the house of Potiphar, a nobleman (Gen 37:28, 39:1).

The story is then interrupted with a narrative about the life of Judah, one of the brothers, but there is a continuity in terms of theme. The story tells how Judah's son marries Tamar. Judah's son (Er) dies. Tamar marries another son (Onan) who also dies. Tamar is left widowed. She leaves the family home and goes to Timnah where she takes off her widow's clothes and puts on the veil of a prostitute and waits. We are back at the theme of clothing, the deceptions in which we cloak ourselves. Shockingly, Judah arrives at Timnah looking for sex. He is fooled by Tamar's veil, as much as he was by Joseph's self-perception and the ornamental coat that he had given Joseph: "He took her for a harlot, for she had covered her face" (Gen 38:14). Judah slept with Tamar and she went her way. But Judah learned to see beyond Tamar's metaphorical veil when he was eventually confronted with his own externalities: his seal, chord, and staff that he had given her as a pledge. Judah recognized them and saw Tamar for the first time in her own uniqueness, neither a widow nor a whore, but a self-determined individual, deserving neither male pity nor to be viewed as a sexual object: "She is more in the right than I . . ." (Gen 38:26).

The narrative then returns to the story of Joseph, who undergoes a similar transformation. He is working in the house of Potiphar when Potiphar's wife tries to seduce him. He resists, leaving his garment in her hand (Gen 39:12). This is a new garment, a replacement for the ornamental coat given to him by his father, but still a barrier, a covering. Potiphar's wife's stripping of Joseph is a revelation of sorts, an arousal of passion, the awakening of Eros.[10] She showed Joseph a terrifying aspect of himself.

Potiphar believes his wife's accusations that it was Joseph who tried to seduce her, his jealousy leading him astray like Othello's (Gen 39:19–20). Like Joseph and his brothers and their father, Potiphar has misperceived reality. We all operate in worlds of our own making, our stories clashing, crisscrossing, rarely matching those of others. The episode of Joseph's seduction by Potiphar's wife marks a turning point within the story, a revelation of Joseph's inner strength. He is no longer the entitled dandy but a man of strength and wisdom.[11]

Joseph is thrown into prison, another pit, now stripped to his authentic core. There he meets a baker and a cupbearer, each of whom, like him, had dreams which troubled them. And it is here that Joseph did something remarkable. For the first time, he showed a genuine interest in someone else. He asked the baker and cupbearer, "Why do you appear downcast today?" (Gen 40:7). The Hebrew reads *madua penechem ra'aim*; "Why are your faces downcast?" Joseph has seen the baker's and cupbearer's faces, individuated, not as a reflection of his own. The Joseph from the start of the narrative would have been incapable of asking such a question. This gesture allowed the cupbearer and baker to confide in Joseph. Joseph told the cupbearer that he will be returned to service, while the baker will be killed, and so it happened (Gen 40:8–19). From this point on, Joseph is on an upward trajectory.

Pharaoh has his own dreams. He dreams of seven thin cows eating seven fat cows, and of seven withered stalks eating seven fat stalks (Gen 41:1–7). His wise men cannot explain the dreams. The cupbearer mentions the young Hebrew he had met in prison. Joseph is released, suited in new clothes, and presented to the king (Gen 41:14). He now understands that dreams are not about imposing order on a chaotic world, but about revealing the inner self so that chaos can be confronted and managed. Joseph explains to Pharaoh that there will be seven years of plenty, followed by seven years of famine. Pharaoh knows immediately and intuitively

---

10. There is a midrashic tradition that Joseph removed his own clothes with the initial intention to sleep with Potiphar's wife. See Kugel, *In Potiphar's House*, 97.

11. On the centrality of this part of the story in later traditions, see Kugel, *In Potiphar's House*, 21.

that this is what was being revealed to him. He appoints Joseph governor to handle the situation. He gives him another outfit (Gen 41:41–2).

As the famine strikes the region, the aging Jacob sends Joseph's brothers to Egypt to buy food. Joseph recognizes the brothers, but they do not recognize him (Gen 47:8). The seeing is, for the moment, all one way. Joseph is once again hidden, this time concealed behind the persona of an Egyptian governor. He accuses his brothers of spying—"You have come to see the land in its nakedness"—an irony, because previously they were incapable of seeing beyond Joseph's clothes and costumes. They were unable to see Joseph when he was young, and they could not see him now standing before them (Gen 42:9).

We too do not see clearly but fill in the gaps of our lived experience with fantasy, how we imagine the world is or how we would like it to be. The brothers explain that they are regular citizens with a father and Benjamin, their youngest brother, back in Canaan. Joseph makes the brothers promise that next time they come to Egypt, they will bring Benjamin back with them. Joseph takes Shimon, one of the brothers, hostage to ensure that the other brothers will fulfill that promise (Gen 42:10–24).

This incident brings history flooding back. It revealed the brothers to themselves. They think back to the brother who pleaded with them and how they paid "no heed" (Gen 42:21). Scales are falling from their eyes. They are coming to terms with who they are and their past. Joseph also has the money returned to the brothers' sacks, which increases their anxiety further when they later discover it (Gen 42:25–28).

Jacob was devastated when the brothers returned home without Shimon, and the news that they could only return to Egypt with Benjamin (Gen 42:35). But the famine in the land of Canaan continued, and the brothers needed to return. Judah, the brother who had initiated the sale of Joseph to the merchants on their way to Egypt, agreed with Jacob to stand surety for Joseph (Gen 43:8). The brothers returned with Benjamin. Joseph, still hiding his identity, entertained them, but secretly had his goblet hidden in Benjamin's sack. Benjamin is accused of theft, but Judah pleads for Benjamin's life (Gen 44:18–34). It is then that we read that "Joseph could not hold himself back any longer" (Gen 45:1). He sends his men out and reveals himself: "I am Joseph. Is my father still well?" (Gen 45:3). There is weeping, recognition, fear, and reconciliation. Joseph gives clothes to his brothers, but to Benjamin he gave three-hundred silver shekels and five changes of clothing (Gen 45:22). Again, we have the symbol of clothing. Is five the average number of personae each one of us has? Jacob is later reunited with Joseph, when he, the brothers, and their families move to Egypt to live under Joseph's patronage.

Life is rarely as neat as this, and even this story of divine planning, does not end like a fairy-tale because Joseph's intervention in the life of Egypt results in the people becoming reliant on the state in the time of famine (Gen 47:14–26). Joseph's descendants likewise become slaves. There is no happy ending, but what the Joseph story reveals is that it is possible to frame a self-narrative which both treats the self as a hero and allows room for the other. The story encourages us to view life as redemptive, as a process of growth and repair, as a call to authenticity.

Joseph reflects the Jewish journey through history, the spoilt son who misunderstands his mission in the world, who is misunderstood in return, who suffers exile, who manifests his faith in God, who discovers the face of the other, who undergoes a return. The story warns of the dangers inherent in wearing a multi-colored coat as a badge of chosenness, rather than a symbol of diversity. The wearer will be misunderstood and will misunderstand himself. It foreshadows the Jewish people's alienation from the family of nations, physical and psychological exile, but also its coming of age, eventual maturity, and the donning of the mantel of responsibility and respect.

Joseph is also every person who reaches the realization that the world does not revolve around her but is nevertheless dependent on her because existence is an intricate network of connection and experience where we each occupy both the periphery and center. Existence does not form an orbit around us. We move through it, navigating its seas, negotiating its terrain. The task is to look beneath externalities, the clothes that we wear, and the clothes worn by others, to find both unity and uniqueness and the means to flourish.[12]

## Facticity

Spinoza, as we have seen, denies freedom of the will. We are buffeted on a sea of desire and emotion, internal and external causes. The only freedom we have is to reorientate ourselves through the application of reason to those causes which arise from within as opposed to without. I

---

12. The Hebrew word for clothing (*Beged*) has the same root as the Hebrew word for deception or betrayal. Clothes cover but also deceive. For this dual meaning in interpretations of Gen 39:12, when Potiphar's wife "seized [Joseph] *be-Bigdo*," see Kugel, *In Potiphar's House*, 97.

imagine a runaway train careering along a mountain track, gravity pulling it steadily downward. There is nothing that we can do to stop it. The
most we can do is to is to pull the switch lever which will move the train
to a different track, that is to another determined fate, when it passes
over. The pulling of the switch lever is analogous to the application of
reason. The new course the train takes once the lever is pulled represents
the trajectory arising from internal causes. Different tracks, different destinies. No freedom. For Spinoza, our salvation comes from embracing
reason and using that to escape our enslavement to the external.

Heidegger takes a different view. He encourages us to find authenticity while recognizing our "thrownness" or *Geworfenheit*; that is, our
past, the forces that have come to shape us.[13] The point here is that we
do not exist in splendid isolation, but are formed from our personal, cultural, theological histories and all the other factors which resulted in our
being. Both Spinoza and Heidegger appreciate the lack of choice we have
in determining who we are. However, for Heidegger, our "thrownness" is
not merely an objective fact about how I came to be here. It influences the
very structure of my thinking, the way I find myself in and feel about any
given moment. In the words of the philosopher John Richardson, I "experience myself as made" and "made by something different to myself."[14]
Heidegger writes of our "facticity" or *Faktizität*. This is the sense that I am
thrown into a condition independent of my projections.[15]

These concepts are alien to technique, the technological worldview
described above for which reason rules supreme. Thrownness and facticity are part of the nature of our being, the place we inhabit in the world,
which explains how we view the projects we live toward. In this engagement, we are limited by the concepts and vocabulary of the cultures in
which we are enmeshed. The philosopher Stephen Mulhall provides an
example:

> No one in twenty-first century Britain can experience the pride
> of a Samurai warrior because the relevant vocabulary is unavail-
> able, "vocabulary" refers not just to a set of Japanese terms but
> to their role in a complex web of customs, assumptions and
> institutions.[16]

13. Heidegger, *Being and Time*, 133.

14. Richardson, *Heidegger*, 111.

15. Richardson, *Heidegger*, 111.

16. Mulhall, *Heidegger's Being and Time*, 80.

How and which things matter to us at any given moment is substantially determined by the society and culture which we find ourselves. Heidegger reminds us that our facticity and thrownness are the result of our psychology, our history, our memory, our origins, and countless other factors. We can rarely fully escape these things.

These insights are important when deciding how to live because we are often taught to believe that we can reshape ourselves anew and find authenticity without reference to anyone but ourselves, but this is almost impossible. We are each born into a specific culture, molded by specific experiences, comprised of a unique arrangement of atoms, and with neurons that connect in specific ways. Our room for maneuver is limited.

We can travel a million miles, but our past, like the sun, will continue to exert a force and keep us in its orbit, even if the gravitational pull is weak. Our pasts, individual and collective, provide a repository of values and narratives by which to make sense of the world. They are the riverbank on which we might stand to observe the flow of endless possibilities beneath our feet before we leap when we decide to, or a place to rest when the water becomes too choppy or difficult to navigate. Moreover, even when we feel that we have escaped our thrownness and facticity, we often discover through self-reflection that, in fact, we are a product of our rebellion against them.

Although Heidegger has named and explicated the phenomena, the biblical tradition is founded on the understanding that we are each rooted in a shared history, a network of beliefs and values, a way of looking at the world. Joseph is a narrative account of how thrownness and facticity operate. He was cast into a pit by his brothers and later into jail after the incident with Potiphar's wife, but he was originally cast into the house of Jacob, and it is this which constitutes his thrownness and shaped him.

Joseph wore many garments and chameleon-like took on many forms; the spoiled youth, the prisoner, the slave, the Egyptian governor, but stripped of his externalities, he was the Hebrew, not just the recipient of a tradition but someone whose vocabulary and worldview was shaped by the values and sense of destiny inherited from his forebears. He knew how to act in each situation because he learned to see beyond the veil.[17] Spinoza wrote of *Conatus*, the internal drive for survival, but in the

17. "R. Huna in the name of R. Mattena taught that, when Joseph was about to sin with Potiphar's wife, he 'saw his father's face and his passion was cooled.'" *Bereishit Rabbah* 1071–73. Joseph's facticity and thrownness were asserting themselves. See also Hazony, *God and Politics in Esther*, 57–58.

Jewish tradition the desire to persevere is not a self-sufficient force, but a response to a "still small voice" calling from the past, present, and future, a call to find the face of the other, to immanence and to participate in a cosmic unfolding.[18] The figure of Joseph highlights the existential nature of the quest. The task is not to smooth out all contours, but to achieve authenticity in a world of chaos and uncertain outcomes.

## The "They"

For Heidegger, the greatest challenge to attaining authenticity is *Das Man*, the disembodied commentary, the "they," the public voice, the force of the collective. The voice of the "they" distracts us and leads to our "falling" or "entanglement" (*Verfallen*).

The term "falling" makes one think of the "fall" of Adam and Eve when they ate of the fruit of the tree of knowledge. Using this analogy, the "they" is the serpent, dictating our concerns, rationalizing our choices, hiding the consequences of living. Heidegger indeed describes what it means to fall prey to the "they": "Temptation, tranquillizing, alienation, and self-entangling characterize the specific kind of being of falling prey."[19]

Heidegger writes that he is not expressing a "negative value judgment" about "falling." It is just the way things are for most of the time. We are immersed in culture, influenced by consensus, vulnerable to the court of public opinion. *Dasein* is "for the most part together with the world that it takes care of." We are lost in public discourse, "guided by idle talk, curiosity and ambiguity."[20] The "they" forms the very structure by which we construct meaning.

The rabbis were particularly concerned by "idle talk." The Talmud warns men not to engage in it with women, including one's own wife.[21] The Talmud also prohibits one from engaging in frivolity in a synagogue.[22] Rabbi Joseph Karo's (1488–1575) legal code, the *Shulchan*

18. On the still small voice, see 1 Kgs 19:11–13.

19. Heidegger, *Being and Time*, 171.

20. Heidegger, *Being and Time*, 171.

21. Mishnah Pirkei Avot 3:17, 5:5.

22. *TB* Megillah 28a–b. See also Prov 10:19, "Where there is much talking, there is no lack of transgressing, but he who curbs his tongue shows sense."

*Aruch*, includes in this rule "humorous or pointless gossip."[23] One might think that idle talk is bad because it is shallow, leads to licentiousness, and distracts from religious duties and other important things in life, but Heidegger offers an additional insight. Idle talk, undirected curiosity, the need for newness, and the need for explanation, reinforce the power of the "they."

In every conversation in which we engage the "they" frame the parameters of debate, the terms of reference, the language that we use. We can only engage in the conversations of our age on climate, equality, gender, lifestyle, religion. We adopt the modes of expression and repeat the platitudes and mantras which we encounter on the internet, read in books, or hear from our family and colleagues. We are rarely the slightest bit original and can only ever be of our time.

The "they" also causes us to take "flight" from the world, to run from death, guilt, and anxiety.[24] Such flight leads to inauthenticity because it involves a hiding from being and the "battle which most belongs to us."[25] We desire always to be at home, secure in our illusions, reassured by the public voice: "Entangled flight into the being-at-home of publicness is a flight before the not-being-at-home, that is, from the uncanniness [*unheimlichkeit*] which lies in *Dasein* as thrown, as being-in-the-world entrusted to itself in its being."[26]

This is not just about the world of media and advertising, celebrity, and escapist glamor, but all aspects of our lives which aim to quell the nagging realization that we are going to die. Think about the world of work with its preoccupation with status, wealth, security, power, control, public approval, and validation. What the "they" want is to obliterate our anxiety, to block the awareness of our inevitable end.

Heidegger discusses our public discourse about death. It is something we speak about all the time, but the conversation skates the surface. We use words like "one dies," which "spreads the opinion that death, so to speak, strikes the they." Through such a "public interpretation of *Dasein*" or "idle talk," people convince themselves that death is something that happens to other people. Even when comforting someone at the end of their life: "The evasion of death which covers over dominates everydayness

23. *Shulchan Aruch*, Orach Chayim 151:1.
24. Heidegger, *Being and Time*, 179.
25. Richardson, *Heidegger*, 39–40.
26. Heidegger, *Being and Time*, 171.

so stubbornly that, in being-with-one-another, those 'closest-by' often try to convince the one who is 'dying' that he will escape death and soon return to the tranquilized everydayness of his world taken care of."[27]

## Resoluteness

Overcoming the "they" and achieving authenticity is difficult, but a first step is to face our anxiety, death, and guilt with resoluteness.[28] These things are generally misunderstood but essential to *Dasein* and reveal aspects of our being of central importance to us.

Let us take anxiety. As a society, we expend huge efforts in trying to eradicate it, but Heidegger would encourage us to look differently at this phenomenon: "Anxiety reveals in *Dasein* its being toward its ownmost potentiality of being, that is, being free for the freedom of choosing and grasping itself."[29] Anxiety is revelatory. It shows up what is important to us.

Anxiety is not for Heidegger anxiety about a particular thing, but a general feeling: "What crowds in upon us is not this or that, nor is it everything, objectively present together as a sum, but the possibility of things at hand in general, that is the world in itself."[30] We are not anxious about but anxious for something indefinite: possibility. The effect of this is that "things at hand"—that is, the objects of the everyday—"sink away." When we allow anxiety to take shape within us, we cease to fall prey to the "public way of being interpreted," the "they" and its petty concerns. A space is created to view that which we care most about. Anxiety "throws *Dasein* back upon that which it is anxious about—its authentic potentiality for being in the world."[31] There are types of anxiety which demand treatment, but there are others which light up the world.

The book of Proverbs teaches: "If there is anxiety in a man's heart, *vayachena* out of his mind" (Prov 12:25). According to the Talmud,

> Rabi Ami and Rabbi Asi dispute the verses' meaning. One said
> it means let him push it (*yashchena*) out of his mind: "one who

27. Heidegger, *Being and Time*, 243.

28. Although the ideas that follow are potentially useful, they should not be taken to discourage the seeking of professional assistance when life becomes too difficult.

29. Heidegger, *Being and Time*, 182.

30. Heidegger, *Being and Time*, 181.

31. Heidegger, *Being and Time*, 181–82.

worries should banish his concerns from his thought." And one
said "he should discuss it with others (*yesichena*)."[32]

*Yesichena* might alternatively refer to meditation or prayer.[33] The juxtaposition of the Talmud and Heidegger reveals an aspect of anxiety which
we do not always appreciate. Meditating on or discussing our anxieties
may prove more beneficial than fleeing them.

Related to anxiety is fear of death, the knowledge that our *Dasein*
can never be complete because death always threatens it. While the "they"
wish to divert us from death, to act authentically we must acknowledge
its presence in every living moment. Death stands behind every possibility and it is ours to own individually. We must also take it to heart that
no one can stand in for us.[34] Death must be encountered alone: "Death is
the ownmost possibility of *Dasein*. Being toward it discloses to *Dasein* its
ownmost potentiality-of-being in which it is concerned about the being
of *Dasein* absolutely."[35]

In chapters 52 and 53 of *Being and Time*, Heidegger describes an
"authentic being-towards-death." This involves recognizing death's inevitability and through it all the other possibilities which characterize *Dasein*. Since death is that which is uniquely mine, it allows me to influence
the way I live now without enthrall to the "they." We should not run from
death but embrace its inevitability, own it: "Authentic being-toward-
death cannot evade its ownmost, non-relational possibility or cover it
over in this flight and reinterpret it for the common sense of the they."[36]
Death creates the freedom to live toward what I may become. It allows
me to embrace what David Brooks has called the "eulogy virtues," which
are those characteristics with which we desire to be eternally associated.[37]

In the Talmud, Rabbi Eliezer taught, "Repent one day before your
death." His students asked him how one can know on which day one
will die. Rabbi Eliezer accepted one cannot know that, but asserted that
because of that, one should "repent today in case he dies tomorrow."[38]
Heidegger sees the awareness of death as a pathway to authenticity, but

32. *TB* Yoma 75a.

33. See Gen 24:63. Isaac went out to *lasuach* in the field. Rashi says that *lasuacch*
means to pray.

34. Heidegger, *Being and Time*, 240.

35. Heidegger, *Being and Time*, 252.

36. Heidegger, *Being and Time*, 249–50.

37. See Brooks, *Road to Character*.

38. *TB* Shabbat 153a. See also Pirkei Avot 2:10.

for Rabbi Eliezer, the key to authenticity is not the awareness of death but the repentance or return to origins (*Teshuvah*) which an awareness of death inspires. Adam and Eve's eating of the fruit led to an awareness of death and exile. The response to such awareness is action aimed at a return.

*Teshuvah* is that existential quality which seeks the totality, turns present into past, and brings the past into the future. Abraham Isaac Kook, who as we noted was a mystic and monist, considered *Teshuvah* to be a literal return to God, an absorption into the totality in which there is no sin.[39] By returning to such a conception of God, "everything has been converted to virtue, from the very beginning."[40] *Teshuvah* also is driven by faith. The medieval Jewish philosopher Bachya ibn Pakuda said of one who trusts in God that "the fear that death may come [to him], immediately increases his efforts and enthusiasm to prepare for his end without concern for the temporal."[41]

Heidegger's insight allows us to see more clearly the place of death in the Judaic religious life. *Teshuvah* responds to death by affirming life and reconfiguring the world, or our perception of it. Death is also a stimulus to living which understands that my life draws its meaning from the community in which I live and future generations: "I call heaven and earth to witness against you this day: I have put before you life and death, blessing and curse. Choose life—if you and your offspring would live" (Deut 30:19). We choose life not just for ourselves but for those who follow.

Heidegger shows guilt too to be a blessing. *Dasein* is generally speaking "lost in the they." It must find itself and can only do this when it is "shown to itself in its possible authenticity." The "voice of conscience" is that which shows *Dasein* to itself.[42] It acts as a call (*Ruf*) or summons (*Anruf*).[43] The summons is to "one's own self."[44] The self, though, does not notice the call. Instead, the voice of conscience strikes at the "they-self," the self that has been conditioned by the public discourse which responds

---

39. Rynhold and Harris, *Nietzsche, Soloveitchik*, 199–202.

40. Kook, *Orot Ha-Teshuvah* 33.79, quoted in Rynhold and Harris, *Nietzsche, Soloveitchik*, 202.

41. Bachya ibn Pakudah, *Duties of the Heart*, 4:5.13. My translation.

42. Heidegger, *Being and Time*, 258.

43. Heidegger, *Being and Time*, 259.

44. Heidegger, *Being and Time*, 262.

by disintegrating: "Because only when the self of the they-self is summoned and made to hear, the they collapses."[45]

What then is the content of this summons or call? The answer is "strictly speaking-nothing. The call does not say anything, does not give any information about events of the world, has nothing to tell." Here again we have the idea of nothingness and the revelation of the *Aleph*, a simple call. The call lacks "any kind of utterance"; "Conscience speaks solely and constantly in the mode of silence."[46] Yet, despite this, the "conscience calls the self of *Dasein* forth from its lostness in the they."[47]

The call also has no regard to the person called. The caller too has a "striking indefiniteness." It "not only fails to answer questions about name, status, origin, and repute, but also leaves not the slightest possibility of making the call familiar for an understanding of *Dasein* with a 'worldly' orientation." The "indefiniteness and indefineability of the caller is not nothing," however. It has a "positive distinction." It "wants to be heard only as such."[48]

Although conscience "calls against our expectations and even against our will," it does not, according to Heidegger, come from the outside or inside. It is also not "a person (God) making himself known" or something merely biological.[49] It is part of *Dasein*. It emerges from the disjoint between our thrownness or facticity, that is the way we find ourselves in the world which limits us, and the possibilities that constitute *Dasein*, and the sense of uncanniness or homelessness that this gives rise to. Conscience, therefore, arises from a lack, the gap between reality and potential. It is "definable by nothing" and speaks in the "uncanny mode of silence." Its effect is to call one "back" to "the reticence of his existent potentiality-of-being."[50]

Heidegger understands that we want to associate such a voice with something beyond *Dasein*, but Heidegger wishes us to resist that urge. He considers it a mistake to think of God as the source of the voice of conscience. People also speak of a world or universal conscience, but for Heidegger such a "public conscience" would be no more than the "voice of the they." To see conscience as a call from the "they" is also a mistake.

45. Heidegger, *Being and Time*, 263.
46. Heidegger, *Being and Time*, 263.
47. Heidegger, *Being and Time*, 264.
48. Heidegger, *Being and Time*, 264.
49. Heidegger, *Being and Time*, 265.
50. Heidegger, *Being and Time*, 266.

Instead, Heidegger contends that conscience is "in each instance mine." It relates only to me, and for that reason should be taken seriously.[51]

Heidegger's conception is different from what we normally think of as guilt. We most often associate guilt with a specific event, as "owing something to someone," as a kind of debt, or alternatively as resulting from our having caused something, and therefore as being responsible for something. Heidegger describes our usual ways of looking at guilt as "vulgar significations."[52] Heidegger considers the usual things we associate with guilt to be surface manifestations, the way we interpret the call. The essence of guilt, however, is the call itself. It is that which brings us "back to thrownness," which wants us to "take notice," to project "oneself upon one's ownmost authentic potentiality for becoming guilty."[53] When we grasp this, we reach beyond the "they-self." The "they-self" demands specifics. It wants only to "calculate infractions" and reacts against the summons by talking "about mistakes all the more vociferously."[54]

We need to resist ascribing information to the call of conscience.[55] We need to understand it as "a call of care from the uncanniness of being-in-the-world that summons *Dasein* to its ownmost potentiality-for-being-guilty."[56] It demands that we take ownership, adopt a position of "resoluteness," avoid the temptation to impose upon my guilt a "they" interpretation, and achieve authenticity.[57] "As authentic being a self, resoluteness does not detach *Dasein* from its world, nor does it isolate it as free floating ego."[58] "Resoluteness means letting oneself be summoned out of one's lostness in the they."[59]

The insight relevant to religious practice that emerges from this discussion, and to which we are already attuned having considered biblical ideas of rebellion, authenticity, and revelation, is that the summons of conscience, true guilt, is contentless. Its root is the incomprehensible infinite. It is delivered through a still small voice, an *Aleph*. It demands authenticity, an overcoming of the "they." The "they" is not just the everyday

51. Heidegger, *Being and Time*, 267.
52. Heidegger, *Being and Time*, 270–71.
53. Heidegger, *Being and Time*, 275.
54. Heidegger, *Being and Time*, 276.
55. Heidegger, *Being and Time*, 276.
56. Heidegger, *Being and Time*, 277.
57. Heidegger, *Being and Time*, 284.
58. Heidegger, *Being and Time*, 285.
59. Heidegger, *Being and Time*, 286.

world in which we inhabit, the popular voice, but those who claim to speak in the name of a nation, religion, or tradition, the collective guilt which wants to talk specifics, to tell me from where my guilt arises and to direct it to specific ends.

This way of considering guilt does not lead us to a nondescript spirituality, but back to our thrownness, and the traditions which emerge from it. Daniel Rynhold and Michael Harris compare Rabbi Joseph B. Soloveitchik's views on guilt to Friedrich Nietzsche's. Nietzsche considered guilt to be perpetual, inescapable, and destructive of psychologic health. Christianity was to blame for turning the adherent's feelings of guilt into "an instrument of torture," so that he feels "guilty and reprehensible to the point that it cannot be atoned for."[60] Guilt [*Shuld*] has its origins in the idea of "debt" [*Schulden*], which would have allowed feelings of guilt to be paid off.[61] But Christianity, with its notion of original sin, had moved beyond the idea of guilt as debt and radicalized and moralized feelings of conscience. Nietzsche wished to overcome feelings of perpetual and inescapable guilt, by adopting Greek ideas of power, autonomy, and art.

In his writing on repentance, Soloveitchik wishes to align the Jewish tradition to the idea of guilt as debt. He observes that according to Rashi, *Kapparah*, the Hebrew word for acquittal, is related to the word *Kofer*, an indemnity payment.[62] Rynhold and Harris explain that within Judaism, there can be no transformation of this idea of guilt into something inescapable or perpetual because "there is no guilt in the Jewish tradition that is not tied to a particular sin or sins."[63] The suggestion is that within Judaism, there is no perpetual and inescapable guilt.

Heidegger appears to address the same concerns as Nietzsche when dealing with guilt. However, in contrast to Nietzsche and Soloveitchik, for Heidegger, as we have seen, the association of guilt with debt is vulgar.[64] Unlike Nietzsche, Heidegger wants us to embrace the perpetual and inescapable guilt, to see it as a summons and call.

60. Nietzsche, *Genealogy* II:22, quoted in Rynhold and Harris, *Nietzsche, Soloveitchik*, 193.

61. Nietzsche, *Genealogy* II:4, addressed in Rynhold and Harris, *Nietzsche, Soloveitchik*, 194.

62. Soloveitchik, *On Repentance*, 50–51, addressed in Rynhold and Harris, *Nietzsche, Soloveitchik*, 194–95.

63. Rynhold and Harris, *Nietzsche, Soloveitchik*, 197.

64. Heidegger, *Being and Time*, 270–71.

Although it is true that Judaism holds no idea of original sin, and that guilt is a response to specific sins which can be atoned for, the fact that the laws are so numerous, detailed, and uncertain means that practicing Jews fall foul of them all the time or worry that we will fall foul of them. To deal with this, practicing Jews feel need to repay the debt, to offer *Kapparah*, continuously. On a phenomenological level, Judaism is capable of generating perpetual and inescapable guilt. Jews, like Christians, do experience the "voice of conscience," a call or summons, which refuses to reveal its name.

In Genesis 32, Jacob is "left alone" by the Jabbok river, and "a man wrestled with him until the break of dawn," an angel. This is an existential struggle, apparently devoid of information or intellectual content, a "summons" to use Heidegger's term. It is a silent encounter, almost. As in Heidegger's account of guilt, the caller and the called struggle to be named. Jacob's name is changed to Israel "for you have striven with beings divine and human, and have prevailed." Jacob asked the angel, the caller, for his name. The angel resisted: "You must not ask my name." Heidegger wrote that the caller "failed to answer questions about name, status, origin, and repute."[65] The same is true of Jacob's angel. The summoner has no name. The primordial call is contentless. Jacob named the place of the struggle *Peni El*, the face of God because "I have seen a divine being face to face, yet my life has been preserved" (Gen 32:23–31). What is left is the experience of being called.

The Judaic tradition recognizes the nothing, the *Ayin*, which stands behind everything, but does not leave it there. The call emerges from the still small voice, from the *Aleph*, and takes on form, as laws, values, insights, through a process of participatory unfolding revelation, involving experience, imagination, interpretation, and community. Institutions and hierarchies emerge. Lines are drawn, domains are protected. Ossification sets in. The "they" take hold. The existential task of *Teshuvah* is to return to origins, the All, the silence before the barest murmur.

Heidegger's black notebooks associate Judaism with *Wuste*, the desert, and the desert with *Verwustung*, devastation. He considers Jews to be rootless, homeless, belonging nowhere and this is their downfall.[66] But we hold that rootlessness is a necessary condition for revelation. Moses told Pharaoh that the "God of the Hebrews" called to them. Moses demanded, "let us go three days into the desert" (Exod 5:19). The Jews were

65. Heidegger, *Being and Time*, 264.
66. Di Cesare, *Heidegger and the Jews*, 99–101.

to hear a new voice, free from *Das Man*, beyond the "they," the society or culture in which they had been enslaved. The desert is where the call was to be encountered.

*Midbar*, the Hebrew word for "desert," contains the same root letters as the word *Dibur*, meaning "word." The desert was not just the place chosen for the divine/human encounter but is the essence of communication. The book of Numbers states that "when Moses went into the Tent of meeting" to speak with God, he heard the voice addressing (*Midaber*) him "from above the cover that was on top of the Ark of the Pact between the two cherubim" (Num 7:89). Rashi explains on this verse that *Midaber* is a reflexive verb form. What Moses heard was "the voice speaking to itself." Moses was eavesdropping on God's self-communication, the sound of the desert, not culturally determined or enframed. From that nonplace between the cherubim, within the desert, wisdom arises, casting its spotlight on the "they" both beyond and within the system, creating the possibility of freedom.

Technique in its constant striving toward a singularity or ultimate superintelligence has little regard for the existential quest, the gap between thrownness and possibility, unhomeliness, the concern for care, silence, the indefinable, anxiety, death, guilt, beyond aspects of *Dasein* unconcerned with cause and effect, lines of code, the algorithmic. Instead, technique adopts Spinoza's rationalism, the passive rational monistic ideal, God as pure self-knowledge. Freedom is unimportant, curtailed, downplayed. The focus is on knowledge, merger, acquisition, conquering, levelling, not authenticity or the face of the other.

This discussion returns us to the Joseph narrative and his existential development, his progression from the inauthentic to the authentic. Joseph starts life imaging himself to be immortal. In the pit and while in prison, he comes face to face with the possibility of his own demise. In his encounter with Potiphar's wife, his grown-up brothers, and the values of his heritage, his own possibilities press in on him as he bears the weight of anxiety and summons. He learns to embrace these values resolutely, to peel away the layers of his external projections, to see the face of the other, to find authenticity, and to assist others—the cupbearer, the baker, Pharaoh, his brothers, and even his father—to do likewise. The Jewish tradition teaches that the world is not transformed by ideas alone. This is the world of action. Resoluteness in divine service:

> One should strengthen himself like a lion to get up in the morning to serve his Creator, so that it is he who awakens the dawn ... And when he lies on his bed he should know before Whom he lies, and as soon as he wakes up from sleep he should rise eagerly to the service of his Creator, May He Be Blessed and Exalted.[67]

Change ultimately only occurs through living differently, and so in the next chapters, I will discuss how the ideas so far addressed relate to living, using the example of the orthodox Judaism into which I am thrown and fallen.

67. *Shulchan Aruch*, Orach Chayim 1:1.

# 9

# The Way

## Halachic Dasein

THOMAS CLARKE'S POEM "IN Praise of Walking" beautifully describes the practice of walking, and the myriad paths that people make when they vein the earth. Robert Macfarlane meditates on Clarke's poem in his magnificent book *The Old Ways*.[1] He writes:

> Paths are the habits of a landscape. They are acts of consensual making. It's hard to create a footpath on your own . . . Paths connect. This is their first duty and their chief reason for being. They relate places in a literal sense, and by extension they relate people . . . Paths are consensual, too, because without common care and common practice they disappear: overgrown by vegetation, ploughed up or built over (though they may persist in the memorious substance of land law). Like sea channels that require regular dredging to stay open, paths need walking . . . By no means all interesting paths are old paths.[2]

*Halachah*, often translated as Jewish law, relates to *Halichah*, walking. Jewish law is not law in the conventional sense, at least not these days. There is no one book which acts like statute. There is no earthly sanction for breach, and much of it is theoretical. Most of it is no longer relevant,

1. Macfarlane, *Old Ways*, 13.
2. Macfarlane, *Old Ways*, 17.

applying to a specific time or place, for example the temple, or to specific roles which no longer exist, such as the priest, king, or prophet.

*Halachah* is the going, or the way. It is a path through time and history, linking one generation to the next, reminding each era of the truths unearthed by its forebears. Paths are consensual, they are not made alone. The paths of *Halachah* are created and deepened by people passing over them, repeatedly, year after year, day after day, each minute and second. They connect one landscape to another, places of meaning, memory. Along them we Jews carry our baggage, heavy or light, under dark clouds or in bright sunshine, seeking the divine, community, world.

Without common care and continuing practice, the paths of *Halachah* become overgrown, submerged, unpassable, lost. They require constant dredging like sea channels. New paths can be as interesting as old paths. From the moment that Abraham discovered God, Jews journeyed. Abraham was commanded to leave his land, his birthplace, and the house of his father. Jacob and his family moved to Egypt. Moses and the people were released from Egypt, zigzagging across the desert for forty years. Rest and stillness were never experienced for long. God is dynamic, itinerant, and so have Jews always been. We move and are commanded to keep moving: "And thou shalt keep the commandments of the LORD thy God, to walk in His ways, and to fear Him" (Deut 8:6). Jews are enjoined to fear, love, and serve God with heart and soul and to "walk in all His ways" (Deut 10:12). Jews promised to "walk in His ways, and keep His statutes, and His commandments, and His ordinances, and hearken unto His voice" (Deut 26:17). This is what is meant to live resolutely, to embrace our thrownness and facticity within the halachic framework.

*Halachah* is not just law. It is paths over sea and land, into caves, and over mountains. The paths of *Halachah* run through space and time, are veins of meaning carved out of granite, under wood, through cityscapes. There is no single method to traverse the way. The paths to be taken will depend on the season and time of travel, the traveler, her proclivities, fitness levels, the other travelers she encounters, the weather, the flora, and the fauna that take her interest, whether she sticks to the well-trodden or forges paths of her own. There are few clear laws of the road or bridleway, but there are those who have traveled some of the way before to guide, save that sometimes even these people are lost. There are also landmarks and signposts, but these are often obscured, or have been twisted the wrong way or blown down in the wind.

There is a science to wandering, a need to be proficient in map and compass, the ability to read the stars, to understand bushcraft, to understand what it takes to survive in the wilderness. There are books that can be mastered and experts who can be consulted. Nowadays we also have the internet giving constant access to knowledge, networked, hyperlinked and infinitely searchable, little effort needed. But what this information can provide is only the bare essentials, the means to continue. As every traveler knows, walking or journeying is not a matter from getting from A to B, but involves the gaining of experience, the acquisition of wisdom, knowing others, the search for essences. It is a call to authenticity.

Science only takes you so far. To journey along the path, one needs an orientation, an openness to the way itself, the spiritual capacity to absorb wisdom, the ability to open the hearts and minds of other wayfarers, to take them with you. Knowing the science of navigation and survival is not enough. And, so it is with *Halachah*.

The ancient Chinese philosophers taught the *Dao*, the Way. They walk their path, as we Jews walk ours, and have articulated well what it is to walk skillfully. For them, right living involves "honing our instincts, training our emotions, and engaging in a constant process of self-cultivation so that eventually—at moments both crucial and mundane—we would react in the right, ethical way to each particular situation."[3]

They also understood the importance of ritual to their training. As Michael Puett and Christine Gross-Loh explain in *The Path: A New Way to Think About Everything*:

> In order to help ourselves change, we must become aware that breaking from our normal ways of being is what makes it possible to develop different sides of ourselves. Rituals—in the Confucian sense—are transformative because they allow us to become a different person for a moment. They create a short-lived alternate reality that returns us to our regular life slightly altered. For a brief moment, we are living in an "as-if" world.[4]

The halachic method spends little time on self-reflection. It is too busy in discussion, building on principles founded in the written Torah, known through transmission, developed through argumentation.[5] Scenario af-

3. Puett, *Path*, 10.

4. Puett, *Path*, 30.

5. On the background of *Halachah* and its transitioning to law, see Chaim, *Halakhah*, 17–28, 143–62.

ter scenario, the world looked at from every angle, no topic too trite or personal—sex, excretion, dirt, dirty laundry, all required to be aired. It aspires to reach to Spinoza's divine perspective, a 360-degree view, before returning to the point of determination and a demand for an answer, on which not everyone will agree, and which will be provisional because when the situation is encountered again, the whole process will need to be repeated and all the challenges once again discussed and sifted.[6]

The halachic method is rational in the sense that it follows reasoned argument based on principles defined and worked through, but it is far from thoroughly scientific. There is often an unresolved tension between the phenomenological, the world as we Jews experience it or how those who came before us experienced it, and the empirical (what is actually happening as a matter of physics and chemistry). The laws of *Kashrut* (kosher food) for example, require knowledge of the workings of dishwashers and detergents, microwaves, and all sorts of materials to determine whether and how things might become unkosher and can become koshered, but the principles of absorption and extraction of non-kosher food into and out of kosher kitchen pots and other utensils is phenomenological, and based on medieval understandings.[7]

The messiness of the system, lack of consistency in approach and inconclusiveness, is a source of frustration, but the complaint ignores the fact that we are not dealing with a law code aimed at ensuring conformity, peace, security, and fairness in the context of a modern state, but an approach to ritual as divine service. It calls for a theology which relates to God as both immanent and transcendent by combining the scientific (immanent) with the experiential (transcendent).

*Halachah* requires us to walk the Way conscious of that which has been revealed by the Torah, both divine otherness and oneness, the God of heaven and earth. Everything we encounter on the way is real and concrete, to be taken at face value. Every facet of the material world makes demands upon us and must be known, scrutinized, theorized, and acted upon according to directives and principles which require forethought, application, and intentionality. At the same time, through the practice of *Halachah*, we nurture the ability to reach beyond the material to the one

6. On the resistance to codification even with respect to the *Shulchan Aruch*, see Chaim, *Halakhah*, 167–85.

7. Forst, *Laws of Kashrus*, 102–10.

in which we all partake, *Dasein*'s ground, the ground on which *Halachah*'s paths stretch across.[8]

The Chinese Master, Laozi (c. fourth or sixth century BCE) captured these ideas in his description of the multi-layered aspect of the Way. Puett and Gross-Loh explain:

> For Laozi, the Way is the original, ineffable, undifferentiated state that precedes everything. It is "a thing inchoate and complete, born before Heaven and Earth." It is that from which everything in the cosmos emerges and to which everything in the cosmos returns. And it exists on many levels. On an earthly level, the Way is akin to the ground. Think of a blade of grass, growing from the earth. As it grows, it becomes more distinct and differentiated, and as it grows taller, it becomes further separated from the Way. This is why a sapling is closer to the Way than a mature oak tree. But when all these things that grow from the earth die, they return once more to the earth, or the Way.[9]

*Halachah* operates in a world of difference, relationship, and practical demands, yet points toward the mystical. It is a ritualistic signifier of the Way in the Daoist sense, a *via mystica*, a path from the world to oneness. As Puett and Gross-Loh state explaining Laozi: "The more we see the world as differentiated, the more removed we become from the Way. The more we see the world as interconnected, the closer we come to the Way."[10]

On this reading, the way is not unlike Heidegger's summons, an indefinable call, but it has an earthly level akin to the real ground on which we walk. Living close to the Way, responding to its summons, has the potential of bringing us back to the "thing inchoate and complete born before Heaven and Earth" and the *Ayin* which precedes that, but it also demands treading the ground of the physical world, the stone, the sand, the grass. *Halachah* does not leave us in a place of undifferentiation, but returns us to the world of separation. Up and down Jacob's ladder God moves, from heaven to earth, and back again.

8. On *Halacha*'s attempt to reach beyond law and to convey a theology and meaning, see Chaim, *Halakhah*, 29–43, 57–123.

9. Puett, *Path*, 91.

10. Puett, *Path*, 94.

## The Threefold Path

The primary statement of Jewish *Dasein*, our place within the world, is the *Shema* found in Deuteronomy 6. It starts, "Hear Israel. The Lord is our God, the Lord is One" (Deut 6:4). "The Lord is One" is the truth elucidated by Spinoza. It raises to consciousness the God of which we are a part. "The Lord is our God" is the truth of being in the world and the narrative of personal meaning explicated by Heidegger. "Hear Israel" is the call to live by both parts of this statement. Taking either part of this statement without the other is to encounter Judaism only partially, to place oneself in conflict with its message.

The *Shema* continues at Deuteronomy 6:5: "You shall love the LORD your God with all your *Lev* and with all your *Nefesh* and with all your *Meod*." What God demands first and foremost is love, not love in the abstract, but love demonstrated by three aspects which I have left untranslated. What is *Lev*, *Nefesh*, and *Meod*? Ibn Ezra (1089–1167), the medieval commentator, saw *Lev* as consciousness, *Nefesh* as corporeal spirit, and *Meod* as effort. Rashi sees *Lev* as involving both positive and negative desires (the *Yetzer ha-Ra* and *Yetzer Tov*), *Nefesh* as requiring Jews to undergo martyrdom rather than give up the love for God, and *Meod* as referring to property or possessions.

I would like to propose a reading of this sentence based on a modification of Spinoza's account of attributes. For Spinoza, we encounter the world in two ways, through thought and extension. These are the only two of God's infinite attributes that we can know. I propose that we add to this scheme the attribute of "mood" or "feeling" because this is the way that we experience the world, i.e., through thought, physicality, and feeling. By feeling, I do not mean specific emotions or passions which as Spinoza explains derive from our thoughts, but the phenomenon to which feelings associate themselves, the underlying felt sense that existence exudes. Heidegger's account of mood, anxiety, and guilt which have no object or content appears to recognize such a basic quality of *Dasein*. The introduction of the attribute of feeling might also provide those attracted to Spinoza's monism with a God that has personality.[11]

My suggestion, then, is that the second sentence in the *Shema* should be taken as a call to love the God of oneness who is also "the LORD your God" through those attributes which we encounter; thought

---

11. On the possibility of viewing God as a person within a pantheistic or panentheistic system, see Melamed, "Concise Grammar of Pantheism."

(*Nefesh*), feeling (*Lev*), and extension or physicality (*Meod*), the act of making, creating, work. Combining Ibn Ezra and Rashi gets us there. Living the Way demands living through these attributes, which are the basic phenomenology of our lived experience with the aim of achieving *imitatio Dei* (imitation of the divine).

In the science of education and holistic and transformative learning, it is common to refer to the development of the heart, head, and hand. The heart is our emotional attachment to the things we learn and the world. The head symbolizes intellectual engagement and the hand represents our direct involvement with the world, artistry, and practical skills. All these aspects are involved in learning and require to be cultivated. The development of emotion through learning also includes love, faith, beauty, trust, gratitude, and aesthetics. Only when we have strong feelings about what we learn do we give significance to it. Physical movement and dexterity have a close connection to learning and are a key aspect of production and artistry.[12] When applied to the *Shema*, *Lev* is heart, *Nefesh* is head, and *Meod* is hand.

Papadopoulou and Birch distinguish between theories of learning which see knowledge as being fixed, propositional, and externally constituted and those which see learning as a mode of being. The latter leads to a much more immersive notion of learning than the former. On the latter approach, "human activity takes place in the lived world of everyday experience."[13] Papadopoulou and Birch describe the phenomenological roots of these ideas by reference to Husserl, Merleau-Ponty (1908–1961), and Heidegger.

Merleau-Ponty is credited with the idea that our experience of the world involves an active mind which "reaches out" into the world and a body which lives the experience. The phenomenological approach focuses on the meaning which arises in the space between our intentional reaching out and the objects we encounter. Our past experiences, personality traits, and our current situation all feed into this encounter.[14]

Merleau-Ponty distinguishes between two types of intentionality: "intentionality of acts" and "operative intentionality." The first type of intentionality is object driven. I identify an object and direct my efforts to achieving it. Operative intentionality is different. It is "felt" more than

12. See Gazibara, "Head, Heart and Hands Learning."

13. Papadopoulou and Birch, "Being in the World," 272–73.

14. Papadopoulou and Birch, "Being in the World," 272–73.

"known." It is the way in which we construct the world. Learning takes place within such construction.[15]

Learning is not therefore only about facts but is "an understanding of the world and the self as part of the world." It is the "result of engagement with social surroundings and the product of interaction with others in different contexts." It "takes place whenever learners engage in social settings and become part of the social and cultural world they inhabit."[16]

The idea of loving God through head, heart, and mind is eminently suited to a transcendent theology and phenomenological approach to learning, one rooted to being in the world. Based on the above meditation, we can see the *Shema* as moving the person of faith from the idea of God as one to the idea of God as other, as encouraging an encounter with every aspect of being through head, heart, and mind. The *Shema* then moves in the subsequent passages to other themes which draw us into the world: the education of children, ritual, justice, return, community, and history (Deut 6:5–9, 11–13, 21; Num 15:37–41).

John Ruskin (1819–1900), the art critic, philosopher, and visionary, also put forward a tripartite division of body (associated with senses and muscles), soul (associated with feeling and resolution), and intellect (associated with understanding and imagination). He writes that "all these parts of the human system have a reciprocal action on one another, so that the true perfection of any of them is not possible without some relative perfection of the others."[17]

Similarly, a religious path which fails to speak to all three aspects of head, heart, and mind, ignores aspects of being and are deficient. The requirement to engage the heart and hand have traditionally been the most neglected. Without them, we can excel only at scholarship. Those who embrace only the heart excel at kindly feeling, but the depths of understanding and ability to transmit them is absent. Those who embrace the hand are reliable laborers, but do not create through knowledge or with intensity. Those who aspire to all three are the true artists.

The danger with the technological worldview is that knowledge is treated as fixed, propositional, and externally constituted. Its ideal is a monistic, all-encompassing singularity. It stops at the first line of the

---

15. Papadopoulou and Birch, "Being in the World," 273–74.

16. Papadopoulou and Birch, "Being in the World," 277.

17. Ruskin, *Works*, 445.

*Shema* and ignores the subsequent passages, the unfolding of divinity as being, constituted by care, meaning and artistry.

## Circular Time

The technological worldview looks to the future. Its goal is utopic, the superintelligence, the singularity, the obliteration of death. The past is inferior to the present and both are inferior to the future, to which they are stepping-stones. History is not relevant, save as a reminder of our ignorance.

For Spinoza, the singularity has already come. From God's perspective, time is the infinite now. Reason allows us to tap into this perspective so "whatever the mind conceives under the guidance of reason it conceives under the same form of eternity or necessity . . . and is affected with the same certainty."[18]

In *Dasein*, time is not linear, but circular. Each moment is connected to the next, a precursor and forerunner, both the same and different to that experienced at the same point the last time around. Heidegger refers to the "common notion of linear time" as the "successive flowing away of the 'now' out of the 'not yet now' into the 'no longer now.'"[19] In this perspective, time is irreversible. In his 1962 Freiburg lecture, "Time and Being," Heidegger similarly described how the "succession of nows . . . disappears into the 'ago' and is already pursued by the 'soon.'"[20]

Our actual experience of time is not like that. As we have seen already, the past forms the present and is shaped and called to by the future. Each tense bleeds into the other. Heidegger gives special place to the future tense in its relationship to the past and present:

> In running ahead *Dasein* is its future, in such a way that in this being future it comes back to its past and present. *Dasein*, conceived in its most extreme possibility of Being, is time itself, not in time . . . Being futural gives time, cultivates the present and allows the past to be repeated in how it is lived. With regard to time, this means that the fundamental phenomenon of time is the future.[21]

18. Spinoza, *Ethics*, IV.PLXII.270.
19. Heidegger, "What Is Called Thinking," quoted in Wolfson, *Heidegger*, 46.
20. Wolfson, *Heidegger*, 46.
21. Heidegger, "Concept of Time," quoted in Wolfson, *Heidegger*, 264.

In fact, time is stationary but gives the impression of movement because of the way past, present, and future are perceived in their interactions. Like an immobile snake ingesting a rodent, time propels us in concertina-like waves through the body of existence. Heidegger writes: "In removing us and bringing towards us, time moves on its way what simultaneity yields and throws open to it: time-space. But time itself, in the wholeness of its nature, does not move; it rests in stillness."[22]

For Joseph B. Soloveitchik, covenantal time, like Heidegger's notion of circular time, looks both forward and back. It provides the individual with a chance to reexperience the past, while looking to the future. It mimics the eternality of God. Time is "not only a formal succession within the framework of calendar time, but the union of the three grammatical tenses in an all-embracing time experience . . . Covenantal man begins to find redemption from insecurity and to feel at home in the continuum of time . . . He is rooted in everlasting time, in eternity itself."[23]

As we have seen, the Jewish philosopher Franz Rosenzweig shared in the developments taking place in German philosophy in the Weimar period and dealt with similar themes to Heidegger, but Rosenzweig was an overt theist who retained a faith in eternity.[24]

Rosenzweig saw the religious calendar as transforming time from a linear to a cyclical progression, or a spiral which repeats yet progresses.[25] The adherent returns constantly to the same point on each lap of the religious calendar, but maturing and aging as he goes:

> In the ever-returning circle of the year, for him his never-ageing relationship of a child to God again and again flows into relationships of a child to the world as he grows from youth to old age, and back again; each preserves and renews itself in the other.[26]

Elliot Wolfson explains that Rosenzweig associates the "eternal God" with "the perpetual process of coming to be"[27] God experiences revelation, creation, and redemption, at one moment. They are the same event continuously becoming. Rosenzweig describes God's redemption as "the

22. Heidegger, "On the Way to Language," quoted in Wolfson, *Heidegger*, 267.

23. Soloveitchik, *Lonely Man of Faith*, 68–69. See Wolfson, *Heidegger*, 43–44.

24. Gordon, *Rosenzweig and Heidegger*, xxii–xxix.

25. Wolfson, *Heidegger*, 57n118.

26. Rosenzweig, *Star of Redemption*, 398.

27. Wolfson, *Heidegger*, 44.

eternal act in which he frees himself from contrasting with something that he himself is not."[28]

Practicing Jews act according to *Halachah* in an effort to live in such eternal time, outside the common way of living time as "between beginning and end." To achieve a sense of eternal time, the "between" must be reversed. Rosenzweig writes: "To reverse a between means to make its after into the before and its before into the after, the end into the beginning, the beginning into the end."[29]

In Kabbalah, the Tetragrammaton, the four-letter name of God (*YHVH*) and God's name, *Ehyeh* (I will be), which appears three times in Exodus 3:14, denote the past, present, and future. Wolfson sees a similarity between the Kabbalah's and Heidegger's treatment of these tenses. In the Kabbalah, there is a

> co-presence of past, present and future symbolized by the Tetragrammaton and the viewing of the name as that which fosters the time-space as the open enclosure of all being, the self-revealing concealment of the self-concealing revelation repeatedly renewed in the site of the moment.[30]

In hurtling us toward the future, the technological worldview disturbs the union between past, present and future, and our experience of the interplay between them. The foundations of *Dasein* start to shake. Our visions and possibilities become constricted. Eternity is put beyond our reach even as the possibility of infinite knowledge is brought into sight. Care is weakened. We become diminished.

Soloveitchik claimed that the religious apprehension of time as cyclic motion or as an eternal repetition, as Kierkegaard envisioned it, is "utterly unintelligible to the scientist who measures spatialized time or to the metaphysician who views time as a directed flow."[31] As Soloveitchik further notes, religious time is also reversible. It is this which allows for conversion and penance.[32]

Religion and the practice of ritual keeps the past and future alive within the present, retains the space for meaning and relationship, the

28. Rosenzweig, *Star of Redemption*, 406.

29. Rosenzweig, *Star of Redemption*, 443.

30. Wolfson, *Heidegger*, 275.

31. Soloveitchik, *Halakhic Mind*, 48.

32. Soloveitchik, *Halakhic Mind*, 48. On time consciousness in Soloveitchik and Rosenzweig, see further Cohen, "Time Consciousness."

potential for depth. The future can be worked toward steadily not with
an eye to conquering the universe but with reverence, humility, gratitude, and love, in the knowledge of our own temporality. In that looking
forward, our past is brought back to us and renewed. Heidegger writes:

> Only a being that is essentially futural in its being so that it can
> let itself be thrown back upon its factical there, free for its death
> and shattering itself on it, that is, only a being that is futural, is
> equiprimordially having-been, can hand down to itself its in-
> herited possibility, take over its own thrownness and be in the
> moment for "its time." Only authentic temporality that is at the
> same time finite makes something like fate, that is, authentic
> historicity, possible.[33]

How the practice of ritual in the Jewish context might renew the past and
present with each new cycle of the religious calendar and bring the Jewish
practitioner to a sense of oneness while embracing difference will be the
subject of the next chapter.

33. Heidegger, *Being and Time*, 366.

# 10

# Meaning in Time

## Unity and Return

### Rosh Hashanah

THE JEWISH NEW YEAR, *Rosh Hashanah*, is intimately connected to *Yom Kippur*, the Day of Atonement, which follows ten days later. These ten days are known as the "ten days of repentance."

The Hebrew Bible refers to *Rosh Hashanah* as the "day of blasting" (Num 29:1; Lev 23:23–32; 25:9). On this day, Jews are commanded to hear the shofar, traditionally a ram's horn, to wake them from their slumber and to return them to themselves.[1]

*Yom Kippur* involves refraining from eating and drinking, wearing leather shoes, washing, putting on perfume, and having sex.[2] *Rosh Hashanah* and *Yom Kippur* orientate us toward the values elucidated in this book. *Rosh Hashanah* is the moment of creation when humanity became separate from God. God is encountered in his transcendence, as the God of heaven. *Yom Kippur* takes us back to the God of oneness, immanence, the God that preceded creation, the God of everything. The Ten Days of repentance transport us from one perspective to another in a reversal of history, to use Rosenzweig's idea.

1. Maimonides, *MT*, Hilchot Teshuvah 3:4 "[The ram's horns] blast is symbolic, as if saying: 'you who slumber, wake yourselves from your sleep . . . examine your conduct, turn in repentance, and remember your Creator!'"

2. *TB* Yoma 73b.

The Talmud states in the name of God:

> On *Rosh Hashanah* say before Me "Sovereignty" (*Malchuyot*), "Memory" (*Zichronot*), and "blasts of the ram's horn (*Shofar*)" (*Shofrot*): Sovereignty so that you should make Me your King; Remembrance so that the Memory of you should rise up before Me. Through what? Through the *Shofar*.[3]

These themes form the core of the *Rosh Hashanah* additional (*Musaf*) service. That service contains a section dedicated to each of these three themes each comprising ten quotations from the Tanach.

### Sovereignty (*Malchut*)

There is nothing in the biblical text which expressly connects God's kingship to *Rosh Hashanah*. The association is made later by the rabbis. The rabbis also named *Rosh Hashanah* as the "anniversary of the creation of the world," reflecting the Jewish eternalizing of time discussed above.[4] Creation, as we have said, is the emergence of difference from the singularity which is God. It is the birth of transcendence, the sense of God as other. Rabbi Naftali Zvi Hurwitz of Ropshitz sees God's name, *Ehyeh*, as referring to God prior to creation, in his singularity, as *Echad*, "one." From that *Echad*, the thirteen attributes emerged by which God made himself known to Moses and which are recited frequently during the High Holy Day period (Num 14:18).[5] The numerical value of *Echad* is thirteen, creating a phenomenological association between oneness and the thirteen attributes which God manifests in his transcendence.[6]

Kingship (*Malchuyot*) is a dualist notion. It divides the world between leaders and their subjects. In the ancient world, kings were divine, a symbol of the ultimate other. The theme of sovereignty is pertinent to *Rosh Hashanah* in that it establishes God as the sole transcendent other. With God enthroned, there is no room for any worldly king or power.

---

3. *TB* Rosh Hashanah 16a and 34b.

4. *TB* Rosh Hashanah 10b. "Rebbe Eliezer said the world was created in Tishrei (when Rosh Hashanah takes place). Rebbe Yehoshua says the world was created in Nissan (when Passover takes place)." A phenomenologist would say that aspects of creation are present in both these festivals.

5. The attributes are: "The Lord! Slow to anger and abounding in kindness; forgiving iniquity and transgression; yet not remitting all punishment, but visiting the iniquity of fathers upon children, upon the third and fourth generations."

6. Hurwitz, *Zera Kodesh*, Nizavim, 366.

There is only humans and God. No earthly force can exercise absolute sovereignty over another human being. We are back at the themes elucidated in chapter 7. Yet the exploration of kingship in the *Rosh Hashanah* service hints at something beyond the dualist sense of king and subject. In the morning service, we sing Rabbi Shimon bar Yitchak's poem "*Hashem Melech*" describing humans and the angels as being united in prayer, heaven and earth brought together. Its stanza reads, "The Lord is King, the Lord was King, The Lord shall be king forever and ever"—the three tenses, reunited in one affirmation.[7]

## Memory (Zichronot)

While God is eternal, creation gives rise to time-space, the division and interlacing of past, present, and future. Time allows for possibility, for a before and after, for memory. But memory cannot be left to remain in the past. It must be allowed to project to the future. Memory confronts us, returns our past to us, allows the past to disclose itself, to direct us forward and backward simultaneously. The call for God to remember encourages us to experience time as God experiences it, without distinction, as a crystal-clear nowness, an eternity in which we each have eternal value.

## Shofar (Shofrot)

There are three types of *Shofar* sound: the *Tekiah*, one long note; *Shevarim*, three medium length notes; and *Teruah*, nine short staccato notes. The length of each *Shevarim* and *Teruah* is the same as that of the *Tekiah*.[8] The *Tekiah* is blown before and after these other notes.[9]

The different sounds of the *Shofar* have been given symbolic meaning, reflecting the wide use of this instrument in ancient Israel. In addition to *Rosh Hashanah*, the shofar was used to mark the jubilee, at the theophany at Sinai, and when the walls of Jericho came tumbling down (Lev 25:9; Josh 6:4; Exod 29:16–19; Judg 3:27; Ps 150:3).[10] It will also be

7. *Koren Rosh Hashana Machzor*, 694–701.

8. *TB* Rosh Hashanah 34a.

9. The Talmud rules that a *Tekiah* must come before and after the *Teruah*. The issue is whether the *Teruah* should be sounded as nine staccato notes or as a *Shevarim*. See *TB* Rosh Hashanah 34b.

10. See also *TB* Rosh Hashanah 34a.

sounded when the messiah arrives (Isa 27:13).[11] These uses are reflected in the meanings attributed to the notes. The *Tekiah* is associated with happiness and mercy, *Teruah* with the sound of war and judgment, and *Shevarim* with weeping. The requirement to surround the *Teruah* and *Shevarim* with a *Tekiah* suggests that mercy must always accompany war, judgment, and the sound of weeping.[12]

The common denominator of these associations is communication. The *Shofar* represents the reaching out of humanity to the divine, and divinity's call to humanity. The commandment of *Shofar* depends on hearing the sound, not on sounding.[13] The *Shofar* has a raw natural sound. It might be envisioned as the Jewish equivalent of the *Om* sound in Hinduism, the sound of the universe, the All. Rabbi Naftali Zvi Hurwitz of Ropshitz describes the shofar's sound as the simple voice from which all language emerges.[14] At the end of days, God himself will sound the *Shofar* (Zech 9:14).

The *Shofar* then is a call through time, a summons, the voice Adam and Eve heard walking in the garden which made them realize they were naked (Gen 3:8).[15] Through the shofar the gap between the transcendent God and historical memory is bridged, and the infinite is given voice within the world.

On both *Rosh Hashanah* and *Yom Kippur*, we recite the *Untaneh Tokef* prayer. It deals with the ephemeral nature of physical existence and the Jewish response to being in the world. It describes the period of the High Holidays as one of judgment. Decisions will be made on who will die, who will be born, but *contra* Spinoza, freedom is asserted with full force. The idea is that we can choose to remake our world with three things: Repentance (*Teshuva*), returning to the source by changing our perception; Prayer (*Tefillah*), pouring out our soul to the One; and Charity (*Tsedakah*) bettering society through acts of giving. These three things correspond to head (*Teshuvah*), heart (*Tefillah*), and hand (*Zedakah*). It is

11. See also *TB* Rosh Hashanah 11b.

12. Moses ben Nahman (1194–1270) (Ramban) on Numbers 9:19–22; see also *TB* Rosh Hashanah 33a–34b; Malbim on Numbers 10:2–3; *Tikunei Zohar*: 20–21, 49a, Malbim on Joel 2:1.

13. Maimonides, MT, *Shofar* 1:1.

14. Hurwitz, *Zera Kodesh*, Nezavim, 366–67. See also Rabbi Levi of Berditchev, *Kedushat Levi* on Genesis 3.

15. See Exod 19:19 where the Hebrew word for walking (*Halichah*) is used in the context of *Shofar*.

a return to the values of the *Shema* discussed above: "with all your heart, soul, and might."

There then follows one of the most beautiful statements of human frailty ever written. Human beings "are like the broken shard, the withering grass, the fading flower, a passing shadow, a dissipating cloud, a wind that blows, a particle of dust, a fleeting dream" but here is the clincher, "God is the King, the living and enduring God."[16] There is only God.

## Yom Kippur

If the focus of *Rosh Hashanah* is the relationship of the individual to God, *Yom Kippur* is a return to the singularity. As discussed, the *Halachah* dictates that on *Yom Kippur* one must refrain from aspects of daily living: eating, drinking, sex, perfume, and wearing leather shoes. The custom is also to wear white as a sign of purity and death.[17] In the world of the singularity, there will be no eating, drinking, or concern with material needs.

There is also just whiteness, no colored garments with which to clothe ourselves, whether ornamental coats, clothes of the prisoner, or rich and mighty (Joseph), or the veil of the widow or prostitute (Tamar). All is transparent.

*Yom Kippur* is Spinoza's festival. We are nothing but thoughts in the mind of God. We immerse ourselves in the liturgy and poetry of the past, containing ideas and images of God to which we might find it difficult to relate, but through which the primordial core shines.

We say the *Viduiy*, the confession, listing all the ways in which we have been human over the last year, and we know that we are nothing, because there is only God, and it is this knowledge which purifies.[18] We see our actions for what they are, illusions, masks, projections onto the world. It is this, and not guilt for individual wrongs, which calls us to

16. *Koren Yom Kippur Machzor*, 843–45; *Koren Rosh Hashana Machzor*, 564–69.

17. *Shulchan Aruch*, Orach Chayim, 610:4: "There are those that write that there is a custom to dress in white clean clothes on *Yom Kippur* [in order] to resemble the ministering angels. There is also a custom to wear a *Kittel* (long white garment) which is white and clean. This garment is used to clothe the dead and brings a person's heart to humility and brokenness" (my translation). Rosenzweig also refers to the Kittel as the "burial garment." Rozenzweig, *Star of Redemption*, 346.

18. *Koren Yom Kippur Machzor*, 588–97, 681–91.

change our perception, to return to the source. This is true *Teshuva* according to Rabbi Kook, as explained above.

Rabbi Shneur Zalman of Liady, the first Rebbe of Habad, taught that in Elul, the month before *Rosh Hashanah* and *Yom Kippur*, God comes down from heaven and makes himself accessible: "the King is in the field." Rabbi Menachem Mendel Schneerson (1902–1994), the last Rebbe of Habad, explained this to mean that "God's essence is in the field."[19] Differences are nullified. God and the world become co-joined.

A central aspect of the *Yom Kippur* service is the late morning additional service (*Musaf*) which recalls the biblical sacrifices and the temple service for *Yom Kippur*. Its content is fundamentally foreign to our contemporary sensibilities—animals, blood, expiation, guilt—and yet it contains profound meaning which resonates still in Jewish souls.

This a day of felt oneness. Just prior to commencing the temple service, we read part of the *Alenu* prayer recited by practicing Jews three times a day. It contains the verse from Deuteronomy 4:39, beloved of Kabbalists discussed earlier: "You shall know and take to heart this day that the Lord is God, in the heavens above and on the earth below. There is no other."[20] The congregation bow as they did in the days of the temple, nullifying any sense of self. There is no other except for God. Jonathan Sacks writes on this that "our body language bespeaks the immediacy of the Divine."[21]

*Musaf* then turns to the description of the temple service; the preparation of the high priest which commences seven days before the festival; the high priest's sacrifices on behalf of himself, his family, and the people; and his intermittent entry into the Holy of Holies—the inner sanctum containing the ark of the covenant—where he would sprinkle blood and intone the Tetragrammaton (*YHVH*). The high priest could only enter the Holy of Holies and pronounce the Tetragrammaton on *Yom Kippur*.

On hearing the Name intoned from outside the Holy of Holies, the people would prostrate themselves and declare "Blessed be the name of His glorious kingdom for ever and all time." This process is repeated three times.[22] The community experiences oneness through this ritual. Describing this part of the service, Rosenzweig writes of idolatry

---

19. Schneerson, *Likkutey Sichot*, 1344.

20. *Koren Yom Kippur Machzor*, 872–73.

21. *Koren Yom Kippur Machzor*, 872.

22. *Koren Yom Kippur Machzor*, 886–93.

disappearing and the community sinking to its knees to "form one single covenant to do God's will with a whole heart."[23]

What is striking about the Holy of Holies is the absence of any image as the object of veneration. Inside the space stood the ark, containing among other things the tablets on which the Ten Commandments were written and the broken tablets. God is encountered through words and the demands they make on those who they address. On the cover of the ark there were two cherubim, winged creatures, facing each other. According to tradition, one had the face of a boy and one a face of a girl. God's presence dwells in the space between them (1 Sam 4:4).

Temples were common in the ancient world. At their center stood the representation of a specific deity. In Judaism, God is what remains when every idol has been smashed; no thing; an emptiness that is full; simplicity. *Yom Kippur* unconceals what lies behind the curtain, the ontological foundation of all existence.

The ancient rights are gone, but the spirit of them lives on. Jews continue to worship a divinity which they take to be the only reality, but in the knowledge that they must operate in relationship, which requires a space where God is hidden. *Yom Kippur* offers the people a moment of insight, but no more.

At the end of *Neilah*, the final service of *Yom Kippur*, as the light fades, the lesson of the day takes on the characteristic of near-mystical insight. The congregation, hungry and tired, but at its most spiritual, call out in unison a mantra of three parts, comprising three sentences taken from Tanach.[24] The first sentence recited once by the leader and then by the congregation is the first line of the *Shema*, the statement of absolute oneness: "Here O Israel, *YHVH* is our God, *YHVH* is One" (Deut 6:4). The second sentence recited three times by the leader and then three times by the congregation is the second line of the *Shema*: "Blessed be the name of the glory of His kingdom for ever and ever."

The third sentence recited seven times by the leader and then seven times by the congregation is "*YHVH* he is *Elokhim*," which translated literally means "*YHVH*, he is God." These words were declared by the crowd that witnessed Elijah's defeat of the false prophets of Ahab on Mount Carmel (1 Kgs 18:39). But what do they mean? We mentioned above the observation that the Hebrew words *Elokhim* and *ha-Teva* (the nature) in

---

23. Rosenzweig, *Star of Remption*, 343–44.

24. *Koren Yom Kippur Machzor*, 1192–95.

Hebrew have the same numerical value. *Elokhim* is sometimes viewed as God's presence in the world. Taken this way, "*YHVH*, he is *Elokhim*" has an uncanny resemblance to the statement *Deus sive Natura*—God or Nature, the catchphrase of Baruch Spinoza, the arch-heretic, the heretic whose truth is not the whole truth because a moment after these words have been voiced, *Yom Kippur* ends and we return to the world of difference, of us and them, of dualism and chaos. We move beyond Spinoza's God back to creation in all its nuance, complication, and meaningfulness.

When a Jew dies, she utters the same three phrases described above. The monistic truth is the truth of death, which is both an end and a beginning. The technological singularity spells the end, but the insight of oneness can also mark a beginning, the gateway through which we pass after *Yom Kippur*, a return to life, to the journey, to the Way.

## Purim

Purim is a one-day rabbinic festival which takes place in the early spring. Its origins are described in the book of Esther, found in Tanach (Esth 9:28). The book is set in Persia where the Jews were exiled during the early second-temple period (c. 500 BCE), but most scholars think that the work was written much later, possibly between 400–200 BCE.[25] Since the festival is of rabbinic origin, it has none of the restrictions of *Shabbat* and other festivals. The laws of the day include the public reading of the book of Esther (*Megilat Esther*), exchanging food parcels between friends, donating money to the poor, and attending a festive meal. The rabbis further dictate that on Purim one should become so inebriated that it is impossible to know the difference between Mordechai (the main male hero) and Haman (the villain).[26] It is also a custom to wear fancy dress.[27]

*Megilat Esther* may have some historical basis but feels very much like a fairy tale or pantomime, starring a king (Ahashverosh), a heroic queen (Esther), a male hero (Mordechai), a villain (Haman), existential and communal danger, farce, and a happy-ever-after ending. But to treat the book in this way would be to miss out on a profound theology.

25. Fishbane, *Esther*, xli.

26. *TB* Megillah 7b.

27. The first to record the custom is R. Yehuda ben Eliezer ha-Levi Minz (c. 1405–1508). *Teshuvot Mahari Minz*, n15. See Sharbat, "Purim Masquerade."

*Purim* is the equivalent of *Yom Kippur*, a pulling back of the curtain, a revealing. *Yom Kippur* approaches the task through introspection and austerity, *Purim* through levity, the breaking of boundaries, and the unshackling of spirit.

The most obvious phenomenological association between *Purim* and *Yom Kippur* is in the name. *Yom Kippurim*, the name of *Yom Kippur* in the Hebrew Bible, can be taken to mean a "day like *Purim*" (Lev 23:27). The *Tikunei Zohar* states that Purim is "called 'Purim' because in the future, people will rejoice on *Yom Kippur*, and affliction will be transferred into joy."[28]

Both *Yom Kippur* and *Purim* raise questions about chance, fate, and destiny. The day on which the law allowing the killing of the Jews to take effect (the thirteenth of the Hebrew month of Adar) was chosen in *Megilat Esther* by drawing lots (*Pur*) (Esth 3:7, 9:26). On *Yom Kippur* a goat is chosen to be sent into the desert to expiate the sins of the people also following the drawing lots (*Pur*) (Lev 16:22). On *Yom Kippur*, the biblical book of Jonah is read. Like Esther, Jonah is initially reluctant to embrace his destiny (Jonah 1:3; Esth 4:11–15). He attempts to run from his mission to berate the people of Nineveh by boarding a ship leaving from Jaffa. There is a storm. The sailors suspect that an angry god is responsible. Jonah reveals that he is a Hebrew. Until this point, like Esther, he had hidden his Jewishness (Jonah 1:9; Esth 7:3–4). In both Jonah and Esther, there is a three-day period prior to fulfillment of the mission (Jonah 2:1; Esth 4:16). (Esther fasts for three days. Jonah prays for three days entombed in the fish). In both stories, the mission is completed successfully.

The rabbis explain that on each festival, half the day should be dedicated to God and half for us.[29] *Purim* and *Yom Kippur* are an exception to this principle. *Yom Kippur* is all for God and *Purim* is all for us. The two days complement each other.

The most striking feature of *Megilat Esther* is the absence of a reference to God. Events on their surface appear to be driven by humans ruthlessly pursuing their own agendas and narrow interests. Haman, Esther, and Mordechai are all involved in plots and subterfuge. Haman plots the demise of his enemies. Esther and Mordechai scheme to secure their own power and protect their people. God is silent. Chance appears to rule. As

---

28. *Tikkunei Zohar* 58b:4.

29. *TB* Beitzah 15b.

described, the day on which the destruction of the Jews was to take place was chosen by drawing lots, not through human design.

Despite this, there is a certain inevitability to the outcome of the story. We know at the outset that the Jews will survive and that Haman will be destroyed. Often traditional religious Jews proclaim that God is acting beneath the surface, pulling the strings, but the work can be read as a rejection, even parody, of traditional conceptions of God. The reference to the "King," when speaking about King Ahasuerus in the book, is traditionally taken as an oblique reference to God, a reminder of his behind-the-scenes presence. Yet one could argue that Ahasuerus is symbolic of a wholly inadequate view of God, and that Purim is an attack on simplistic ideas about God's providence and institutional religion.

King Ahasuerus is portrayed in the book of Esther as a weak individual, ruled to a large degree by his emotions, and capable of manipulation by all and sundry. At the start of the book, he removes Vashti, the Queen, on the advice of his advisor, Memucan, for exerting her independence and standing up to him. After Vashti is removed, Ahasuerus chooses Esther to be his wife following a beauty parade. Associating Ahasuerus with God would suggest that God is whimsical and suggestible and chose Israel, represented by Esther, for superficial reasons.

Observe too how Haman, Mordechai, and Esther seek to manipulate Ahasuerus to do their bidding based on their own prejudices and interests. Haman is driven by a paranoid hatred of the Jew: "There is a certain people, scattered and dispersed among the other peoples . . . whose laws are different from those of any other people and who do not obey the King's laws; and it is not in Your majesty's interest to tolerate them" (Esth 3:8). Haman wants the King to issue an edict to have them destroyed.

Mordechai meanwhile cares most about his own people. He directs Esther in how best to approach "the King." Based on such advice, Esther invites the King to several parties to "butter him up," like many adherents attempt to do to God through prayer. Esther eventually points the finger at Haman, the villain. He and his ten sons are hung, but that does not end the killing.

The law allowing the Jews to be killed could not be undone, only a new edict allowing self-defense could be issued. We are told at the end of the story that the Jews killed more than 75,000 people (Esth 9:15–16). We treat all this as a great victory, but blood has been spilled on a terrible scale. There is an element of mockery here. The King has set up a system which works against the desired outcome, but which cannot be undone but only manipulated imperfectly. If Ahasuerus is symbolic of God, God it seems can only work in defined parameters.

The symbolism of Ahasuerus taking off his ring and handing it first to Haman, to allow him to issue the edict for the destruction of the Jews, and eventually to Esther to allow the decree to be removed, also corresponds to how religious people often relate to God (Esth 8:2). God not only listens to them, but places power in their hands. Rabbi Joseph B. Soloveitchik writes in *Halakhic Man*:

> Even the Holy one, blessed be He, has, as it were, handed over his imprimatur, His official seal in Torah matters, to man; it is as if the Creator of the world himself abides by man's decision and instruction . . .[30]

Handing over power in this way involves great risk. Humans are incapable of acting dispassionately with all knowledge of the facts. They cannot see things from every angle. They cannot fully understand another person's being. The idea that Ahasuerus symbolizes God demonstrates the inadequacy of traditional conceptions of God.

The book of Esther, however, does more than subtly undermine traditional notions of God. It promotes an alternative awareness, a sense of the non-dualist God of Jewish mysticism, the God of Spinoza, of absolute being, evident just beneath the surface of our lived experience. The name Esther relates to the Persian word *Stara* meaning star, but also to the Hebrew word *"Astir"* meaning, "I will conceal" or "hide."[31] Purim recognizes the world as farce and fancy dress and encourages us to look beneath the surface. This is the primary way *Purim* and *Yom Kippur* are similar. They both lead temporarily to Spinoza's God.

We can now understand the rabbis' instruction to drink until one does not know the difference between Haman and Mordechai.[32] What is being urged is a return to monism. Rava, the sage credited with the edict, observes elsewhere that wine and "incense" enhance perception.[33] Without wanting to encourage alcohol or drugs, one of the attractions of these substances is the ability to dissolve ego, the sense of difference. On *Purim*, Jews are urged to drink until they see no difference between Haman and Mordechai because on one level, within the totality, there really

---

30. Soloveitchik, *Halakhic Man*, 80.

31. Hazony, *God and Politics in Esther*, 195.

32. *TB* Megillah 7b.

33. *TB* Yoma 76b.

is no difference. In the Talmud, Rava takes a critical stance toward both Haman and Mordechai.[34] They are of equal worth.

Jewish mystics play on this non-dualistic theme. For Rabbi Yehudah Loew ben Bezalel of Prague (the Maharal) (1609), Amalek, the tribe of Haman, is characterized by its material dualistic outlook. Amalek cannot recognize the unity of being and is unable to see the world as connected. This failure amounts to nothing less than a denial of God's oneness: "Amalek has so far removed himself from reality that he has made himself a thing apart . . . for as long as Amalek exists in the world, it cannot be said that 'God is One and His Name is One.'"[35] While the Hebrew Bible and Jewish tradition has encouraged Jews to view themselves as distinct from other peoples, that same tradition has espoused the idea that, in reality, everything is one. Mordechai and Haman are different sides of the same coin.

There is also an element of existential discovery within the *Purim* story. Characters hide behind clothes and personas and must find their way without direct communication from God. Some have identified thematic and linguistic parallels between the book of Esther and the Joseph narrative.[36] Both deal with the theme of authenticity, the path that selves travel when free from divine or societal coercion. Both Joseph and Esther are strangers in strange lands and must choose whether to identify with their heritage, their thrownness, or throw it off.[37]

Many cultures permit the occasional releasing of the pressure valve and encourage people to let off steam. Medieval Christianity had the carnival and the *festum fatuorum*, the Feast of Fools, during which the world was turned upside down for four days. Priests would play dice and bray like donkeys, drink alcohol, and deliver nonsensical sermons. The church recognized the need for permissive licentiousness for a short period to protect morality for the remainder of the year.[38] Purim is the Jewish equivalent. However, it fulfills not just a social need but a theistic one, the need for the removal of boundaries, to see reality for what it is, a

34. Eliach, "Mordecai the Villain."

35. Maharal, *Or Chadash*, 91, see also 105.

36. Hornung, "Nature and Import."

37. For the first time since the Exodus, in Persia becoming a Jew was a choice that every individual would need to make. See Hazony, *God and Politics in Esther*, 165. See also *TB* Shabbat 88a. Rava taught that the Jews accepted the covenant involuntarily at Sinai and voluntarily in the days of Ahasuerus.

38. De Botton, *Religion for Atheists*, 64–65.

virtual reality, an expression of oneness, but like *Yom Kippur*, the seeing is temporary. We are allowed only the merest glimpse (and not too much debauchery). Singularity gives way to world.

## Particularist Universality

### Succot

The festival of Tabernacles or *Succot* takes place five days after *Yom Kippur*. The festival lasts for seven days (eight outside Israel). The main commandments associated with the festival are the taking and shaking of the four species (a palm (*Lulav*), myrtle (*Hadassim*), willow (*Aravot*), and citron (*Etrog*)) and dwelling in the *Succah*, a booth covered with organic material such as leaves or branches uprooted from the ground (*Sechach*).

*Succot* is both an agricultural festival, "the Feast of Ingathering at the turn of the year," and a commemoration of the Exodus from Egypt (Exod 34:22; Lev 23:41–43; see also Deut 16:13–15). The *Succah* is a reminder of the huts used by the Israelites in the desert or of the clouds of glory that accompanied the Israelites.[39] The commentators see the clouds as representing God's presence, the *Shechinah*.[40] *Succot* is much more clearly rooted in history than *Yom Kippur* or *Rosh Hashanah*.

In the period leading up to *Succot*, there has been a movement from the God of creation (*Rosh Hashanah*), back to the monistic God of pre-creation (*Yom Kippur*). In *Succot*, we meet the God of history, of a specific tribe. It is as if once we have understood creation and the oneness of God, we are free to form an identity through narrative, to travel as a people. The idea of oneness, however, is never far away. *Succot* has both particularist and universalist aspects, which might be said to give rise to a particularist universality, a realm where oneness and individuality meet.[41]

*Succot* is a reminder of the Jewish story, but the result of that particularism is a desire to look outward, to move beyond safe enclaves, to take risks. Through its focus on oneness, *Yom Kippur* allowed us to look beyond the temporal. This resulted in a lifting of a burden, a newfound

39. *TB* Succah 11b. R. Akiva takes the former view. R. Eliezer takes the latter view.

40. Sforno on Numbers 9:15, and Tanchuma on Numbers 12.

41. On the term see Wolfson, *Heidegger*, 224–25. Wolfson comments on a description by Gershom Scholem of Luria's system that "totality and individuality cannot be easily separated inasmuch as the former is manifest through the latter, and the latter through the former."

freedom and ability to roam. Hence, the halachic injunction to leave the apparent security of our homes and to sit in a flimsy hut covered with nature uprooted from its source. *Succot* marks the end of the summer. Nature is turning. Decay is in the air. *Succot* is a living toward death in the Heideggerian sense. It embraces change, the uncertainty of the harvest, the removal of physical protection from the elements. But there is a sense of overwhelming joy, *Simchah*. Joy is at the heart of the festival.[42]

The ability to feel comfortable with the temporal is the essence of faith and the source of happiness, which the sages count as the supreme value of *Succot*. *Succot* was the time of the great water-drawing festival which occurred within the temple during this period. The Talmud states: "One who has not witnessed the celebration of the water-drawing festival has never seen *Simchah*, real joy."[43] On the intermediate *Shabbat* of the festival, Jews read the book of Ecclesiastes, discussed in chapter 7. Its message is that happiness is to be found in the here and now, accepting that which we cannot control. It displays some of the stoicism beloved of Spinoza, coupled with a deep faith. The wisdom of Ecclesiastes is universal.

As indicated, once secure in ourselves, we can reach out to others. The Bible commands seventy bulls to be offered during *Succot* as well as other sacrifices (Num 29). The rabbis maintain that these sacrifices are brought on behalf of the seventy nations of the world.[44] Care seeks to expand. We are back at Joseph who having found himself is able to turn to the task of sustaining his family and Egypt during the famine. Joseph indeed is one of the "seven shepherds", who, according to the Jewish mystics, visit the *Succah* during the festival.[45]

Heidegger observes how we project our own lives onto other people, but the other is not an object within our *Dasein*, but an entity which "has itself the same kind of Being as *Dasein*."[46] Only when we retreat from the self, do we cease from projecting that self onto other people, and allow

---

42. Deut 16:13–15: "You shall rejoice in your festival, with your son and daughter, your male and female slave, the Levite, the stranger, the fatherless, and the widow in your communities. You shall hold a festival for the LORD your God seven days, in the place that the LORD will choose; for the LORD your God will bless all your crops and all your undertakings, and you shall have nothing but joy."

43. *TB* Succah 51a.

44. *TB* Succah 55b.

45. For the custom, see *Zohar* 3:103b:8–9.

46. Heidegger, *Being and Time*, 121.

the other to be as she is and to enter our world. Under the *Succah*, the self-retreats, absorbed metaphorically into the *Shechinah*. An intimate love gives way to a broader mysticism, a move toward nature, infinity, oneness. The world is brought under the canopy of the *Succah*. The world within God. The four species are united and shaken in each direction. God within the world. We experience *Shlemut*, wholeness.

On each day of *Succot*, Jews make a procession around the *Bimah*, the platform from where the Torah is read, and except for *Shabbat*, hold the four species in their hands. This ritual of *Hakafot* (circuits) is based on a similar practice of circling the altar on *Succot* in temple times.[47] The circle is the symbol of eternity, wholeness, inclusivity, the universal. The ritual enacts circular time.

The festivals of *Shemini Azeret* and *Simchat Torah* follow immediately after *Succot*.[48] They enact another circle; namely, the completion of the yearly communal reading of the Torah. During the Torah reading which forms part of the festival's synagogue service, Deuteronomy is completed, and Genesis is immediately begun, the end and beginning, the end which is in the beginning, and the beginning which is in the end (Isa 44:6; 46:10). The circle of learning, like God, is infinite. There can be no gap. In this system, philosophy is not just thought, but lived.

## Chanukah

*Chanukah* is a post-biblical winter festival, commemorating the rededication of the temple in Jerusalem at the time of the Maccabean/Hasmonean revolt against the Seleucid Greeks in about 200 BCE. It lasts for eight days and is celebrated by lighting the *Menorah*, an eight-branched candelabra, with an additional raised branch on which the *Shamash* (service candle) stands. The *Shamahsh* is lit each night and used to light the other candles. On the first night, we light one candle; on the second, two candles; and so on.[49]

*Chanukah* is a low-maintenance festival. Since the festival is of rabbinic origin, like Purim, it has none of the restrictions of *Shabbat* and other festivals. There are laws about lighting the *Menorah*, a few additions

47. *TB* Succah 45a.

48. In Israel, *Shemini Azeret* and *Simchat Torah* are held on the same day. In the diaspora, *Simchat Torah* falls the day after *Shemini Azeret*.

49. *Shulchan Aruch, Orach Hayim* 671:2.

to be made to the prayer and synagogue service, but that is it. There are though several customs, including a custom to eat food cooked with oil like doughnuts and latkes, playing dreidel (a spinning top with painted letters on the side), and giving gifts (primarily of money).[50]

The genius of *Chanukah* lies in how the rabbis turned it from a celebration of a military victory into a spiritual one. After dealing with the laws of *Chanukah*, the Talmud asks, "What is *Chanukah*?"[51] The answer is the celebration of a miracle. When the Hasmoneans emerged victorious over the Greeks, they searched and found only one cruse of oil sufficient to light the temple *Menorah* for one day. The miracle was that it lasted for eight days. The rabbis instituted those eight days as the festival of *Chanukah*. The festival came to be seen as a celebration of Judaism's victory over Greek Hellenism, the restrictions it imposed on Jewish ritual and the Greek's immoral practices, including exercising naked, *gumnos*, which gives us our contemporary word "gym" (1 Macc 1:14–17; 2 Macc 4:7–17).

Phenomenologically, *Chanukah* is linked to *Succot* (including *Shemini Azeret*). Both of these festival periods last for eight days, both celebrate Jewish particularism (sitting in *Succot* following the Exodus from Egypt in the case of *Succot* and Judaism's victory over Greek Hellenism in the case of *Chanukah*), and both involve an outward looking aspect.[52] *Succot* requires Jews to sit outside the home for seven days. *Chanukah* requires the *Menorah* to be lit in public at the time that people return from the market to "publicise the miracle."[53] There is both a looking inward and desire to engage with the family of nations, an encounter with a transcendent God of a particular people and the God of everything, which has been the subject of this book.

Judaism did not in fact defeat Hellenism. At the time, many Jews sought an accommodation with Greek culture.[54] Even the rabbis were not consistent in their attitude toward Hellenism and the Greek language. A view in the Talmud grants a special status to sacred scrolls written in Greek (although not everyone agreed).[55] And even when negative atti-

50. For other customs see *Shulchan Aruch* 671:1.

51. *TB* Shabbat 21b.

52. This is true only in Israel. In the diaspora, *Succot* and Shmini Azeret/Simchat Torah together last for nine days.

53. *TB* Shabbat 21b. *Mishnah Berurah* 672.1.

54. Gruen, *Heritage and Hellenism*, 292–97.

55. *TB* Shabbat 115a discusses whether sacred scrolls written in translation may be read or rescued from a fire on *Shabbat*. The *Mishnah* suggests that scrolls in any

tudes toward Hellenism increased, there were rabbinic-sponsored Greek translations of the Bible, such as the Bible of Aquila.[56] Through Hellenism, many Jews came to embrace universal values and some sought to combine Hellenistic ideas about God with biblical notions.[57] In the Hellenistic Jewish diaspora, the Bible came to be viewed through a Hellenistic lens.

In this context, the figure of Joseph became a focus of literary attention, one which was not always positive. Hellenistic Jews no doubt related to Joseph's predicament as a Hebrew enmeshed in a foreign culture, struggling to find and express his identity.[58]

In the context of *Chanukah*, the universal finds its most obvious expression in the symbol of light. The lighting of the candles signifies a Jewish miracle, yet light is a metaphor for universal wisdom and understanding, including in ancient Greek literature. In the sixth book of Plato's *Republic*, the sun represents the Form of the Good in whose light all existence is revealed.[59] The Psalmist similarly declares: "In Your light shall we see light" (Ps 36:9). The *Bhagavad Gita* pronounces: "The Ultimate Truth is declared as the illuminator of all that illuminates."[60] Light contains all colors, but these become apparent only when it is refracted. Light therefore conceals, as well illuminates. Chanukah understands the universality of light, but also that beauty lies in individuation, the refraction of the light of wisdom through a specific tradition.

---

language can be read and rescued. The Talmud records a debate. One view is that scrolls written in Greek, and a handful of other languages, can be rescued even though they cannot be read.

56. Alexander, *Rabbis*, 245.

57. Collins, *Jewish Cult and Hellenistic Culture*, 21–26.

58. Gruen, *Heritage and Hellenism*, 73–109. 4 Macc 2:1–6 sees the story of Joseph's resistance to Potiphar's wife's advances as demonstrating the ability of reason to prevail over passion. Philo of Alexandria (c. 25 BCE), the Hellenistic Jewish philosopher, is also interested in Joseph, writing about him in *On Joseph* and *On Dreams*. In *On Joseph*, Joseph is seen as the model citizen and given sympathy because of his brothers' ill treatment of him. In *On Dreams*, he is criticized for his vanity.

59. Plato, *Republic*, 507b–9c.

60. *Bhagavad Gita* 13:18.

## Freedom

## Pesach

Passover (*Pesach*) is the seven-day (eight-day in the diaspora) celebration of the birth of the Jewish nation following its escape from Egyptian servitude. It takes place in the spring. Each year on the first night (and on the second night in the diaspora), Jewish families gather round the *Seder* table to read the *Haggadah*, which describes the story of the Exodus, and to perform the rituals associated with the day, the most important in post-temple times being eating *Matzah* (unleavened bread) and *Maror* (bitter herbs) (Exod 12:26–27; 13:14; Deut 6:20–22). During Pesach all *Chametz* (leaven) must be removed from one's home. It should not be eaten, found, owned, or seen (Exod 12:15, 19–20; 12:15; 13:3, 7).

Peach is called *Zeman Cherutenu*, the time of our freedom. It charts the journey from the Jewish people's slavery in Egypt to the Exodus.[61]

We have seen that Spinoza tells us that we have no freedom of the will. We can determine only through the application of reason whether to be determined by internal causes or external causes. Heidegger similarly tells us that we are bound by our thrownness and our facticity. By exercising resoluteness, we can own these aspects of our existence and move forward authentically.

The Exodus story does not, on careful reading, suggest the possibility of absolute freedom. Indeed, the point appears to be that we all need to serve somebody, whether gods, God, or a no-god. Moses, as God's servant, encouraged the Jews to serve God. The alternative was to serve Pharaoh, the slave master and his gods. There is no power vacuum to be occupied by the self. The force of the Exodus story, as reenacted at *Pesach*, is its role in allowing us to choose the power that ultimately has authority over us.

Pesach is relevant not just to ancient times, but to now. It should sensitize us to all forms of abuse and servitude, physical and ideological, the force of the "they," the tides of everyday opinion on which we are pulled, the all-consuming drive toward efficiency, the technological, and the daily whittling down of freedom. There are three preconditions to achieving freedom: the ability to ask questions, the belief that we can be free, and acting as free people act. It involves being different and embracing our unique histories and destinies.

---

61. Melamed, *Peninei Halakhah*, 1:2.6.

## Questioning

Freedom begins with the asking of questions. Where there are no questions, there is no possibility for change. A slave has no right to question, and no language from which to formulate a question. The *Haggadah* opens with questions (the Four Questions), encourages questions from each individual according to her background and inclination (the Four Sons), and is an incomplete work, waiting for the next generation to add its own questions and its incomplete answers (Exod 12:26–27; 13:14; Deut 6:20–22).[62]

Slavery, like the idea of the technological singularity, treats humans as cogs in a machine, without will or worth save as a means to some external material end. Slavery strips us of a sense of independence and the freedom to manifest our creativity, while making us blind to what is happening to us. The ultimate slave is unaware of his servitude. He is passive in his suffering and sees no alternative world beyond the system. An encounter with values outside the system leads to an appreciation of what is taking place within it. It is a tear which lets the light in, a first step toward liberty. As long as we can ask the question "Why?" the possibility of freedom remains open.

## Believing in Freedom

Freedom also entails belief in the possibility of freedom. While scientists debate the possibility of free will, there is evidence that believing in freedom is essential for people to be able to exert control over their actions. Studies tell us that those who do not believe in free will are more likely to act dishonestly, to behave aggressively, and to conform to other people's thoughts and opinions. Furthermore, when people feel that they have little control over their actions, they tend to feel more distant from what they perceive to be their true or authentic selves, and generally less satisfied.[63] At the start of the Exodus story, we witness the elders' cynicism about ever achieving freedom after Moses's interference (Exod 5:20–21).

62. Melamed, *Peninei Halakhah*, 15:3–4: "This is the main reason for the unique mitzvot of the Seder night: eating matza, the paschal sacrifice, and bitter herbs (*Maror*). They cause the children to ask, '*Ma nishtana?*' 'Why is this night different?'"

63. Feldman, "Agency Beliefs Over Time," 304–17. See also Smilansky, *Free Will*, and Vohs and Schooler, "Value of Believing in Free Will," 49–54: "Exposure to deterministic messages increases the likelihood of unethical actions." Not everyone agrees.

By the end, the entire people had the courage to sacrifice a lamb, the symbol of an Egyptian God, and to place its blood on their doorposts (Exod 12:7).

### Acting Like a Free Person

The next stage of achieving freedom is acting like a free person. In ancient Greece and Rome, aristocratic families gathered to hold a meal, drink wine, and to debate, scheme, show off and enjoy each other's company. This was the symposium. The Seder mirrors this institution, but is designed for every person, and not just the aristocratic few.[64] It also demands that we choose who we want to serve.

What then were the people being asked to choose to serve with their new-found freedom? The answer is God encountered as oneness and God encountered as other. In other words, the God of everything but encountered through a specific history. We have seen this dichotomy several times now.

While tending his father-in-law's flocks in Midian, Moses hears God speaking out of a "blazing fire" (Exod 3:2). God introduces himself as "the God of your father, the God of Abraham, the God of Isaac, and the God of Jacob" (Exod 3:6). This is the God of relationship which has "seen" and "knows" his people's suffering in Egypt, the God who "has come down" to save the people and take them to the promised land (Exod 3:8). Slavery negates individuation. The God of Israel guarantees it. Yet, this is also the episode where God reveals himself as "*Eheyeh Asher Eheyeh*," as *YHVH*, as the ineffable God of becoming (Exod 3:14, 18). Pharaoh did not recognize such a God (Exod 5:2).

On the intermediate *Shabbat* of *Pesach*, we read the Song of Songs. The book portrays a pastoral romance, a relationship between a young man and his betrothed, each trying to find the other, coming together, losing each other, holding back from intimacy. The *Zohar* claims that "whatever was, is, or ever will be . . . is all in the Song of Songs."[65] In that book, the singularity is approached, but never quite reached. The lovers are of one mind but remain distinct: "I am my beloved's and my beloved is mine" (Song 6:3). There is a conjoining without obliteration. This is the relationship of the Jewish people to their God.

---

64. See Kulp, *Schechter Haggadah*, 12, 196.

65. *Zohar* 2:144a.

In his *Orot Hakodesh*, Abraham Isaac Kook describes four kinds of song corresponding to four types of individual. The first song is sung by an individual who finds in her own soul all that is necessary. The second song is that sung by nations, through which individuals can transcend their own concerns. The third song is the song of humankind, which transcends all national interests. The fourth song comprises the entirety of existence, through which all elements come together.

Kook goes on to describe an additional song. It is sung by an individual with the ability to absorb and reflect everything. In this individual,

> all of the songs come together at all times and in all hours, and this perfection in its fullness ascends to become a holy song: a song to God, a song to Israel . . . This should be the aspiration of Israel and every Jew, and citizen of the world.[66]

The ultimate ideal is difference in unity and unity in difference.

## Shavuot

We have mentioned three preconditions to achieving freedom. The next step is having a system of values and practices by which to live and a place from which to reflect on the present condition. For the Jewish people, this system of values and place is Torah. This is the theme of *Shavuot*.

*Shavuot* is a one-day festival (two days in the diaspora) which takes place seven weeks after *Pesach*. The Hebrew Bible requires Jews to count seven weeks from the second day of *Pesach* until *Shavuot*. (Deut 16:9–10; Exod 34:22). There is nothing in the Bible which expressly links *Shavuot* to the giving of the Torah at Sinai. The rabbis drew the connection. The Jews left Egypt and journeyed to Mount Sinai where they received the Torah. That journey was said to have taken seven weeks.[67] There is also a custom of staying up the whole night on the first night of the festival to learn Torah.[68] The *Zohar* describes *Shavuot* as a marriage of two aspects of the divine, the male and female. The Jewish people stay up all night with the bride to rejoice and ready the bride.[69] On *Shavuot* day, there is a

66. Kook, *Orot* II:444–45, quoted in Fishbane, *Song of Songs*, 304.

67. *TB* Pesachim 68b; see also *TB* Shabbat 86b. The festival also marks the wheat harvest and the bringing of first fruits to the temple (Exod 23:16; Num 28:26; Deut 10:1–11).

68. I.e., after nightfall on the eve of the festival. Jewish days commence at nightfall.

69. *Zohar* I:8a. Another tradition claims the custom is an atonement for the Jews

public reading of the Ten Commandments from the Torah.[70] I would like to explore further the theme of Torah.

The Mishnah rules that there are several commandments which have no limit, including "the study of Torah."[71] Torah learning includes the study of the written Torah and the Oral Torah, including the Mishnah and Talmud. Maimonides describes the obligation as follows:

> Every Jew is required to learn Torah whether he is poor or rich, whether healthy or suffering pain, whether a young man or one who has grown weak; even if he is a poor man who makes his living collecting charity by going from door to door, even if he is a husband and has young children, he must set for himself times for learning Torah during the day and night as it says: "And you shall study it day and night" (Joshua 1:8).[72]

The obligation is both beautiful and burdensome. It is beautiful in fixing education at the center of the religious life, in making Judaism into a conversation across time, between different generations and groups, and in more recent times between the sexes. It is burdensome because, at least within Jewish orthodoxy, the obligation to learn Torah is all-encompassing. There is so much to know and very few moments where the obligation does not apply.[73] With the rise of technology and the internet, Jewish learning is more accessible than it has ever been. There are also now countless programs of learning available in numerous languages and at every time of day and night.[74] There is a pressure to know and a danger

---

having overslept on the morning of the giving of the Torah. *Shir Hashirim Rabbah* 1:57.

70. *TB* Megillah 31a.

71. Mishnah Peah 1:1.

72. Maimonides, *MT*, Hilchot Talmud Torah, 1:8.

73. E.g., Someone who is in the seven days of mourning for a close family member is not obligated to learn Torah (*Shulchan Aruch*, Yoreh Deah, 384:1), but even then there are certain things which can be learned, such as the book of Job, Jeremiah, and the laws of mourning (*Shulchan Aruch*, Yoreh Deach, 384:4).

74. In the 1920s, Rabbi Moshe Menachem Mendel Spivak, and later Rabbi Meir Shapiro, proposed the idea of learning one folio page of the Babylonian Talmud each day, in what became known as the *Daf ha-Yomi* cycle. Every seven-and-a-half years, the cycle culminates in a *Siyum ha-Shas* (completion of the sixty volumes). There are currently thousands of Jews from all walks of life following this programme globally on websites, through apps, live classes, and on their own. But *Daf ha-Yomi* is not the only cycle. Numerous other cycles also operate for example in Tanach, Maimonides's *Mishneh Torah*, and the *Zohar*.

within the Jewish orthodox world of Torah learning leaving no room for anything else.

There have been attempts both within and without orthodoxy to formulate a concept of Torah that includes all activity and knowledge, and which might be used to encourage creativity and invention through engagement with its texts, yet Torah learning within the orthodox world has largely resisted such universalizing tendencies. Furthermore, while there have always been those who have sought to combine Torah with making a living, or science, or worldly wisdom, in traditional circles Torah tends still to be viewed as something separate from such disciplines and has always held prime position in the knowledge hierarchy.[75]

The different formulations of what counts as Torah study parallels the ideas of God as transcendent and immanent discussed in this book. An idea of Torah as including all knowledge fits with an outlook that sees God as everything. The idea that Torah is limited to the oral and written laws more closely aligns to a transcendent God who reveals himself to a specific people. As we have seen, that tension is never completely resolved within the traditional context. Those of us who aspire toward a more universal, monistic Judaism will gravitate toward a more universal, all-encompassing view of Torah in which all knowledge and experience is drawn into its domain.

However, we should recognize the inherent danger of such an exercise. It is the danger of the singularity, of levelling all existence, of eroding all boundaries, individuation, uniqueness. Instead, as with our conceptions of God, we are compelled to embrace two notions of Torah, Torah as everything and Torah as the heritage of a specific people.

The experience of learning Torah reflects such dialectic. Torah learning is a form of contemplation, an immersion in texts and concepts through the application of an emotional-intellectual discipline which is wholly different to that applied in the university or laboratory. It is a form of meditation, but one directed at the world of human interaction and objects. Practical *Halachah* emerges from the system. Halachah is rooted in physicality, but has an eye on the infinite which lies beyond. It is simultaneously an encounter with being in the world and a call to oneness: a form of worship, communal ordering, and a spiritual exercise. One way to universalize Torah is by applying its method to all areas of learning so that all learning is approached with emotional intensity and reverence.

75. See Lamm, *Torah Umadda*. The inclusivist model is described on pp. 161–67.

Torah, however, is fraught on every level. It stimulates an aggressive battle of opinions and takes no prisoners. Images of war and violence frame the talmudic debates.[76] Nothing is taken as read. Nothing is permitted to settle for long. Everything is a target for reexamination. It gives rise to conflict between those who know and those who do not, between those who practice, and those who do not. Through it, families and communities are brought into a state of tension and debate. It arises from and gives rise to an obsession and compulsiveness, forever making demands on those who fall within its influence.

This is anxiety of a unique kind, not the anxiety of Heidegger toward death, but an anxiety born out of love, a summons out of history, a call to lose oneself in an act of self-nullification, into the Torah's depths, the world with all its messiness and chaos, not a world of objects to be conquered, but one to be mentally ordered and sanctified. Torah scholars are said to bring peace to the world, but in fact Torah challenges the world, uproots certainty, and generates anxiety.[77] Yet, Torah has a mysterious capacity to inspire a love of learning and humanity, care for the world, and search for infinity which expands beyond the Torah's traditional confines. Peace will result when we learn to deal with the conflict of knowledge, opinion, and differing lifestyles peaceably.

Torah has a role in challenging the technological worldview because it is a reminder that true learning is not just about knowledge acquisition, but human engagement, wisdom, culture, and value. This is not to say that Torah learning has remained fresh and vigorous. It has not. It has obsessed with feats of memory, focused on regurgitation rather than innovation, become disconnected from all other knowledge and activity, and has been used to shut out diverse viewpoints.[78]

However, it is discovering a new vibrancy and dynamism. This is made possible, in part by technology, which has allowed easy access to the traditional sources, often in translation, and exposure to diverse opinions and cultures from across humanity. Social and intellectual developments are also leading to broader engagement, greater creativity, and greater openness, and will continue to do so. The increasing participation of women in Torah study at the highest levels is one example of innovation,

---

76. Rubenstein, *Culture of the Babylonian Talmud*, 55–64.

77. *TB* Berachot 19a: "R. Elazar said on behalf of Rabbi Chanina: Torah scholars increase peace in the world . . ."

78. For a critique of contemporary orthodoxy, see Cardozo, *Jewish Law as Rebellion*, 65–67, 108–9, 110–12, and 159–10.

which will give rise to new approaches and insights, and is likely to re-shape Judaism, including orthodox Judaism, in unexpected ways.

Coronavirus has accelerated the above developments, created a rup-ture in synagogue attendance and ritual, allowed people to enter alien environments through Zoom and other platforms and exposed them to new ideas, dented institutions, empowered the grassroots, created space for a reevaluation, and shown us all what we care about most. But anyone seeking to remake Judaism must deal from the outset with the primacy of Torah learning embedded in the tradition.

How then do we deal with the burden of Torah learning, the com-mandment constantly weighing on our shoulders? The answer is authen-tically, through a recognition that just as the commandment to learn Torah is without end, there must be an infinite number of ways to per-form that commandment. Every individual has her language, *Conatus*, *Elan Vital*, *Dasein*, mode of flourishing, way to learn, teach, and walk. All voices need to be heard (although not necessarily followed). Everything will be brought to bear on Torah study, and the insights gained will reflect on every aspect of life. God, as we have seen repeatedly in this book, is to be found both in the totality and in the individuals that comprise such totality.[79] In the next chapter, we will see how such ideas relate to the weekly *Shabbat*.

79. This idea has been made persuasively by Tal Keinan. See Keinan, *God Is in the Crowd*, 205–54.

# 11

## Eternal *Shabbat*

### Origins

As with the festivals, *Shabbat* orientates us toward two aspects of God, the immanent and the transcendent. We are commanded to keep *Shabbat* because God rested on the seventh day. In *imitatio Dei*, we return on that day to our source: living in eternity, rest, nothingness, bliss, the God of oneness (Exod 20:8–11; Gen 1:32–2:3). We are also commanded to keep *Shabbat* because God brought us out of Egypt (Deut 5:12–15). *Shabbat* stands us in relationship to our past, present, and future, and others in their unique holiness, the God of otherness.

These two aspects impact the way the material world is taken. On the one hand, the world is the realm of being, a place in which we seek the face of others in authenticity, a ladder on which we climb (the transcendent view espoused by Heidegger). On the other, it is an illusion, part of the divine unfolding, a garment hiding the absolute unity of everything (the immanentist view espoused by Spinoza). Both aspects find expression in the experience of *Shabbat*.

### The Sympathy of Things

We live in a world of objects. They do not exist separate from us but form part of our lives, our *Dasein*. They contain memories, arouse emotions, express our creativity, and when shaped into tools permit us to create.

Our relationship to objects has changed. Once craftspeople made things with care, using ingenuity and skill. Each item was individually crafted with head, hand, and heart. The industrial revolution of the nineteenth century marked a change in our relationship to objects. It brought with it the technological worldview which prizes practicality and efficiency above all else. Things are made to fulfill a purpose. The quicker and cheaper an item can be made, the more profit can be generated. As with all ideas that seek to explain the world and direct us toward a single end, other values fell by the wayside. Everything was pressed into the service of this overarching goal.

The history of the idea of the singularity runs through this period. The lives of workers became valued by the hours they worked and how much they could produce. The objects themselves also changed. Standardization became the norm. Design followed function and ease of manufacture. The relationship between the artisan and the consumer broke down. Work became the blood and sweat of distant others. We started to purchase carelessly and blind to origins, with ease. Objects became stripped of meaning.

Thankfully, there were some who retained the ability to ask questions. Where are we going? What kind of world are we creating? William Morris (1834–1896), the designer and architect, and John Ruskin, who we have already mentioned, founded the Arts and Crafts Movement in about 1860. It flourished in America and England, encouraging people back to the aesthetic and handmade. Ruskin saw art as having a moral value and bemoaned the modern ability to produce without effort.[1] No longer could the artisan take pride in his personal handiwork. Ruskin thought we had taken a retrograde step, valuing results without effort. He wrote: "It is only good for God to create without toil; that which man can create without toil is worthless: machine ornaments are no ornaments at all."[2]

## To Hand

Heidegger has much to say about objects. He writes that we encounter objects in two ways; as "present-at-hand" or as "ready-to-hand." When we engage with an object as present-at-hand, we view it as distinct from

1. Triggs, *Arts and Crafts Movement*, 13.
2. Ruskin, *Stones of Venice*, 1.454.

its history, surroundings or meaning. We consider the object scientifically, taking interest in distinct aspects of its physical makeup, such as
its chemical composition. In contrast, when an object is ready-at-hand it
forms part of our world of meaning, part of our *Dasein*.

Heidegger gives the example of a hammer. As an object present-at-
hand it consists of metal and wood, is heavy or light, varnished or raw.
It has a certain weight and measurement. When the hammer is ready-
to-hand, it is a tool: not only equipment with a specific function, but
something which creates in a specific way in a specific context. The hammer holds meaning to us. It has a history and shares an intimacy with
us through the task being performed. As ready-to-hand, the hammer I
hold is always pointing toward some purpose beyond itself, an "in order
to" do something else, and that something else also points further afield,
beyond the object of production.[3] For example, work may be dependent
on leather, "Leather in turn is produced from hides. These hides are taken
from animals which were bred and raised by others."[4]

By considering an object's chain of meaning, we come to understand
what it means to be a particular *Dasein*, in this case that of a carpenter. As
explained by Cerbonne, a hammer is "something with-which to hammer
in nails in-order-to hold pieces of wood together towards the building of
something for the sake of *Dasein*'s self-understanding as a carpenter."[5]
In this mode of readiness-to-hand we see the hammer in the context in
which it is used, as equipment.

Heidegger explains that our engagement with a tool, such as a hammer as ready-to-hand, is primordial. This is the natural way we engage
with all items in the world. This way of engaging comes prior to our scientific or technological way of understanding the world. Heidegger wants
to make us realize that something has been lost by the turn toward the
scientific and technological. He wants to return us to this primordiality:
"Hammering does not just have a knowledge of the useful character of
the hammer; rather, it has appropriated this utensil in the most adequate
way possible."[6]

We encounter an object's utility by actually using it. It is not something we know theoretically:

3. Heidegger, *Being and Time*, 68.

4. Heidegger, *Being and Time*, 70.

5. Cerbone, *Heidegger*, 40.

6. Heidegger, *Being and Time*, 69.

The less we just stare at the thing called hammer, the more we take hold of it and use it, the more original our relation to it becomes and the more undisguisedly it is encountered as what it is, as a useful thing. The act of hammering itself discovers the specific "handiness" [*Handlichkeit*] of the hammer.[7]

*Handlichkeit* is ready-to-hand.

But there is a barrier to our ability to see in things a readiness-to-hand. This is because when we are engaged with equipment in a ready-to-hand manner, there is no gap in the experience. The hammer, in our case, is an extension of our hand. We are in the flow of the act of hammering. We are not conscious of the hammer or the manifold meanings it holds for us, the "towards" to which it reaches. We only come to see the hammer when something goes wrong, when we step back, or when the tool breaks or goes missing:

When something at hand is missing whose everyday presence was so much a matter of course that we never even paid attention to it, this constitutes a breach in the context of references . . . discovered in circumspection. Circumspection comes up with emptiness and now sees for the first time what the missing thing was at hand for . . . and at hand with . . .[8]

Totality obscures, seamlessness blinds us. We see only when there has been a breakdown. As Graham Harman explains:

Equipment in action operates in an inconspicuous usefulness, doing its work without our noticing it. When the tool fails, its unobtrusive quality is ruined. There occurs a jarring of reference, so that the tool becomes visible as what it is: The contexture of reference and thus the referential totality undergoes a distinctive disturbance which forces us to pause. There is thus a double life of equipment—tool in action, tool in disrepair.[9]

Harman explains that Heidegger considered that it is not just that tools cannot be grasped when they are working properly. Even when broken, an aspect of them is always concealed: "The wrench as reality and the visible or tactile wrench are incommensurable kingdoms, solitary planes without hope of intersection."[10]

7. Heidegger, *Being and Time*, 69.
8. Heidegger, *Being and Time*, 74.
9. Harman, *Tool-Being*, 45.
10. Harman, *Tool-Being*, 21.

Judaism can relate to these ideas. The infinite totality cannot be comprehended. Existence shows itself only in absence, the void left after God withdraws into himself through the process of *Zimzum*. We are able to perceive only when infinity contracts, after homogeneity has been disturbed, questions have been asked, mistakes have been made, tablets of the law have been smashed, in the desert, in exile, in overcoming. Leonard Cohen's 1992 song, "Anthem," well captures the revelatory character of brokenness. Things that are broken allow light to enter. We might add that this light is only partial and conceals as much as it reveals.

## Halachah and Heidegger

Through *Shabbat*, we recognize with Heidegger our inability to see when immersed in things all-consuming, the everyday. When the world works, we do not see hammers or nails, individuals or ourselves for what they or we are.

But with *Shabbat* we do not need to wait for something to break before seeing. The day itself has a revelatory quality which unconceals the world, even as it reconnects us with the eternal.

*Shabbat* is about our relationship to objects, people, and creativity. Immediately after the detailed description of the *Mishkan*, the portable tabernacle which the Jews were commanded to build in the desert, the Jews are reminded to keep *Shabbat* (Exod 31:12–13; 35:1–3). The rabbis learn from this juxtaposition that the cessation demanded by *Shabbat* applies to all of the creative activities (*Melachot*) required to build the *Mishkan*.[11] There are thirty-nine such primary *Melachot*. These include writing, sowing, and building. The thirty-nine *Melachot* give rise to countless related activities (*Toldot*) having the same features as the primary *Melchaot*, which are also forbidden on *Shabbat*.[12]

The laws of *Shabbat* share with Heidegger a common interest in hammers. One of the *Melachot* of *Shabbat* is *Makeh be-Patish* (striking with a hammer) associated with the final hammer blow in making an item or other completion of a process.[13] The Talmud records opinions

11. See Rashi on Exod 31:12–13 and 35:1–3; Ramban on Exod 31:13.

12. *TB* Shabbat 61a; *TB* Shabbat 73a–75b. Although the number thirty-nine is set in stone, the precise categories covered is a matter of debate. See Bin-Nun, "Textual Source for the 39 *Melachot*."

13. Shabbat 75b.

that this form of labor includes assembling a bed, chiselling, or making a hole in a chicken coop.[14] Maimonides sees any activity which completes an action as a *Toldah* of the head *Melachah* of striking with a hammer. Such activities include glassblowing or the making of a hole in wood or metal.[15] *Boneh*, the prohibition of building on *Shabbat*, is closely related to *Makeh be-Patish* and often seen as an alternative prohibition. For example, inserting a handle into a hammer head might constitute the *Melachah* of *Boneh*, rather than *Makeh be-Patish*.[16]

There is also a general rabbinic prohibition of moving objects designated as *Mukzah* on *Shabbat*. The Talmud considers the concept of *Mukzah* as deriving from an incident related in the biblical book of Nehemiah. Nehemiah was a Jewish governor who returned to Israel in the fifth century BCE, following the Babylonian exile. Together with the scribe, Ezra, he sought to encourage the Jewish community living in the land of Israel, who had become lax in its religious practices, to return to its tradition. Nehemiah writes:

> At that time I saw men in Judah treading winepresses on the sabbath, and others bringing heaps of grain and loading them onto asses, also wine, grapes, figs, and all sorts of goods, and bringing them into Jerusalem on the sabbath. I admonished them there and then for selling provisions. Tyrians who lived there brought fish and all sorts of wares and sold them on the sabbath to the Judahites in Jerusalem. I censured the nobles of Judah, saying to them, "What evil thing is this that you are doing, profaning the sabbath day!" (Neh 13:15–22)

Nehemiah is shocked that the people were so oblivious to the sanctity of *Shabbat* that they could engage in routine commerce. He also berated the leaders for allowing this to occur. The talmudic rabbis understood this admonition as referring to a general disrespect for the sanctity of the day rather than a direct infringement of any of the thirty-nine *Melachot*.

The talmudic discussions introducing the law of *Mukzah* suggest that the concept is something of a moving feast:

> The Sages taught: Initially, they would say three utensils may be moved on *Shabbat*: A knife for cutting a cake of dried figs, and a combined spoon and fork to clean dirt from a pot, and a small

---

14. *TB* Shabbat 47a, 102b. For a history of the law, see Gilat, "Hammering," 150–51.

15. Maimonides, *MT*, Shabbat, 10:16.

16. Melamed, *Peninei Halachah*, Shabbat 15, 6.

knife that is on the table. They permitted, and then they permitted again, and then they permitted again, until they said in the
last Mishnah: All utensils may be moved on *Shabbat* except for
a large saw and the blade of a plough.[17]

*Mukzah* was therefore initially intended to be a flexible category that
could be expanded or contracted depending on the requirement of the
age. According to this teaching, the sages initially limited any engagement with objects on *Shabbat* to a handful of household implements, but
as time went by the rabbis became less restrictive.

The laws of *Mukzah* were eventually codified and are today extremely intricate. They require the adherent to consider all the objects
that may be encountered on *Shabbat*, and the uses to which they are put.
The questions that arise include, can one use a *Mukzah* item, even if it
is not being used for one of the thirty-nine *Melachot*? Can one move a
*Mukzah* item if she requires the place that the item occupies? Can one
move an item to prevent it being damaged? Can one move an item just for
fun? In addressing each one of these questions, the adherent might encounter an object's present-at-hand and readiness-at-hand qualities—the
memories associated with each item, what it is he or she wants from the
item, its function and meaning.

This is a practice in mindfulness, with a focus on an object's week-
day use as well as status on a day considered eternal in which certain uses
are prohibited. The exercise instills a realization that *Shabbat* is unique,
different to a workday, that objects have a sanctity, are to be protected.
This, according to Maimonides, is the purpose of the laws of *Mukzah*.
On Shabbat, the way we walk, the manner in which we converse, the way
we act should all be different.[18] The other reason for such laws is to be a
protective fence, to prevent the performance of activities forbidden by
the Torah on *Shabbat*.[19]

The rabbis ruled that certain items were inherently not *Mukzah*
and add to the enjoyment of *Shabbat*.[20] Such items include food and holy

17. *TB* Shabbat 123b.

18. Maimonides, *MT*, Hilchot Shabbat 24:12–13.

19. Melamed, *Peninei Halachah*, Shabbat, 23, 1–2. The Ra'avad, for example, claims
that laws of *Mukzah* aim at preventing a violation of the *Shabbat* law (*Toldah*) of carrying an article from a private domain to a public domain. See *Mishnah Berurah*, 308:1,
intro.

20. For a short overview of the categories of *Mukzah* see *Mishnah Berurah*, 308:1,
intro.

books. Many authorities include items such as clothes and jewelry under this category. There is no restriction attached to any of these items.[21]

Other items are used for permissible activities such as chairs and pillows. These can be used for their primary purpose, or moved for their place or to avoid damage, but cannot be moved for no reason at all or for fun. A restriction still applies to them.[22]

The status of objects which have both a permitted and forbidden use are determined by how they are used most of the time.[23] Objects which have as their primary purpose a forbidden act can still be used for a permitted act provided there is no other object to hand that can fulfill that function. Such an object can also be used if one needs the place in which it stands but cannot be moved to prevent damage and cannot be moved at will. A common example is the hammer already considered. A hammer is *Mukzah* because of *Maka be-Patish*, striking with a hammer, as we have seen. This is one of the thirty-nine *Melachot*. A hammer, however, can have a different function. It can, for example, be used to crack a nut which is permitted on *Shabbat*.[24]

*Dasein* reshapes *Halachah*, and *Halachah* reshapes our *Dasein*. On *Shabbat*, the hammer is no longer equipment for us, linked to our past, present, and future. It is also not an object of scientific investigation. It has a function wholly other. It becomes holy, subject to a new way of understanding in which the hammer remains rooted in the world but is now an object which makes demands on us, rather than us making demands on it, and which seeks to instill within the mind of the observer a consciousness of the divine.

The fourth category of *Mukzah* consists of items which are completely forbidden in all circumstances. They have no permitted function, save where designated prior to *Shabbat*. Examples of such items include scraps of wood, money, ashes, and broken utensils. This fourth category also includes items of great value which one would never use for a mundane permitted activity. Such items include works of art, fine musical instruments, and specialized tools.[25]

21. Melamed, *Peninei Halachah*, Shabbat 23:9.

22. Melamed, *Peninei Halachah*, Shabbat 23:9.

23. Melamed, *Peninei Halachah*, Shabbat 23:8; *Mishnah Berurah* 308:1:10.

24. Melamed, *Peninei Halachah*, Shabbat 23:7; *Mishnah Brurah* 308:12.

25. Melamed, *Peninei Halachah*, Shabbat 23:4. *TB* Shabbat 123b, 157a; *Shulchan Aruch*, 308:1.

The laws of *Shabbat* force an engagement with every item and ask us to consider its purpose, manner of its use, its meaning, function, and religious status. Through such exercise, *Dasein* is restored. Even objects which are mass-produced are given weight and value under such inter-rogation. The rabbis of the Talmud understood handicraft and creative labor. They were artisans, scribes, physicians, merchants, blacksmiths, builders, and shoemakers.[26] They supported guilds and strongly encour-aged vocational training.[27] The Talmud states that he who fails to teach his son a trade, teaches him robbery.[28] They were immersed in the world of objects. They understood creativity, toil, and the holiness of things.

Harman explains Heidegger's view of the process by which we ex-tract items from the totality of existence through the meaning we impose upon them: "It is only I, almighty *Dasein*, who am able to insinuate cracks into this totalizing machinery, liberating single fragments from what would have been a single homogeneous effect."[29] Harman expands Hei-degger's insight to enlist all objects into the process of meaning-making, slicing existence into pieces with their sharp edges. The world is "made of pieces that resist one another, that forever caress each other or wage war with one another."[30]

By ceasing creative activity, by distancing ourselves from certain objects, by viewing objects through the lens of *Halachah* and distanc-ing ourselves from the meaning they usually hold for us, we remind ourselves of the totality of which all objects partake, the *Shabbat* that inheres beneath the surface of everything. The world, however, is never obliterated. *Shabbat* is also a time of worldly pleasure, of good food, and of physical intimacy.[31] The material affirms itself and thank goodness it does. As Harman writes, "If the existence of the single world-system were the full story about reality, we would reside in a universe of absolutely simple action, thoroughly devoid of individual beings."[32]

26. See Friedman, "Ideal Occupations"; Maimonides, *MT*, Hilchot Talmud Torah 1:9.

27. Wischnitzer, "Notes to a History," 249–52. See also Ayali, "Labor as a Value," 7–59.

28. *TB* Kiddushin 29a.

29. Harman, *Tool-Being*, 33.

30. Harman, *Tool-Being*, 34.

31. *Shulchan Aruch*, Orach Chayim 280:1. *Mishnah Brurah*, Orach Chayim 242:1. See also Isa 58:13 and *TB* Shabbat 118a.

32. Harman, *Tool-Being*, 43.

For Raymond Tallis, the hand, as the proto-tool, and more specifically the wholly opposable thumb, gave rise to human consciousness. The thumb instigated a transition from "primate consciousness, which for all its complexity is not turned back on itself in any sustained way, to human self-consciousness, in which objects and subjects are explicitly differentiated."[33] As opposed fingers manipulate objects there is a "self-fingering" or "meta-fingering" in which "the hand addresses itself."[34] We self-refer. Humans are also unique among the primates in making things, in acting as an agent who wills things to happen. Human awareness is also collectivized. We share, record, and transmit our knowledge, and are linked psychologically; our ability to point contributed to the creation of a common world.[35]

The injunction to cease from creative activity on *Shabbat* returns us to a primordial state, prior to self-consciousness, before the desire to fidget and make took hold, and before we formed ourselves into societies dedicated to that task.

## Boredom

*Shabbat* then is a reminder of eternity. It contains a fullness and emptiness, a stripping away, a chance simply to be, circumscribed by law, a holy enclosure in time, but it is also a cessation of creativity, an enforced boredom of sorts.

In his 1929 lecture course, the "Fundamental Concepts of Metaphysics," Heidegger describes three kinds of boredom: (1) being bored by something; (2) being bored with something; and (3) profound boredom. That is, is boredom without any obvious reason.

Heidegger's example of the first type of boredom is all too familiar. He describes the torment of sitting in a railway station waiting for a train:

> It is four hours until the next train arrives. The district is uninspiring. We do have a book in our rucksack, though—shall we read? No. Or think through a problem, some question? We are unable to. We read the timetables . . . We look at the clock—only quarter of an hour has gone by. Then we go out onto the local road. We walk up and down, just to have something to do. But

33. Tallis, *Aping Mankind*, 217.

34. Tallis, *Aping Mankind*, 217.

35. Tallis, *Aping Mankind*, 220–21.

it is no use. We walk up and down . . . Then we count the trees along the road . . . draw all kinds of figures in the sand, and in so doing catch ourselves looking at our watch again—half an hour—and so on.[36]

His description is reminiscent of Simon and Garfunkel's 1966 song "Homeward Bound," the ennui and longing generated by sitting in a railway station, smoking, reading magazines, and waiting, the bland sameness of it all, yearning for home.

This boredom has little to do with waiting. We are capable of waiting without being bored, such as when we wait in anticipation for an event or film to start. Being bored by something is "a peculiar being affected in a paralyzing way by time as it drags and by time in general, a being affected which oppresses us in its own way."[37] One way of looking at this is that in situations such as the railway station, items in the world do not meet our demands in the manner we expect. We cannot simply purchase the ticket, proceed to the platform, and jump on the train. Our path is blocked. The station cannot be put to a use which absorbs us. We become anonymous to the world. The world ignores our presence. We become cognizant of time, which appears to drag. We are left in limbo, feeling empty.[38]

Heidegger sees the second category of being bored as more "original" or "deeper" than the first category. He asks us to envisage a dinner party; the food, the table, the company. There is "lively discussion," music. We might say that it was all "very nice" and "terribly charming," but at the end of the day we are left with a feeling which voices itself in the sentiment, "I was bored, after all, this evening, on the occasion of this invitation."[39] In this second category, the guest is left empty not by something which has left her in limbo (as in the rail station example), but by a feeling of disconnectedness. Heidegger describes this as a slipping away from ourselves.[40] We are so immersed in the party that it becomes our entire world. We become cut off "from any sense of the past and the future."[41] With those tenses out of sight, we act in ways expected of the occasion without regard to who we really are. We act inauthentically.

36. Heidegger, *Fundamental Concepts*, 93.

37. Heidegger, *Fundamental Concepts*, 98.

38. Hammer, *Philosophy and Temporality*, 166–68.

39. Heidegger, *Fundamental Concepts*, 109.

40. Heidegger, *Fundamental Concepts*, 118.

41. Hammer, *Philosophy and Temporality*, 176.

It is only after the event that we appreciate how we were simply "going through the motions," lost in the moment. In this type of boredom, time does not drag, but appears to stand still.[42]

The third type of boredom, "profound boredom," does not relate to any specific situation, although it is the kind of mood which might creep up on us "walking through the streets of a large city on a Sunday afternoon."[43] This type of boredom tells us something about *Dasein* in general. It relieves us of our everyday personality and generates a feeling of indifference: "It makes everything of equally great and equally little worth"[44] Like Heidegger's depiction of anxiety in *Being and Time*, profound boredom in "Fundamental Concepts of Metaphysics": "reveals to *Dasein* that it itself is responsible for its own being." It forces us to define ourselves as "something in particular." Boredom attunes us to being, to identify what we care about.[45]

The Hebrews struggled with boredom in the desert. They remembered the fish, the cucumbers, the melons, the leeks, the onions, and the garlic that they enjoyed in Egypt. However, they complained, "now our soul is dried away; there is nothing at all; we have nought save this manna to look to" (Num 11:5–6). According to the rabbis, the Hebrews experienced the same type of boredom at Sinai, fleeing on a three-day journey to escape the endless instruction. They were "like a child who comes out of school, fleeing as fast as possible."[46]

Things have not changed. We hate being bored. We desire to fill every moment with something, checking our phones, looking at the news, at videos of fluffy kittens, people eating cold oranges in the shower. We seek the voice of the "they," distraction from our death. We crave diversion, feel the need always to be active, to fashion, to conquer, to know.

An aspect of such boredom is the need always to advance what we perceive to be our role in the world. Heidegger considered this urge to be a sign of a lack of self-worth; "Have we become too insignificant to ourselves, that we require a role? Why do we find no meaning for ourselves,

---

42. Heidegger, *Fundamental Concepts*, 122.

43. Heidegger, *Fundamental Concepts*, 135.

44. Heidegger, *Fundamental Concepts*, 137.

45. Hammer, *Philosophy and Temporality*, 183–84.

46. Tosafot *TB* Shabbat 116a. See also Brown, *Spiritual Boredom*.

i.e., no essential possibility of being? Is it because an indifference yawns at us in all things, an indifference whose grounds we do not know?"[47]

Coronavirus stripped us of our roles. It forced us into months of waiting, to experience Heidegger's lonely railway station, where the world was no longer an instrument of our personal or collective designs. We were bored by. We were bored with. The world was no longer there for us. We touched profound boredom on a truly global scale. As plagues always do, it brought us face to face with *Dasein*, called us to take responsibility for our own beings. What is it that we care about? Where is it that my self-worth resides?

The *Shabbat* experience has a similar effect. Experiencing *Shabbat* during coronavirus was like experiencing a *Shabbat* within *Shabbat*, the particular within the universal. On *Shabbat*, the roles we generally perform are forbidden or forgotten. I am not a lawyer. My friend is not a dentist, teacher, or producer. We encounter oneness, a boredom of sorts. Existence is undifferentiated, but this is not an indifference "which yawns at us," to use Heidegger's words, but an encounter with oneness.

The use of technology, including computers, phones, and tablets, are forbidden on *Shabbat* under orthodox *Halachah* as these function in ways which either fall within, or are too similar to, certain of the thirty-nine prohibited categories of work. There are numerous discussions about the extent of such prohibitions and whether technologies might be developed which do not infringe these prohibitions, but there is no dispute that *Shabbat* must remain a day unlike every other. Anything secular or unconnected to the holiness of the day is not permitted or discouraged. I think that, apart from limited exceptions, *Shabbat* should remain technology-free for as long as possible.

In forging our halachic paths, we should keep in mind that *Shabbat* is a bulwark against technique, the worldview we have been discussing. Heidegger observes that the technological worldview experiences time as separate instants which marches forward in even steps toward ever greater progress. The past is rendered pointless. He observed that, as this view takes hold, *Dasein* risks falling into a profound boredom in the face of which we fail to take responsibility. We lapse into passivity. Authenticity becomes difficult to locate.[48] We become devoid of purpose. In response, we do not seek to rediscover ourselves, but find ways to make

47. Heidegger, *Fundamental Concepts*, 77.
48. See Hammer, *Philosophy and Temporality*, 185–87.

ourselves appear more interesting than we really are. Heidegger asks, "Why must we do this? Perhaps because we ourselves have become bored with ourselves?"[49]

The Hebrew word to return is *Lashuv*, which relates to the word *Shabbat*. *Shabbat* returns us to ourselves. It reconnects us with the past, with our families and the communities to which we belong. *Shabbat* stops in its tracks the human desire to conquer and sets us free, if only momentarily, from those forces which desire to control and nullify us.

*Shabbat*, complete cessation, like profound boredom, reveals. To exist, purely to exist, in a place outside the normal flow of time where no authority can make demands, except the authority of the infinite, shows up our individual and societal possibilities, the great expanse of human potential. *Shabbat* allows us to be bored not by or with something but in a profound way. It values us in our uniqueness. It connects us with others. Unlike the technological worldview, it provides an experience of the All, without seeking to obliterate us.

We rest so that we can flourish individually and labor creatively. *Shabbat*, meaning "rest," is also connected to the Hebrew word *Lashevet*, "to sit" or "dwell." For Heidegger dwelling is a kind of sitting back, a retreat from the world as *Dasein*, which allows the world to show itself objectively. He writes:

> In order for knowing to be possible as determining by observation what is objectively present, there must first be a deficiency of having to do with the world and taking care of it. In refraining from all production, manipulation, and so on, taking care of things, it places itself in the only mode of being-in which is left over, in the mode of simply lingering with . . . This looking at is always a way of assuming a definite direction toward something, a glimpse of what is objectively present . . . This looking itself becomes a mode of independent dwelling together with beings in the world. In this "dwelling" [*Aufenthalt*]—as refraining from every manipulation and use—the perception of what is objectively present takes place.[50]

Levinas too deals with the theme of dwelling, referring to the "home" as being the condition for human activity. It is where each person comes from, where a person "abides in the world as having come to it from a

49. Heidegger, *Fundamental Concepts*, 77.
50. Heidegger, *Being and Time*, 61.

private domain, from being at home with himself, to which at each moment he can retire."[51]

Returning, homecoming, dwelling, holding back, and observing
then are related themes, and all feature in the meaning of *Shabbat*. *Shabbat* allows us to linger, it is a dwelling, a place of comfort, and a refraining from manipulation which connects us with eternity but also brings
objects into view, a precursor to scientific investigation and creativity.

So, we dwell and rest so that we can observe the world objectively,
so when we return to action, we can make, but what is it that we want to
create? Not machines, not a world comprising only data without end, but
human beings. Ruskin, that wise prophet of the industrial age, saw this
clearly when he wrote:

> And the great cry that rises from all our manufacturing cities,
> louder than their furnace blast, is all in very deed for this—that
> we manufacture everything there except men; we blanch cotton,
> and strengthen steel, and refine sugar, and shape pottery; but
> to brighten, to strengthen, to refine, or to form a single living
> spirit, never enters into our estimate of advantages.[52]

Our task then should always be to form living spirits, our own spirit and
those of others. This is the essence of *Shabbat* and worthy goal of all human endeavor.

## Havdalah

*Shabbat*, we are taught, is an intimation of the future world, a taste of the
singularity to come, but only an intimation. It is never reached. For at
dark, at the appearance of three stars, we take wine, a candle, spices, and
recite the *Havdalah*, and bless the One who separates between the holy
and the less holy, us and others, light and darkness. Unity disintegrates,
individuation reinstates itself. The dam waters held back by *Shabbat*
come crashing back, obligation inundates, the jobs undone, the bills un-
paid, the field to be sown or harvested, objects to be fashioned and made.
Each person returns to their labor, their problems, difficulties, dreams,
and responsibilities, *Dasein*. This is what it means to be human.

But to live as a Jew is to live in the awareness of *Shabbat*, the ever-
present presence, the absence of the presence, the All and the Other.

51. Levinas, *Infinity and Totality*, 1.152.
52. Ruskin, *Works*, II.XVI.VI.196.

We exist suspended between these aspects of the divine, our encounter with them mediated through our reason and humanity, our laws and our teachings, the philosophies we encounter—in my case, in these pages, in Spinoza and Heidegger reconnected, reframed, reconciled in part, in an effort to gather sparks.[53]

53. This is a reference to the Lurianic Kabbalah discussed above.

# 12

# Onward

NONE OF US KNOWS where things are heading, where technology will take us, how we will deal with the threats that confront us, make use of the opportunities that await, or how we will evolve and develop as a species. We are in the realms of guesswork, speculation, and fantasy, the sphere of imagination. However, we should take such speculations seriously because they reveal what most concerns us and forces us to confront what we most care about and want from the future.

In this book, I have focused on one notion associated with the future, the idea of the singularity or superintelligence. I have tried to show how this idea relates to earlier eschatology and our hankering after a God, an absolute unifying entity in which we are all a part, and how it raises some serious questions about the future and the place of religion.

I have claimed that Spinoza's rational monism provides the philosophical roots of the idea of the singularity and explored the attraction of that outlook for those of us with a scientific mindset who also have a sense of the spiritual. But I have also shown how Spinoza's ideas run the risk of narrowing our focus on the purely practical and scientific. Philosophical criticisms levelled against technology apply equally to Spinoza's thought. Oneness, whether expressed philosophically, politically, technologically, or theologically, always runs the risk of totalizing, levelling, and obliterating difference. In every one of these spheres, we benefit from a sense of the transcendent, the idea that we need relationship, others, the ultimate other, to challenge us, to open existence up for us, to take us out of ourselves, to wake us from our own delusions, to care for, and to make us whole. I have shown Heidegger to be a valuable resource in opening-up this way of thinking.

From these philosophical encounters, I have tried to frame a theology for myself, a midrash, rooted in my own personal thrownness within orthodox Judaism and my reaction against that fed by the manifold streams and influences that make up my world. My intention has been to pique the interest of people like me but also of people with different backgrounds from my own, because I think my tradition has given voice in a unique way, through its great unfolding, to the interplay of unity and difference, the sense of oneness and otherness that comprises all experience in this realm of being which Heidegger called *Dasein*. This is the paradox of immanence and transcendence, thinking of God as the All, yet seeking the face of the other.

The sense of God as immanent and transcendent emerges from the nature of existence itself, which reveals as it conceals and conceals as it reveals. When we isolate an object, we can observe its physical properties, understand its chemistry, feel its texture, but we lose sight of its connection and emergence out of the whole. Something is missing. By the same token, when we experience the totality, we are incapable of understanding an object in its uniqueness, as a thing of meaning, scientifically, unfixed and apart. Heidegger illustrates this process in his discussions of readiness-at-hand (objects in flow) and present-at-hand (objects as subjects of scientific investigation).

The task of seeing things in two ways at the same time, to constantly toggle between immanence and transcendence, is not just about perspective, but a matter of ethics and part of the project in which I think the Jewish tradition has been engaged. Human beings are not just facts, but worlds unto themselves, capable of overreaching themselves, meaning making, imagining alternatives. *Dasein* involves care, being with others which includes entering and resolving conflict. Levinas speaks of the face of the other who makes demands on us. The absolute continuously seeks to pull us into its gravitational field, keeping us rooted, but it also seeks to level, to homogenize, to remake the world in its uniform image. We sense its presence, but constantly push against it, resist its totalizing effect.

The Jewish tradition has also understood that this is not just about intellect but living out a philosophy through seeking justice, engagement with texts, looking out, looking in, seeking, running, returning, following old ways and new ways over familiar and unfamiliar terrain, discovering, living, following a shared destiny, creating destinies, and rebelling.

*Shabbat* and the Jewish Year which I have explored in summary provides a framework in which the message is articulated and given expression by the people. For what end? To improve ourselves and to improve the world, to find the infinite in the finite and the finite in the infinite. There is a sense of constant movement and advancement. We move in circles, but each return is different. We create spirals.

All this is directly relevant to our advancing technology. Ruskin, Morris, Heidegger, and Ellul followed by many others could see where this is heading. Technology seeks absolute power, to bring order to chaos, to make humans more predictable, less complex, algorithmic, instances of a particular kind, to eradicate difference.

I am not for a moment suggesting that we seek to reverse this process which is carrying us along at break-neck speed, but I do think that for now we should resist the singularity by acting in ways which promote our humanity, which overreach ourselves. This involves expressing gratitude and love in the ways that Zohar Atkins has suggested. It involves acting heroically for the other, reaching beyond boundaries, combining knowledge with wisdom and a sense of responsibility, believing in freedom, acting to enhance others' freedom, striving to do justice, to create, to feel, to stand up to the "they," to shun consumerism, to withhold from spending, to explore something someone is not trying to foist on you, to avoid the obvious, to leave technology behind occasionally, to practice ritual, to cherish disagreement, to explore a tradition, to use our hands to make, draw, play music, and touch, to use our minds to think about how objects acquire meaning and delve and dream, and to use our hearts to create, intuit, and feel the pain and happiness of strangers and those close by.[1] Our mistake has been to associate knowledge with virtue. Knowledge flows into receptacles already made. We need to make ourselves first. Virtue should precede knowledge. These messages are particularly pertinent to those on the coal face, designing, developing, programming, and promoting the technologies of the future.

For me, *Halachah* is a way to overreach myself. It is bulwark against technique, a path free of the market, of the forces of the state, of the ambitions of industry, and results in no obvious material reward. It is a resource to navigate the world, the path of a living tradition and lived theology. It is not there to make or acquire or aggrandize, but an expression of something wholly other but rooted in worldly care. It is not without

1. On the need to embrace wider interests and respect the heart and hand over the head, see Goodhart, *Head Hand Heart*; and Sax, *Revenge of Analog*.

flaws. It can be too demanding to keep perfectly. It can have problematic outcomes. Relatively few Jews see it as the only way, but view it as one of myriad ways. Each of us who feel its pull will find our own way.

I also see the value in asserting our differences not just because it is nice to live in a world of respect and harmony, but because the things that make us different are essential to the attainment of personal and collective knowledge and understanding, and to being human. In life, we all start our inquiries through the traditions and numerous identities which are first thrust upon us, looking out from the windows of the house in which we are born. We do not engage the world purely rationally or objectively, but from within a framework of prior allegiances and commitments not of our choosing. Our life is spent testing, abandoning, or refining these. It is that act of engagement which liberates, which precedes technical or other knowledge, and which informs how we develop and use such knowledge.

During the Enlightenment, some sought to create a union of faiths founded on reason, an ambition closely aligned to technique. Moses Mendelssohn, the father of the Jewish Enlightenment, understood that this was not a messianic dream but a nightmare.

He ends his *Jerusalem* with a plea which is as applicable today as it was then, and relevant to moderating the forces of technology. He begs leaders not to

> feign agreement where diversity is evidently the plan and pur-
> pose of Providence. None of us thinks and feels exactly like his
> fellow man: why then do we wish to deceive each other with
> delusive words? . . . Let no one in your states be a searcher of
> hearts and a judge of thoughts; let no one assume a right that
> the Omniscient has reserved to himself alone! If we render unto
> *Caesar* what is *Caesar's*, then do you yourselves render unto *God*
> *what is God's! Love truth! Love peace!*[2]

2. Mendelssohn, *Jerusalem*, 138–39. I am grateful to Professor Edward Breuer for reminding me of this passage.

# Bibliography

Alexander, Philip. "The Rabbis, the Greek Bible and Hellenism." In *The Jewish-Greek Tradition in Antiquity and the Byzantine Empire*, edited by James K. Aitken et al., 229–46. Cambridge: Cambridge University Press, 2014.

Altmann, Alexander. *The Book of Doctrines and Beliefs*. Philosophia Judaica. Oxford: East and West Library, 1946.

Anderson, Jeff. "The Social Function of Curses in the Hebrew Bible." *Zeitschrift Für Die Alttestamentliche Wissenschaft* 110 (1998) 223–37.

Arkush, Allan. *Moses Mendelssohn and the Enlightenment*. SUNY Series in Judaica. Albany: State University of New York Press, 1994.

Armond, Kate. "Cosmic Men: Wyndham Lewis, Ernst Haeckel, and Paul Scheerbart." *Journal of Wyndham Lewis Studies* 4 (2013) 41–62.

Armstrong, Karen. *Buddha*. New York; Penguin, 2001.

Atkins, Zohar. *An Ethical and Theological Appropriation of Heidegger's Critique of Modernity: Unframing Existence*. New York: Palgrave Macmillan and Springer International, 2018. Kindle.

Ayali, Meir. "Labor as a Value in the Talmudic and Midrashic Literature." *Jerusalem Studies in Jewish Thought* 1 (1982) 7–59.

Azize, Joseph, and Noel Weeks, eds. *Gilgameš and the World of Assyria*. Ancient Near Eastern Studies. Leuven: Peeters, 2007.

Baltzer, Klaus, and David E. Green. *The Covenant Formulary in Old Testament, Jewish and Early Christian Writings*. Oxford: Blackwell, 1971.

Barabasi, Albert-László. *Linked*. Cambridge: Perseus, 2002.

Baxter, Donald L. M. "Oneness, Aspects, and the Neo-Confucians." In *The Oneness Hypothesis: Beyond the Boundary of Self*, edited by Philip J. Ivanhoe, 90–95. New York: Columbia University Press, 2018.

Becker, Ernest. *The Denial of Death*. London: Souvenir, 2020.

Beltrán, Miquel. *The Influence of Abraham Cohen De Herrera's Kabbalah on Spinoza's Metaphysics*. Iberian Religious World 2. Leiden: Brill, 2016.

Ben-Pazi, Hanoch. "Joseph." In *Levinas Faces Biblical Figures*, edited by Yael Lin, 166–82. Lanham, MD: Lexington, 2014.

Berman, Joshua. *Ani Maamin: Biblical Criticism, Historical Truth, and the Thirteen Principals of Faith*. Jerusalem: Magid, 2020.

Bin-Nun, Yoel. "The Textual Source for the 39 Melachot of Shabbat." *TheTorah.com*, 2013. https://www.thetorah.com/article/the-textual-source-39-melachot-shabbat.

Blau, Yitzchak. "Idolatry and Martyrdom." *Torah u-Madda Journal* 17 (2016) 35–45.

Bor, Harris. "Enlightenment Values, Jewish Ethics, the Haskalah's Transformation of the Traditional Musar Genre." In *New Perspectives on the Haskalah*, edited by Shmuel Feiner et al., 48–63. London: Littman Library of Jewish Civilization, 2001.

———. "Jewish Mysticism in a Modern Orthodox Prism." *Le'ela* 45 (1998) 10–15.

———. "Moral Education in the Age of the Jewish Enlightenment." PhD diss., University of Cambridge, 1997.

Bostrom, Nick. "Existential Risks: Analyzing Human Extinction Scenarios and Related Hazards." *Journal of Evolution and Technology* 9 (2002).

———. "Letter from Utopia." *Studies in Ethics, Law and Technology* 2 (2008) 1–7.

———. *Superintelligence: Paths, Dangers, Strategies*. Oxford: Oxford University Press, 2017.

Bowler, Peter J. "Monism in Britain: Biologists and the Rationalist Press Association." In *Monism Science, Philosophy, Religion, and the History of a Worldview*, edited by Todd H. Weir, 179–96. Palgrave Studies in Cultural and Intellectual History. New York: Palgrave Macmillan, 2012.

Boyarin, Daniel. *A Radical Jew: Paul and the Politics of Identity*. Berkeley: University of California Press, 1994.

Bridle, James. *New Dark Age: Technology, Knowledge and the End of the Future*. London: Verso, 2018.

Brill, Alan. *Judaism and Other Religions: Models of Understanding*. New York: Palgrave Macmillan, 2010.

Brooks, David. *The Road to Character*. London: Penguin, 2016.

Brown, Erica. *Spiritual Boredom: Rediscovering the Wonder of Judaism*. Woodstock, VT: Jewish Lights, 2009.

Burdett, Michael S. *Eschatology and the Technological Future*. Routledge Studies in Religion. London: Routledge, 2014.

Burkeman, Oliver. "This Column Will Change Your Life: Why Are Ethicists So Unethical?" *Guardian*, November 16, 2013. https://www.theguardian.com/lifeandstyle/2013/nov/16/change-your-life-unethical-ethicists.

Cardozo, Nathan L. *Jewish Law as Rebellion*. Jerusalem: Urim, 2018.

Cerbone, David R. *Heidegger: A Guide for the Perplexed*. London: Continuum, 2008.

Chu, Ted. *Human Purpose and Transhuman Potential: A Cosmic Vision of Our Future Evolution*. San Rafael, CA: Origin, 2013.

Clarke, Desmond M. "Descartes' Proof of the Existence of Matter." In *The Blackwell Guide to Descartes' Meditations*, edited by Stephen Gaukroger, 160–70. Blackwell Guides to Great Works 2. Oxford: Blackwell, 2005.

Clarke, Timothy. *Aristotle and the Eleatic One*. Oxford: Oxford University Press, 2019.

Cohen, Jonathan. "The Halakah, Sacred Events, and Time Consciousness in Rosenzweig and Soloveitchik." *Shofar* 35 (2016) 69–94.

Cohen, Richard A. *Out of Control: Confrontations between Spinoza and Levinas*. SUNY Series in Contemporary Jewish Thought. New York: State University of New York Press, 2016.

Collins, John J. *Jewish Cult and Hellenistic Culture: Essays on the Jewish Encounter with Hellenism and Roman Rule*. Leiden: Brill, 2005.

Corby, James. "Making Nothing Happen: Yeats, Heidegger, Pessoa, and the Emergence of Post-Romanticism." *Humanities* 1 (2012) 117–44.

Coyne, Jerry. "Why Are Faitheists So Nasty?" *Why Evolution Is True*, July 14, 2014. https://whyevolutionistrue.com/2014/07/14/why-are-faitheists-so-nasty/.

Dan, Joseph. *Kabbalah a Very Short Introduction.* Very Short Introductions 162. New York: Oxford University Press, 2007.

Davis, Julia. "Need Delimited: The Creative Otherness of Heidegger's Demigods." *Continental Philosophy Review* 38 (2005) 223–39.

Dawkins, Richard. *The God Delusion.* London: Black Swan, 2007.

De Botton, Alain. *Religion for Atheists.* London: Penguin, 2012.

Deleuze, Gilles. *Expressions in Philosophy: Spinoza.* New York: Zone, 1990.

Descartes, René. *Selected Philosophical Writings.* Translated by John Cottingham et al. Cambridge: Cambridge University Press, 1988.

Di Cesare, Donatella. *Heidegger and the Jews: The Black Notebooks.* Cambridge: Polity, 2018.

Dor-Shav, Ethan. "Ecclesiastes: Fleeting and Timeless Solomon's Confrontation with Mortality." *Azure* 18 (Autumn 2004) 67-87.

Drabinski, John E., and Eric S. Nelson. Introduction to *Between Levinas and Heidegger,* edited by John E. Drabinski et al., 1–12. Albany: State University of New York Press, 2014.

Dreyfus, Hubert L., and Mark A. Wrathall, eds. *A Companion to Heidegger.* Blackwell Companions to Philosophy 29. Malden, MA: Blackwell, 2005.

Eliach, Ayalon. "Mordecai the Villain: The Untold Story of Drinking on Purim." *Haaretz,* February 26, 2015. https://www.haaretz.com/jewish/.premium-the-untold-story-of-drinking-on-purim-1.5329077.

Elie, Paul. *The Life You Save May Be Your Own: An American Pilgrimage.* New York: Farrar, Straus and Giroux, 2003.

Ellul, Jacques. *The Technological Society.* Translated by John Wilkinson. New York: Knopf, 1964.

Enders, Marjus. "Meister Eckhart's Understanding of God." In *A Companion to Meister Eckhart,* edited by Jeremiah M. Hackett, 359–88. Leiden: Brill, 2012.

Engel, Amir. *Gershom Scholem: An Intellectual Biography.* Chicago: University of Chicago Press, 2017.

Feldman, Gilad, et al. "Agency Beliefs Over Time and Across Cultures: Free Will Beliefs Predict Higher Job Satisfaction." *Personality and Social Psychology Bulletin* 44 (2018) 304–17.

Fishbane, Michael A. *Esther.* JPS Torah Commentary. Philadelphia: Jewish Publication Society, 2001.

———. *Song of Songs.* JPS Torah Commentary. Philadelphia: Jewish Publication Society, 2015.

Forst, Binyomin. *The Laws of Kashrus: A Comprehensive Exposition of Their Underlying Concepts and Applications.* New York: Mesorah, 1993.

Fraenkel, Carlos. "Maimonides' God and Spinoza's *Deus sive Natura.*" *Journal of the History of Philosophy* 44 (April 2006) 169–215.

Friedman, Hershey H. "Ideal Occupations: The Talmudic Perspective." *Jewish Law,* 2001. http://www.jlaw.com/Articles/idealoccupa.html.

Friedman, Richard Elliott. *The Hidden Face of God.* San Francisco: Harper, 1996.

Garrett, Aaron. "The Lives of the Philosophers." *Jahrbuch Für Recht Und Ethik* 12 (2004) 41–56.

Garver, Eugene. *Spinoza and the Cunning of Imagination.* Chicago: University of Chicago Press, 2018.

Gilat, Y. "Hammering as One of the Principal Labours Forbidden on the Sabbath." *Proceedings of the World Congress of Jewish Studies* 1 (1965) 149–51.

Gillespie, Alexander. *The Causes of War*. Vol. 3, *1400–1650 CE*. Oxford: Hart, 2017.

Godínez, Héctor Sevilla. "The Being of Nothingness." *Philosophy and Theology* 29 (2017) 147–67.

Goff, Philip. *Consciousness and Fundamental Reality*. Philosophy of Mind Series. New York: Oxford University Press, 2017.

Goldenberg, David M. *The Curse of Ham: Race and Slavery in Early Judaism, Christianity, and Islam*. Woodstock: Princeton University Press, 2005.

Goldstein, Rebecca. *Betraying Spinoza: The Renegade Jew Who Gave Us Modernity*. Jewish Encounters. New York: Schocken, 2006.

Golinkin, David, and Joshua Kulp. *The Schechter Haggadah: Art, History and Commentary*. Jerusalem: Gefen, 2019.

Goodhart, David. *Head Hand Heart: The Struggle for Dignity and Status in the 21st Century*. London: Allen Lane: 2020.

Goodman, Lenn E. "What Does Spinoza's Ethics Contribute to Jewish Philosophy?" In *Jewish Themes in Spinoza's Philosophy*, edited by Heidi M. Ravven et al., 17–89. Albany: State University of New York Press, 2002.

Goodman, Martin. *Rome and Jerusalem*. London: Allen Lane, 2007.

Gordon, Peter Eli. *Rosenzweig and Heidegger: Between Judaism and German Philosophy*. Berkley: University of California Press, 2003.

Gould, Stephen Jay. *Rocks of Ages: Science and Religion in the Fullness of Life*. New York: Ballantine, 2002.

Gratton, Peter. "Spinoza and the Biopolitical Roots of Modernity." *Modernity* 18 (2013) 91–102.

Green, Arthur. *Ehyeh: A Kabbalah for Tomorrow*. Woodstock, VT: Jewish Lights, 2011.

Greene, Joshua. *Moral Tribes: Emotion, Reason and the Gap between Us and Them*. London: Atlantic, 2015.

Gruen, Erich S. *Heritage and Hellenism: The Reinvention of Jewish Tradition*. Hellenistic Culture and Society 30. Berkeley: University of California Press, 1998.

HaCohen, Meir Simcha. *Meshech Chochmah*. Riga, 1927.

Halmi, Nicholas. "Coleridge's Ecumenical Spinoza." In *Spinoza Beyond Philosophy*, edited by Beth Lord, 188–207. Edinburgh: Edinburgh University Press, 2015.

Hammer, Espen. *Philosophy and Temporality from Kant to Critical Theory*. Modern European Philosophy. Cambridge: Cambridge University Press, 2011.

Harari, Yuval Noah. *Homo Deus: A Brief History of Tomorrow*. London: Random House, 2017. Kindle.

———. *Sapiens: A Brief History of Mankind*. London: Vintage, 2011.

Harman, Graham. *Tool-Being: Heidegger and the Metaphysics of Objects*. Chicago: Open Court, 2002.

Harris, Michael J. *Faith without Fear: Unresolved Issues in Modern Orthodoxy*. Elstree, UK: Vallentine Mitchell, 2015.

Harris, Sam. *Waking Up: A Guide to Spirituality without Religion*. London: Random House, 2014.

Harrison, Victoria S. "Oneness: A Big History Perspective." In *The Oneness Hypothesis: Beyond the Boundary of Self*, edited by Philip J. Ivanhoe, 39–52. New York: Columbia University Press, 2018.

Hazony, Yoram. *God and Politics in Esther*. Cambridge, Cambridge University Press, 2015.

————. *The Virtue of Nationalism*. New York: Basic Books, 2018.

Hefter, Herzl. "Idolatry: A Prohibition for Our Time." *Tradition* 42 (2009).

Hegel, Georg Wilhelm Friedrich. *Lectures on the History of Philosophy*. 3 vols. Translated by Elizabeth S. Haldane and Frances H. Simson. London: Paternoster, 1896.

Heidegger, Martin. *Being and Time*. Translated by Joan Stambaugh. SUNY Series in Contemporary Continental Philosophy. Albany: State University of New York Press, 1996.

————. *The Fundamental Concepts of Metaphysics: World, Finitude, Solitude*. Translated by William McNeill et al. Studies in Continental Thought. Bloomington: Indiana University Press, 1995.

————. "Only a God Can Save Us." In *Heidegger: The Man and the Thinker*, edited by Thomas Sheehan and translated by W. Richardson, 45–67. Chicago: Precedent, 1981.

————. *The Question concerning Technology, and Other Essays*. Translated with introduction by William Lovitt. London: Harper Perennial, 1977.

————. "What Is Metaphysics?" In *Basic Writings*, edited and translated by David Farrell Krell, 89–111. New York, HarperCollins, 1993.

Hicks, Stephen. *Explaining Postmodernism: Skepticism and Socialism from Rousseau to Foucault*. Brisbane: Connor Court, 2019.

Hirschensohn, Chaim. *Mosge Shave v-ha-Emet: Five Sections in Religious Philosophy*. Jerusalem: Defus ha-Ivri of Yechiel Werker, 1932.

Horkheimer, Max, and Noeri Adorno. *Dialectic of Enlightenment: Philosophical Fragment*. Edited by Gunzelin Schmid Noerr. Translated by E. F. N. Jephcott. Cultural Memory in the Present Series. Stanford: Stanford University Press, 2002.

Hornung, Gabriel. "The Nature and Import of the Relationship between the Joseph Story in Genesis and the Book of Esther." PhD diss., Harvard University, 2016.

Hurwitz, Naftali Zvi. *Zera Kodesh*. New York: Klagsbrun, 2017.

Ihde, Don. *Heidegger's Technologies: Postphenomenological Perspectives*. Perspectives in Continental Philosophy. New York: Fordham University Press, 2010.

Isaeva, Natalia V. *From Early Vedanta to Kashmir Shaivism: Gaudapada, Bhartrhari, and Abhinavagupta*. SUNY Series in Religious Studies. Albany: State University of New York Press, 1995.

Israel, Jonathan I. *Radical Enlightenment Philosophy and the Making of Modernity, 1650–1750*. Oxford: Oxford University Press, 2001.

Jacobs, Louis. *Seeker of Unity: The Life and Works of Aaron of Starosselje*. London: Vallentine Mitchell, 2006.

————. *We Have Reason to Believe*. London: Vallentine Mitchell, 1995.

James, Susan. "Narrative as the Means to Freedom: Spinoza on the Uses of Imagination." In *Spinoza's "Theological-Political Treatise": A Critical Guide*, edited by Yitzchak Y. Melamed et al., 250–67. Cambridge Critical Guides. Cambridge: Cambridge University Press, 2010.

Jammer, Max. *Einstein and Religion Physics and Theology*. Princeton: Princeton University Press, 2011.

Kasher, Asa, and Shlomo Biderman. "Why Was Baruch de Spinoza Excommunicated?" In *Skeptics, Millenarians and Jews*, edited by David S. Katz et al., 98–141. Brill's Studies in Intellectual History 17. Leiden: Brill, 1990.

Kasher, Hannah. "Maimonides on the Intellects of Women and Gentiles." In *Interpreting Maimonides: Critical Essays*, edited by Charles H. Manekin and Daniel Davies, 46–64. Cambridge: Cambridge University Press, 2018.

Keinan, Tal. *God Is in the Crowd: Twenty-First-Century Judaism*. New York: Random House, 2018.

Kimelman, Reuven. "Abravanel and the Jewish Republican Ethos." In *Commandment and Community: New Essays in Jewish Legal and Political Philosophy*, edited by Daniel H. Frank, 195–217. Albany: State University of New York Press, 1995.

Kolnai, Aurel. *The Utopian Mind and Other Papers: A Critical Study in Moral and Political Philosophy*. Edited by Francis Dunlop. London: Athlone, 1995.

Konacheva, Svetlana. "Vision of God and Thinking of Being: Vladimir Lossky and Martin Heidegger." *Horizon* 7 (2018) 312–36.

Kook, Abraham Isaac. *Kevatsim Miketav Yad Kodsho*. 2 vols. Jerusalem: Makhon le-Hotzaat Ginzei ha-Reayah, 2006, 2008.

———. *Abraham Isaac Kook: The Lights of Penitence, The Moral Principles, Lights of Holiness, Essays, Letters and Poems*. Translated by Ben Zion Bokser. New York: Paulist, 1978.

Kraemer, Joel L. *Maimonides: The Life and World of One of Civilization's Greatest Minds*. New York: Doubleday, 2008.

Kugel, James L. *How to Read the Bible: A Guide to Scripture, Then and Now*. New York: Free Press, 2008.

———. *In Potiphar's House: The Interpretive Life of Biblical Texts*. San Francisco: HarperSanFrancisco, 1990.

Kurzweil, Ray. *The Age of Spiritual Machines: How We Will Live, Work and Think in the New Age of Intelligent Machines*. London: Orion Business, 1999.

———. *The Singularity Is Near: When Humans Transcend Biology*. London: Duckworth, 2018.

Kwek, Dorothy H. B. "Power and the Multitude: A Spinozist View." *Political Theory* 43 (2015) 155–84.

Lamm, Norman. *Torah Umadda: The Encounter of Religious Learning and Wordly Knowledge in the Jewish Tradition*. Northvale, NJ: Aronson, 1990.

Lebens, Samuel. "Nothing Else." *European Journal for Philosophy of Religion* 11 (2019).

Lessing, Gotthold Ephraim. "The Parable of the Three Rings." In *The Three-Ring Parable: Tales of Aarne-Thompson Type 920E*, edited and translated by D. L. Ashliman. Pittsburgh: University of Pittsburgh Press, 1999–2008.

Levan, Yigal. "The Wars of Joshua: Weaning Away from the Divine." In *War and Peace in Jewish Tradition: From the Biblical World to the Present*, edited by Yigal Levin et al., 37–50. Florence: Taylor and Francis, 2011.

Levi Ben Gershon (Ralbag). *Biur ha-Milot*. 1325–38. https://mg.alhatorah.org/Full/Shemot/32.32#eon6.

Levi of Berditchev. *Kedushat Levi*. Munkatch, 1939. https://www.sefaria.org/Kedushat_Levi%2C_Exodus%2C_Shemot.1?lang=biandwith=Aboutandlang2=en.

Levinas, Emmanuel. "Difficult Freedom: Essays on Judaism." In *Spinoza's Challenge to Jewish Thought: Writings on His Life, Philosophy and Legacy*, edited by Daniel B. Schwartz, 233–37. Waltham, MA: Brandeis University Press, 2019.

———. *Totality and Infinity: An Essay on Exteriority*. Translated by Alphonso Lingis. Pittsburgh: Duquesne University Press, 1969.

Loew ben Bezalel, Yehudah. *Ohr Chadash*. Warsaw, 1874.

Loewenthal, Naftali. *Hasidism beyond Modernity: Essays in Habad Thought and History.* London: Littman Library of Jewish Civilization, 2020.

Loëwy, Michael. *Redemption and Utopia: Jewish Liberation Thought in Central Europe; A Study in Elective Affinity.* Translated by Hope Heaney. London: Athlone, 1992.

Lord, Beth. *Spinoza's Ethics: An Edinburgh Philosophical Guide.* Edinburgh Philosophical Guides Series. Edinburgh: Edinburgh University Press, 2010.

Lovelock, James. *Gaia: A New Look at Life on Earth.* Oxford: Oxford University Press, 2009.

Lucas, Julian. "Man, Woman, and Robot in Ian McEwan's New Novel." *New Yorker,* April 22, 2019. https://www.newyorker.com/magazine/2019/04/22/man-woman-and-robot-in-ian-mcewans-new-novel.

Macfarlane, Robert. *The Old Ways: A Journey on Foot.* London: Penguin, 2013.

Maimonides, Moses. *The Guide for the Perplexed.* Translated by Michael Friedländer. London: Routledge, 1904.

———. *Introduction to Mishnah Tractate Sanhedrin.* Translated by J. Abelson. Brooklyn: Society for Preservation of Hebrew Books, 1906.

———. "Letter to the Jews of Yemen." In *Epistles of Maimonides: Crisis and Leadership,* 91–208. Translated and notated by Abraham Halkin and discussions by David Hartman. Philadelphia: Jewish Publication Society, 1993.

———. *Mishneh Torah, Yad ha-Hazakah.* Translated by Simon Glazer, 1927.

Mark, Zvi. *Mysticism and Madness: The Religious Thought of Rabbi Nachman of Bratslav.* Kogod Library of Judaic Studies 7. London: Shalom Hartman Institute, 2009.

Marshall, Eugene. *The Spiritual Automaton: Spinoza's Science of the Mind.* Oxford: Oxford University Press, 2013.

Matt, Daniel C. "The Concept of Nothingness in Jewish Mysticism." *Tikkun* 3 (1987) 43–47.

McEwan, Ian. *Machines Like Me.* London: Vintage, 2019.

Melamed, Eliezer. *Peninei Halakhah.* https://www.sefaria.org/texts/Halakhah/Peninei%20Halakha.

Melamed, Yitzhak Y. "A Concise Grammar of Pantheism." Paper delivered at the Templeton Pantheism Workshop, Rutgers University, June 2018.

Mendelssohn, Moses. *Jerusalem; or, On Religious Power and Judaism.* Translated by Allan Arkush. Hanover, NH: University Press of New England, 1983.

Michaelson, Jay. *Everything Is God: The Radical Path of Nondual Judaism.* Boston: Shambhala, 2009.

Mieroop, Marc van de. *Cuneiform Texts and the Writing of History.* New York: Routledge, 1999.

Morrow, Jeffrey L. *Three Skeptics and the Bible: La Peyrere, Hobbes, Spinoza, and the Reception of Modern Biblical Criticism.* Eugene, OR: Pickwick, 2016.

Mulhill, Stephen. *Routledge Philosophy Guidebook to Heidegger and Being and Time.* Routledge Philosophy Guidebooks. London: Routledge, 2013.

Nadler, Allan. "Romancing Spinoza." In *Spinoza's Challenge to Jewish Thought: Writings on His Life, Philosophy and Legacy,* edited by Daniel B. Schwartz, 244–45. Waltham, MA: Brandeis University Press, 2019.

Nadler, Steven. *A Book Forged in Hell: Spinoza's Scandalous Treatise and the Birth of the Secular Age.* Princeton, NJ: Princeton University Press, 2011.

———. *Spinoza: A Life.* Cambridge: Cambridge University Press, 2009.

———. *Spinoza's Heresy: Immortality and the Jewish Mind.* Oxford: Clarendon, 2001.

———. *Think Least of Death: Spinoza on How to Live and How to Die*. Princeton: Princeton University Press, 2020.

Nancy, Jean-Luc. *The Inoperative Community*. Theory and History of Literature 76. Minneapolis: University of Minnesota Press, 1991.

Nassar, Dalia. "Spinoza in Schelling's Early Conception of Intellectual Intuition." In *Spinoza and German Idealism*, edited by Yitzchak Melamed et al., 136–55. Cambridge: Cambridge University Press, 2012.

Negri, Antonio. "Potency and Ontology: Heidegger or Spinoza." In *Spinoza for Our Time: Politics and Postmodernity*, 55–68. Translated by William McCuaig. New York: Columbia University Press, 2013.

Neusner, Jacob, and Tamara Sonn. *Comparing Religions through Law: Judaism and Islam*. London: Routledge, 1999.

Nordenhaug, Erik S. "Technology and the End of History: Jacques Ellul and Martin Heidegger on the Eschatological Dimension of the Technological Society." PhD diss., Emory University, 1994.

Oakley, Francis. *Kingship: The Politics of Enchantment*. Oxford: Blackwell, 2006.

Oltermann, Philip. "Heidegger's 'Black Notebooks' Reveal Antisemitism at Core of His Philosophy." *Guardian*, March 13, 2014. https://www.theguardian.com/books/2014/mar/13/martin-heidegger-black-notebooks-reveal-nazi-ideology-antisemitism.

Papadopoulou, Marianna, and Roy Birch. "Being in the World: The Event of Learning." *Educational Philosophy and Theory* 41 (2009) 270–86.

Pekuda, Bachya ibn. "Duties of the Heart." *Sefaria*. https://www.sefaria.org/Duties_of_the_Heart?lang=bi.

Pilkington, Ed. "The Future Is Going to Be Very Exciting." *Guardian*, May 2, 2009. https://www.theguardian.com/technology/2009/may/02/google-univeristy-ray-kurzweil-artificial-intelligence.

Pinker, Steven. *Enlightenment Now: The Case for Reason, Science, Humanism and Progress*. London: Penguin, 2019.

Plato. *The Republic*. In *Complete Works*, edited with introduction and notes by John M. Cooper, 971–1223. Indianapolis: Hackett, 1997.

Pollock, Benjamin. *Franz Rosenzweig and the Systematic Task of Philosophy*. Cambridge: Cambridge University Press, 2015.

Popoveniuc, Bogdan. "Pro and Cons Singularity: Kurzweil's Theory and Its Critics." *Proceedings of the Virtual Reality International Conference* (2013) 1–6.

Prochnik, George. *Stranger in a Strange Land: Searching for Gershom Scholem and Jerusalem*. London: Granta, 2017.

Proudhon, Pierre-Joseph. "Away with Authority." In *Ni Dieu Ni Maître*, edited by Daniel Guérin et al. Oakland: AK, 2005.

Puett, Michael, and Christine Gross-Loh. *The Path: A New Way to Think about Everything*. London: Penguin, 2017.

Rabinovitch, Nahum E. "The Way of Torah." *Edah Journal* 3 (2003) 1–34.

Rakeffet-Rothkoff, Aaron. "The Law of the Land in Halakhic Perspective." *Tradition: A Journal of Orthodox Jewish Thought* 13 (Fall 1972) 13–25.

Rees, Martin J. *Our Final Hour: A Scientist's Warning: How Terror, Error, and Environmental Disaster Threaten Humankind's Future in This Century—on Earth and Beyond*. New York: Basic Books, 2003.

Richardson, John. *Heidegger*. Oxford: Routledge, 2012.

Robinson, James T. "On or Above the Ladder? Maimonidean and Anti-Maimonidean Readings of Jacob's Ladder." In *Interpreting Maimonides: Critical Essays*, edited by Charles H. Manekin and Daniel Davies, 85–98. Cambridge: Cambridge University Press, 2018.

Roelofs, Luke. "The Unity of Consciousness Within Subjects and Between Subjects." *Philosophical Studies* 173 (2017) 3199–221.

Rosenzweig, Franz. *Star of Redemption*. Translated by Barbara E. Galli. Madison: University of Wisconsin Press, 2005.

Rosling, Hans, et al. *Factfulness: Ten Reasons We're Wrong about the World—and Why Things Are Better than You Think*. London: Sceptre, 2018.

Ross, Tamar. *Expanding the Palace of Torah: Orthodoxy and Feminism*. Waltham, MA: Brandeis University Press, 2004.

Rovelli, Carlo. *Reality Is Not What It Seems*. London: Penguin, 2017.

———. *Seven Brief Lessons on Physics*. London: Penguin, 2016.

Rubenstein, Jeffrey L. *The Culture of the Babylonian Talmud*. Baltimore: Johns Hopkins University Press, 2003.

Ruskin, John. *The Works of John Ruskin*. Edited by Edward Tyas Cook et al. Cambridge: Cambridge University Press, 2010.

Rynhold, Daniel, and Michael Harris. *Nietzsche, Soloveitchik, and Contemporary Jewish Philosophy*. Cambridge: Cambridge University Press, 2018.

Sacks, Jonathan. *Dignity of Difference*. London: Continuum, 2002.

———. *Future Tense: A Vision for Jews and Judaism in the Global Culture*. London: Hodder and Stoughton, 2009.

———. *The Great Partnership: God, Science and the Search for Meaning*. London: Hodder and Stoughton, 2011.

———. *Morality: Restoring the Common Good in Divided Times*. London: Hodder and Stoughton, 2020.

———. *Not in God's Name: Confronting Religious Violence*. London: Hodder and Stoughton, 2015.

———. *Radical Then, Radical Now: On Being Jewish*. London: Continuum, 2003.

Saiman, Chaim N. *Halakhah: The Rabbinic Idea of Law*. Princeton: Princeton University Press, 2018.

Sarna, Nahum M. *Understanding Genesis: Heritage of Biblical Israel*. New York: Schocken, 1970.

Sax, David. *The Revenge of Analog: Real Things and Why They Matter*. New York: Public Affairs, 2016.

Scarborough, Milton. *Comparative Theories of Nonduality: The Search for a Middle Way*. London: Bloomsbury, 2009.

Schaffer, Jonathan. "Monism: The Priority of the Whole." *Philosophical Review* 119 (2016) 31–76.

Schleiermacher, Friedrich. *On Religion: Speeches to Its Cultured Despisers*. Translated by John Oman. Montana: Kessinger, 2008.

Schneerson, Menachem Mendel. *Likkutey Sichot*. Vol. 4. Brooklyn: Kehot, 1998.

Scholem, Gershom. *Major Trends in Jewish Mysticism*. New York: Schoken, 1995.

———. *On the Kabbalah and Its Symbolism*. New York: Schoken, 1996.

Schorsch, Jonathan. *Jews and Blacks in the Early Modern World*. Cambridge: Cambridge University Press, 2014.

Schwartz, David, B. *The First Modern Jew: Spinoza and the History of an Image.* Princeton: Princeton University Press, 2014.

Schwartz, Dov. "Fascination and Rejection: Religious Zionist Attitudes toward Spinoza." *Journal of Israeli History* 14 (1993) 147–68.

Schwartz, Yossef. "Meister Eckhart and Moses Maimonides: From Judeo-Arabic Rationalism to Christian Mysticism." In *A Companion to Meister Eckhart*, edited by Jeremiah Hackett, 189–214. Leiden: Brill, 2012.

Scruton, Roger. *The Uses of Pessimism and the Danger of False Hope.* London: Atlantic, 2012.

Seeskin, Kenneth. "No One Can See My Face and Live." In *Negative Theology as Jewish Modernity*, edited by Michael Fagenblat, 48–61. Bloomington: Indiana University Press, 2017.

Senka Gazibara. "'Head, Heart and Hands Learning': A Challenge for Contemporary Education." *Journal of Education Culture and Society* 4 (2013) 71–82.

Shapira, Amnon. *Jewish Religious Anarchism, Chapters in the History of an Idea, from Biblical and Rabbinic Times, through Abravanel and up to the Modern Era.* Jerusalem: Ariel University, 2015.

Shapiro, Marc B. *Changing the Immutable: How Orthodox Judaism Rewrites Its History.* Oxford: Littman Library of Jewish Civilization, 2015.

———. "Hayyim Hirschensohn, Can One Kill an Am Ha'aretz on Shabbat? Physical Punishments and Lots More." *Seforim Blog*, November 9, 2014. https://seforimblog.com/2014/11/r-hayyim-hirschensohn-can-one-kill-a/.

———. "Is Modern Orthodoxy Moving towards an Acceptance of Biblical Criticism?" *Modern Judaism* 37 (2017) 165–93.

———. *The Limits of Orthodox Theology.* Oxford: Littman Library of Jewish Civilization, 2004.

Sharbat, Yosef. "Purim Masquerade: Unmasking the Origins." Paper presented at Rabbi Isaac Elchanan Theological Seminary, 2012. https://www.yutorah.org/lectures/lecture.cfm/817663/Rabbi_Yosef__Sharbat/Purim_Masquerade:_Unmasking_the_Origins.

Shmalo, Gamliel. "Orthodox Approaches to Biblical Slavery." *Torah u-Madda Journal* 16 (2012–13) 1–20.

Siedentop, Larry. *Inventing the Individual: The Origins of Western Liberalism.* London: Allen Lane, 2014.

Smilansky, Saul. *Free Will and Illusion.* Oxford: Oxford University Press, 2000.

Smith, James K. A. *How (Not) to Be Secular: Reading Charles Taylor.* Grand Rapids: Eerdmans, 2014.

Sokol, Sam. "Slammed by COVID-19, Ultra-Orthodox Try to Fathom What God Hath Wrought." *Times of Israel*, May 13, 2020. https://www.timesofisrael.com/slammed-by-covid-19-ultra-orthodox-jews-try-to-understand-what-god-hath-wrought/.

Solomon, Sheldon, et al. *The Worm at the Core: On the Role of Death in Life.* London: Penguin, 2015.

Soloveitchik, Joseph B. *Halakhic Man.* Philadelphia: Jewish Publication Society, 1991.

———. *The Halakhic Mind: An Essay on Jewish Tradition and Modern Thought.* New York: Seth, 1986.

———. *Lonely Man of Faith.* New York: Doubleday, 2006.

Sommer, Benjamin D. *Revelation and Authority: Sinai in Jewish Scripture and Tradition.* New Haven: Yale University Press, 2015.

Sonsino, Rifat. "Characteristics of Biblical Law." *Judaism* 33 (1984) 202–9.

Spinoza, Benedict. *Ethics*. Translated by George Eliot. Edited and introduced by Clare Carlisle. Princeton: Princeton University Press, 2020.

———. *Theological-Political Treatise*. Edited by Jonathan Israel. Cambridge Texts in the History of Philosophy. Cambridge: Cambridge University Press, 2007.

Spiro, Melford E. "Utopia and Its Discontents: The Kibbutz and Its Historical Vicissitudes." *American Anthropologist* 106 (2004) 556–68.

Strogatz, Steven H. *Sync: The Emerging Science of Spontaneous Order*. London: Penguin, 2004.

Stuart, James D. "Descartes' Proof of the External World." *History of Philosophy Quarterly* 3 (1986) 19–28.

Tallis, Raymond. *Aping Mankind*. Routledge Classics. Oxford: Routledge, 2016.

Taylor, Charles. *A Secular Age*. Cambridge: Harvard University Press, 2007.

Teitelbaum, Mordechai. *The Rabbi of Liady and the Habad Movement* (Heb). Warsaw: Tushiyah, 1913.

Tirosh-Samuelson, Hava. "In Pursuit of Perfection: The Misguided Transhumanist Vision." *Theology and Science* 16 (2018) 200–22.

Triggs, Oscar Lovell. *The Arts and Crafts Movement*. New York: Parkstone, 2009.

Ulam, Stanislaw M. "John Von Neumann." *Bulletin of the American Mathematical Society* 64 (1958) 1–49.

Vinge, Vernor. "The Coming Technological Singularity: How to Survive in the Post-Human Era." Paper presented at Vision 21: Interdisciplinary Science and Engineering in the Era of Cyberspace, San Diego, December 1, 1993. https://ntrs.nasa.gov/archive/nasa/casi.ntrs.nasa.gov/19940022856.pdf.

Vohs, Kathleen H., and Jonathan W. Schooler. "The Value of Believing in Free Will." *Psychological Science* 19 (2009) 49–54.

Weir, Todd H. "The Riddles of Monism: An Introductory Essay." In *Monism Science, Philosophy, Religion, and the History of a Worldview*, edited by Todd H. Weir, 1–44. Palgrave Studies in Cultural and Intellectual History. New York: Palgrave Macmillan, 2012.

Wessely, Naphatli Herz. *Divrei Shalom v'Emet: 4 Mikhtavim* (Heb). Berlin, 1784.

Whipple, Tom. "Ethics Professors Are No More Ethical Than The Rest of Us." *Times*, March 25, 2019. https://www.thetimes.co.uk/article/ethics-professors-don-t-walk-the-walk-d7n6097m8.

Wiedemann, Thomas. *Greek and Roman Slavery*. London: Croom Helm, 1988.

Wilkinson, Robert. *Nishida and Western Philosophy*. Abingdon: Taylor and Francis, 2009.

Williams, Florence. *The Nature Fix: Why Nature Makes Us Happier, Healthier, and More Creative*. New York: Norton, 2017.

Williams, Rowan. *Being Human: Bodies, Minds, Persons*. London: SPCK, 2018.

Wischnitzer, Mark. "Notes to a History of the Jewish Guilds." *Hebrew Union College Annual* 23 (1950) 245–63.

Wolf, Gary. "Ray Kurzweil Pulls Out All the Stops (and Pills) to Survive the Singularity." *Wired*, March 24, 2008. https://www.wired.com/2008/03/ff-kurzweil/.

Wolfson, Elliot R. *The Duplicity of Philosophy's Shadow: Heidegger, Nazism, and the Jewish Other*. New York: Columbia University Press, 2018.

———. *Heidegger and Kabbalah: Hidden Gnosis and the Path of Poiesis*. New Jewish Philosophy and Thought. Bloomington: Indiana University Press, 2019.

———. "Secrecy, Apophasis, and Atheistic Faith in the Teachings of Rav Kook." In *Negative Theology as Jewish Modernity*, edited by Michael Fagenblat, 131–60. Bloomington: Indiana University Press, 2017.

Wolin, Richard. *Heidegger's Children: Hannah Arendt, Karl Löwith, Hans Jonas, and Herbert Marcuse.* Princeton: Princeton University Press, 2015.

Yudlowsky, Eliezer. *Coherent Extrapolated Volition.* San Francisco: Singularity Institute, 2004.

Zalman, Schneur. *Tanya.* Otsar HaChasidim Lubavitch. https://www.sefaria.org/Tanya%2C_Part_One%2C_The_Book_of_the_Average_Men.1.1?lang=biandwith=Aboutandlang2=en.

Zarader, Marlène. *The Unthought Debt: Heidegger and the Hebraic Heritage; Cultural Memory in the Present.* Stanford: Stanford University Press, 2006.

Zelnick-Abramovitz, Rachel. "Not Wholly Free: The Concept of Manumission and the Status of Manumitted Slaves in the Ancient Greek World." *Mnemosyne* 266 (2005) 335–44.

# Subject Index

# Ancient Documents Index